Public relations research:
an international perspective

In drawing together the work of leading academics in Europe and in the United States, this volume presents a truly global view of the current themes in public relations research.

The chapters presented in this book reveal the imaginative and wide ranging nature of scholarly enquiry now being brought to bear on public relations. The book contains comparative studies of public relations practice in different countries and explores issues such as the relationship between PR and journalism, the history of PR and the moral role of the public relations practitioner.

Public relations research: an international perspective provides a fascinating insight into the state of public relations and will be of great interest to both academics and advanced students of public relations, communication science, marketing and management science.

Public relations research: an international perspective

Editors

Danny Moss

Co-director
Centre for Corporate and Public Affairs
Manchester Metropolitan University

Toby MacManus
Senior Lecturer
Department of Communication and Marketing
Bournemouth University

Dejan Verčič
Director
Pristop Communications Group
Ljubljana, Slovenia

INTERNATIONAL THOMSON BUSINESS PRESS
I⨀P®An International Thomson Publishing Company

London • Bonn • Boston • Johannesburg • Madrid • Melbourne • Mexico City • New York • Paris
Singapore • Tokyo • Toronto • Albany, NY • Belmont, CA • Cincinnati, OH • Detroit, MI

Public Relations Research: An International Perspective

Copyright © 1997 Danny Moss, Toby MacManus and Dejan Verčič

First published by International Thomson Business Press

I(T)P®   A division of International Thomson Publishing Inc.
The ITP logo is a trademark under licence

British Library Cataloguing-in-Publication Data
A catalogue record for this book is available from the British Library

First edition 1997

Typeset by J&L Composition Ltd, Filey, North Yorkshire
Printed in the UK by TJ International Ltd, Padstow, Cornwall

ISBN 0–415–10995–7

International Thomson Business Press   International Thomson Business Press
Berkshire House   20 Park Plaza
168–173 High Holborn   13th Floor
London WC1V 7AA   Boston MA 02116
UK   USA

Contents

List of figures   vii
List of tables   viii
Contributors   ix
Preface   xv
Acknowledgements   xviii

Part I American perspectives of public relations

1 A situational theory of publics: conceptual history, recent
   challenges and new research   3
   James E. Grunig

2 Requisite variety in public relations research   49
   Larissa A. Grunig

Part II German-Austrian perspectives of public relations

3 Public relations and reality: a contribution to a theory of
   public relations   89
   Gunter Bentele

4 Community public relations in Germany – East and West
   state-of-the-art and development   110
   Barbara Baerns and Anja Kutscher-Klink

5 Towards a typology of MA and PhD theses projects in
   public relations   122
   Benno Signitzer

Part III UK perspectives of public relations

6 Public relations or simply product publicity? An exploration of the role of public relations in the UK retail sector 135
Danny Moss, Gary Warnaby and Louise Thame

7 Business and organizational consequences of the moral role of the public relations practitioner 159
Jon White

8 A comparative analysis of public relations in Austria and the United Kingdom 170
Toby MacManus

Part IV Central and Northern European perspectives of public relations

9 Towards a metaphorical theory of public relations 199
Henrik Rebel

10 Legitimacy and strategy of different companies: a perspective of external and internal public relations 225
Inger Jensen

11 Communication: magical mystery or scientific concept? Professional views of public relations practitioners in the Netherlands 247
Betteke van Ruler

12 Towards fourth wave public relations: a case study 264
Dejan Verčič

Concluding remarks 280
References 282
Index 307

Figures

7.1 The task of the public relations practitioner 164
9.1 The psychological system of self (personality) 205
9.2 A model of corporate identity 207
9.3 Image, identity and ideality in perspective 216
9.4 The cognitive relations between images, attitudes and values 217
9.5 The role of images in the personological model 220
10.1 Legitimate field of activities 230
10.2 Communicative relationships 231
10.3 The strategic concepts of companies: the balance between economic and substantive objectives 232
10.4 The reference of legitimacy to systems or life-world 235
10.5 The dependency of employee involvement on identification 242
10.6 Analytical matrix I 243
10.7 Analytical matrix II 245

Tables

6.1 Research findings: summary of characteristics of the
    public relations function   149
6.2 Research findings: summary of characteristics of the
    public relations function   150
6.3 Research findings: summary of characteristics of the
    public relations function   151
8.1 Hofstede's cultural dimensions for Austria, the UK and
    Sweden   178
8.2 Response to question 1   183
8.3 Percentage of 'no' responses to question II by UK and
    Austria   187
11.1 Essence and contribution compared   258
11.2 Description of communication, compared with a
    description of the essence of communication policy   261
12.1 Probabilities of communication behaviour obtained on
    the Slovenian sample   270
12.2 Control sample   270

List of contributors

Dr Barbara Baerns

Professor Dr Barbara Baerns is Head of the Center of Public Relations Studies in the Institute of Media and Communications Research at the Department of Communications Science at the Free University of Berlin. Having obtained her Doctorate in 1967 from the Free University of Berlin, Barbara Baerns completed a second Doctoral thesis in 1982 leading to recognition of *venia legendi* status (Rhur University of Bochum). She is political editor of the *Neue Hannoversche Presse* and the *Neue Rhur/NeueRhein Zeeitung*. She has also worked in the Department of the US Information Centre Hannover and was head of the Public Relations Department of Coca Cola (Coca Cola Central Europe) in Essen.

Günter Bentele

Günter Bentele is a full professor at the University of Leipzig and holds the first chair of public relations to be appointed in Germany. He is the author, co-author, editor and co-editor of 23 books and has written more than 80 scientific articles in the fields of communications theory, film and media semiotics, journalism and public relations. Among his latest publications is 'PR Ausbildung in Deutschland' (Public Relations Education in Germany) written with Peter Szyszka in 1995. Günter Bentele is currently President of the Deutsche Gesellschaft fur Publizistik und Kommunikationswissenschaft (DGPuK) (German Association for Public Communication and Communication Studies).

James E. Grunig

James E. Grunig is a professor of public relations in the College of Journalism of the University of Maryland, USA. He has published x List of contributors

over 150 articles, books, chapters, papers and reports. His most
influential publications include: *Managing Public Relations* (co-
authored with Tod Hunt) and *Excellence in Public Relations and
Communications Management* (editor). He has won the three major
awards in public relations: the Pathfinder Award for Excellence in
public relations research, awarded by the Institute of Public Relations
Research and Education; the Outstanding Educator Award from the
Public Relations Society of America (PRSA); and the Jackson, Jackson and Wagner Award for behavioural science research made by the
PRSA Foundation. James Grunig directs a $400,000 research project
for the International Association of Business Communicators
Research Foundation on excellence in public relations and communications management.

Dr Larissa Grunig

Dr Larissa Grunig, associate professor, teaches public relations and
communications research on the faculty of the College of Journalism
at the University of Maryland, USA. In 1989, Dr Grunig received the
Pathfinder Award for excellence in research, sponsored by the Institute of Public Relations Research and Education (USA). She was
founding co-editor of the *Journal of Public Relations Research* and
has written more than one hundred articles, book chapters, monographs, reviews and conference papers on public relations, activism,
science writing, feminist theory, communications theory and research.

Inger Jensen

Inger Jensen is an associate professor at the University of Roskilde in
Denmark where she is Head of Business Studies and Public Relations
Studies. She was one of the initiators of the Master's Degree Programme in Public Relations at the University. She is also President of
CERP – Education Research Committee and has published a number
of articles and has contributed papers to a large number of conferences on public relations.

Anja Kutscher-Klink

Anja Kutscher-Klink, MA is a public relations assistant with Partner
für Berlin-Gesellschaft für Hauptstadtmarketing MBH. She was born
in Bremen in 1968, took her school-leaving exam (Abitur) in 1987
and then studied media and communication science, information
science, and business administration at the Free University of Berlin
from 1988 to 1994. Her main subject areas were public relations,
marketing and information management and her Master's dissertation

was 'Public Relations for Communities in East and West Germany. State of the Art and Criticism'. She has had practical training in a community press office and in the section for the promotion of trade and industry of the World Trade Centre in Bremen.

Toby MacManus

Toby MacManus is a senior lecturer at the Department of Communication and Marketing, Bournemouth University, UK. He lectures in public relations and marketing, and is currently engaged in research about international public relations. He has written several papers and articles on European, cultural and sociological aspects of public relations, and contributed to the teaching of the MA programme in European Public Relations at the Free University of Berlin, and Hogeschool Eindhoven. From 1991–1994 he was President of the CERP Education Research Committee.

Danny Moss

Danny Moss is currently co-Director of the Centre for Corporate and Public Affairs at the Manchester Metropolitan University (MMU) and is Course Leader for both the full-time and part-time Master's Degrees in Public Relations at the University. Danny Moss has lectured on public relations in a number of countries including at the University of Orebro in Sweden, Ball State University in America as well as presenting papers at conferences in Malaysia, Hong Kong, Australia and China. Prior to moving to the MMU in 1992, he held the post of Director of Public Relations programmes at the University of Stirling for some six years where he was responsible for the introduction of the first dedicated Master's Degree in Public Relations in the UK and for the development of a distance learning version of this Master's Degree which was the first such programme to be developed in Europe. Danny Moss is the co-founder and organizer of the International Public Relations Research Symposium which is held annually at Lake Bled in Slovenia. He is also a member of the Academic Council of Educators for the International Public Relations Association and helped to prepare the IPRA Gold Paper No.10 *Customer Satisfaction and Quality in Public Relations*. Danny Moss has had a number of articles published in UK and European journals and is the author of several books including *Public Relations in Practice: A Casebook* and is working on two further books on public relations which are due for publication in the next twelve months.

Henrik-Jan Rebel

Henrik-Jan Rebel studied political science at the Calvinist Free University in Amsterdam, majoring in political theory, philosophy of science and methodology. After several teaching assignments in sociology and social philosophy, he had to fulfil his military service as a journalist at the Dutch MoD. In the aftermath he was offered a research assignment at the MoD for the study of public opinion in problems of war and peace and for the evaluation of governmental communication. After more than ten years of research for the government he moved to Nijenrode Business University as a researcher in marketing communication. He received a Ph.D. in political psychology at the University of Utrecht, writing a dissertation on modelling personal opinions. Finally, he was appointed at the Hogeschool van Utrecht (at the School for Communication Management as a senior lecturer in communication theory and co-ordinator of applied communication research.

Benno Signitzer

Benno Signitzer is an Associate Professor in the Department of Journalism and Communications at Salzberg University, Austria. He is Head of the Department's public relations and organizational communications courses. He is a member of the Confederation of European Public Relations (CERP) Education and the International Council of the International Public Relations Association (IPRA). He has published a number of books and articles including *Using Communication Theory: An Introduction to Planned Communication*, (co-authored with Sven Whindahl).

Louise Thame

Louise Thame graduated from Manchester Metropolitan University in 1994 with a BA (Hons) Degree in Retail Marketing. She now works as a consultant for the Reton Group, a specialist retail management consultancy based in London. Louise Thame assisted Danny Moss and Gary Warnaby with the field research for their chapter on the role of public relations in the UK retail sector.

Betteke van Ruler

Dr Betteke van Ruler is chair of the Department of public relations at the faculty of Communication and Journalism of the Hogeschool Van Utrecht, the Netherlands. She lectures in public relations, public information and communication science. She has published many articles on public relations and Communication management. Her dissertation was on the critical role of Communication theory-in-use for public relations and Communication management. She is currently engaged in research on public affairs. Betteke van Ruler is a member of the ICA, CERP, BvC, and the VVO.

Dejan Verčič

Dejan Verčič is a director of Pristop Communications Group, Ljubljana, Slovenia, the only full-service public relations firm in Slovenia. Within the Pristop Group he is director of the PR Institute, the research arm of the firm. He holds an MSc. Degree in Communications Science from the University of Ljubljana and is currently a doctoral student in the Organizational Psychology programme at the London School of Economics. Dejan Verčič is also the co-founder of the International Public Relations Symposium which is held annually at Lake Bled in Slovenia.

Gary Warnaby

Gary Warnaby is a Senior Lecturer in the Department of Retailing and Marketing at the Manchester Metropolitan University, where he is currently the course leader of the part time version of the MA in Public Relations. He is currently working with Danny Moss on research into the strategic role of public relations in organizations and has published a number of articles on the subject of strategy and strategic management.

Dr Jon White

Jon White is a consultant in management, organizational development and public affairs. Previously he worked at Cranfield University School of Management, where he was responsible for the School's teaching and research activities in public relations, public affairs and corporate communications. Jon White has written extensively on public affairs, public relations and corporate communications and has published *How to Understand and Manage Public Relations* (Business Books 1991), *Excellence in Public Relations and Communications Management* (Lawrence Erlbaum and Associates 1992), with James Grunig and others, and more recently, *Strategic Communications Management: Making Public Relations Work*, with Laura Mazur (Addison-Wesley 1995). He has also written a number of management case studies. He holds a doctorate from the London School of Economics and Political Science, where he also teaches corporate communications. In addition to his connection with City University, he is an associate of the BNFL Corporate Communications

Unit at the University of Salford, and a visiting teacher for the Judge Institute of Management Studies at the University of Cambridge. He has research links with the University of Maryland, San Diego State and Syracuse Universities in the United States.

Preface

In the late 1980s, The Public Relations Society of America (PRSA) asked a group of academics and practitioners to identify the literature that defines the profession. In 1988, The Task Force of PRSA Research Committee published the initial works to be codified in what was termed the Public Relations Body of Knowledge. The 'Body of Knowledge' was updated in 1990 and 1993. However, on closer examination, it becomes clear that this so-called body of knowledge of public relations, contains few, if any, references to work conducted outside the United States and thus reflects a predominantly North American bias.

This North American bias in the works included in the 'Body of Knowledge' to date is perhaps understandable, given that American Universities have dominated the teaching of, and research into, the subject of public relations until relatively recently. However, since the Second World War the practice of public relations has developed and become dispersed around the globe, albeit that the pace of development has been extremely varied with some countries, such as the UK, demonstrating much more sophisticated patterns of practice than, for example, other parts of Europe or the Far East. The formal teaching of public relations as a discipline in UK and other European Universities is a relatively recent phenomenon, commencing only in the late 1980s. Although there has been a rapid expansion in the number of courses in public relations and in the number of academics working in this field in Europe over the past ten years, it would perhaps be unrealistic to expect to find a significant body of research to have emerged in such a short period.

However, a considerable amount of scholarly work has been undertaken throughout Europe over the past ten years which has laid the foundations for the development of a substantive and distinctive

European body of knowledge about the concept and practice of public relations. The problem has been that much of this work has tended to take place in a very fragmented manner, with relatively little co-operation between the academics and practitioners working in each respective European country. Moreover, the work that has been undertaken in the public relations field has reflected the very different research traditions within Europe which has, if anything, compounded the problems of creating a unified 'body of knowledge'. As a result, it is impossible to claim that a single coherent 'European body of knowledge' about public relations yet exists in Europe.

The fact that, until recently, US academics and practitioners have dominated research and writing in this field, has also prevented much of the work that has been undertaken in Europe from receiving due recognition. The fragmented development of the discipline in Europe is also evidenced in the lack of cross-referencing of the work of different researchers in any of the European, let alone, US public relations texts. Furthermore, although European academics and practitioners are in touch with the work of their colleagues in the USA, the reverse cannot be said to be the case.

Therefore, at present, it would be impossible to attempt to publish a comprehensive European public relations body of knowledge – only a collection of national bodies of knowledge. The fragmented nature of the academic base underpinning the practice in Europe has also undoubtedly hindered attempts to gain recognition for public relations as a true profession: medicine is medicine wherever it is practised; whether the same can be said for public relations is very hard to say.

It was the recognition of the need to bring together the various strands of research into public relations being undertaken in Europe that lay behind the organization of the first International Public Relations Symposium, which was held in Bled, Slovenia in July 1994. Nearly one hundred participants – both academics and practitioners – attended the Symposium, representing some twelve European countries. The Symposium was also attended by a small number of academics from the USA. A selection of the best papers presented at the Symposium are contained as chapters in this volume.

Because of the diversity of themes found within the chapters we have chosen to group them by region or country rather than attempting to find what would inevitably prove a more tenuous basis for linking individual chapters together. The very diversity of the subject matter on which the chapters contained in this volume focus, serves to illustrate the rich multi-diciplinary domain of public relations and the variety of research interests pursued by scholars working in this field.

We believe that students and scholars of public relations will find the chapters contained in this volume will help to stimulate their interest in further exploration of the many dimensions of this still emerging disciplinary field, and we hope that they may suggest new directions in which research to extend our understanding of the theory and practice of public relations can be developed.

Ultimately, it is our intention that this book should mark a further step towards the creation of what will become an extensive European body of knowledge in the field of public relations which will help enrich the existing predominantly North American bias within the literature.

In organizing the chapters selected for inclusion in this book we have divided them into four sections. In each case, a brief introduction has been provided to the chapters contained in that section. These four sections represent American, Austro-German, Central and Northern European and UK perspectives of public relations.

Acknowledgements

We would like to thank the organizations listed below for their generous support of the first Public Relations Research Symposium held at Lake Bled in Slovenia in July 1994. Without their support it would not have been possible to organize what was the first symposium devoted to public relations research to be held in Europe. The chapters contained in this monograph have been drawn from amongst the papers presented at the Symposium.

PRISTOP Communications Group, Slovenia
Republic of Slovenia Ministry of Science and Technology
Government of the Republic of Slovenia, Public Relations and Media
   Office
Adriatic d.d., Slovenia
HIT d.o.o, Slovenia
Krka, p.o., Slovenia
Mobitel d.d., Slovenia
SKB banka, Slovena

We must also acknowledge the work of both Andrew Newman and Gary Warnaby of the Manchester Metropolitan University who contributed to the editing and preparation of the text, particularly with regard to a number of the chapters submitted by European authors.

Part I

American perspectives of public relations

The first section of the book contains chapters by two of the most prolific and eminent academics currently working in the field of public relations – Jim and Larissa Grunig of the University of Maryland. Both these chapters reflect the established traditions of research which these two academics have been pursuing for a number of years and build on the research themes that have provided the basis for many of the studies of public relations that have been conducted by both students and academics working in this field in recent years.

Jim Grunig's chapter revisits the origins of his 'situational theory of publics' and reviews the evolution of this theory about how and why people communicate and how these different communications behaviours affect the outcome of communications programmes. The chapter explores how the concepts of 'public opinion' and 'publics' have been defined in the literature and explores how theories for segmenting the general population into relevant groups for communication puposes have evolved. It reviews Grunig's original situational theory of publics and goes on to discuss the more recent refinements which he has made to the original theory both in terms of conceptual and methodological improvements. Here Grunig distiguishes between the internal and external dimensions of the three original independent variables in the theory – problem recognition, level of involvement and constraint recognition. Grunig also draws on theories of cognitive psychology to extend our understanding of the effects of communication by identifying new types of cognitive structures for publics associated with the theory. The chapter concludes by reporting on the results of several new studies conducted in the US to test these new concepts.

This chapter also provides a valuable summary of the current level of understanding of the behaviour of publics and offers valuable insights into how the situational theories can be used to help explain the communications behaviour of specific groups of people with whom an organization may need to communicate.

Larissa Grunig's chapter examines the research approach used by the research team in course of carrying out the so-called 'Excellence study' sponsored by the International Association of Business Communicators (IABC) in the USA during the early 1990s. Larissa Grunig points to the use of a variety of research methodologies in conducting this essentially comparative study of public relations practice within over three hundred US and European organizations. The paper reflects on the experience gained by the researchers in course of conducting the exellence study and argues that the notion of requisite variety (Weick 1978) holds important implications for the composition of research teams undertaking research amongst a diverse range of organizations. The paper concludes by highlighting the implications for researchers engaging on basic or applied research projects in public relations.

Thus, this chapter offers some useful guidance to those involved in the design and management of public relations research projects. It advocates the need for greater sensitivity to the way in which different research approaches can be combined to provide a more rounded and complete picture of the phenomena under investigation and highlights some of the potential dangers inherent in relying too heavily on a single set of paradigmatic assumptions with respect to any given discipline. Here Larissa Grunig calls for greater recognition of the need for requisite variety in research teams engaged in the study of contemporary public relations practice and argues that such an approach can foster a healthier respect for alternative explanations of the phenomena under investigation.

1 A situational theory of publics: conceptual history, recent challenges and new research

James E. Grunig

PUBLIC RELATIONS AND PUBLIC OPINION

The concept of public opinion has been an enduring part of public relations theories ever since Bernays (1923) took the concept from late 19th and early 20th Century sociologists and psychologists and applied it to public relations in his classic book, *Crystallizing Public Opinion*. In his words:

> The character and origins of public opinion, the factors that make up the individual mind and the group mind must be understood if the profession of public relations counsel is to be intelligently practiced and its functions and possibilities accurately estimated. . . . The public relations counsel works with that vague, little-understood indefinite material called public opinion. Public opinion is a term describing an ill-defined, mercurial and changeable group of individual judgements. Public opinion is the aggregate result of individual opinions – now uniform, now conflicting – of the men and women who make up society or any group of society.
>
> (1923: 61)

Cutlip and Center (1958) opened their chapter 'Persuasion and Public Opinion', in an early edition of their classic textbook, with the summary statement: 'The power of public opinion must be faced, understood, and dealt with. It provides the psychological environment in which organizations prosper or perish' (1958: 58). In the first paragraph of the chapter, they added that the basic objective of public relations 'is either to *change* or *neutralize* hostile opinions, to *crystallize* unformed or latent opinions in your favour, or to *conserve* favourable opinions' (1958: 59). More recently, Sauerhaft and Atkins (1989:13) defined public relations as 'the art and science of informing, influencing, changing, or neutralizing public opinion'.

In essence, then, public opinion is both a cause and effect of public relations activities. The power of public opinion affects management decisions, and it is the role of public relations professionals to identify that opinion and to communicate and explain it to management. In addition, the stated objective for most public relations programmes is to affect public opinion. For such an important concept, however, it is surprising that few public relations practitioners understand the nature either of 'publics' or of 'opinions' and that even fewer have a practical way of identifying publics and measuring their opinions. Most practitioners seem to equate public opinion with the content of the media and cling to the notion that if they can change the content of the media they will have affected public opinion. Although most contemporary practitioners talk about the need to measure the effects of what they do, few in practice ever do research.[1] Those that do research generally commission commercial firms to do surveys of attitudes of the general population – surveys that in my opinion have relatively little value in the planning or evaluation of public relations programmes (see J. Grunig and Hunt 1984, Chapter 9). That most public relations research is survey research should not be surprising, because in practice the survey research industry has come to equate the concept of public opinion with the results of polls of the general population.

The current superficial understanding of public opinion by both public relations practitioners and pollsters stands in stark contrast to the long history of theoretical discussion and applied research devoted to the subject. Price (1992) opened the first chapter of his book, *Public Opinion*, by stating:

> Public opinion is one of the most vital and enduring concepts in the social sciences. It is widely applied in psychology, sociology, history, political science, and communication research, both in academic and applied settings. Few concepts have engendered as much broad social concern, scientific interest, or intellectual debate. Certainly very few have roots that run as deeply into Western thought.
>
> (1992: 1)

What is a public?

The study of public opinion has centred on two questions: What is the (or a) public? What is the nature of the 'opinions' that the public or multiple publics hold? Price (1992) pointed out that the concept of public opinion originated as a sociological concept at the turn of the century by theorists such as Gabriel Tarde, John Dewey, Walter Lippmann, and Herbert Blumer: ' . . . public opinion was commonly viewed in the early 1900s as a special kind of social-level product – not a collection of separate public opinions but instead the opinion of *a* public' (Price 1992: 23). The opinion of a public, then, was something developed through discussion and debate. Publics, in this early theory, formed around issues – publics that waxed and waned as problems and issues changed. Publics also differed in the extent to which they were active or passive (attentive, active, or elite) (1992: 24–43). The more active the publics, the more likely they were to have well-organized opinions and to use those opinions to guide their behaviours.

With the advent of survey research in the 1930s, according to Price, it became difficult to measure the opinions of 'fluid and complexly structured' publics. Thus, the classic concept of a public gave way to the simpler concept of 'an aggregate "one person, one vote" conception' (1992: 34). The concept of public opinion, therefore, was replaced by measures of *mass opinion*. Concepts such as a 'general public'[2] and 'mass publics,' which would have been oxymorons to the classic theorists, began to dominate both professional and lay thinking about public opinion. Price pointed out that the pioneers of public opinion polling justified this move in democratic terms: 'The commitment to viewing the public as inclusive of all members of society was a populist, democratic decision' (1992: 36).

The populist notion that most people have opinions on most issues persists in the mind of many public relations practitioners today – and especially in the minds of their client organizations. Thus, practitioners and their clients either fear that media coverage will move mass opinion against them or hope that if they 'get their message out' that mass opinion will support them. As a result, public relations programmes typically are unfocused, and the expectations for their effects are unrealistic.

Writing recently in the Washington Post, columnist Richard Harwood (1994) pointed out the folly of these expectations and the shortcomings of most polls of the general population. Harwood contrasted polls showing that about two-thirds of the people interviewed in the United States, Canada, Britain, and France thought that 'things were going badly in their countries.' At the same time, polls showed that 85 percent of the people in the United States 'were quite satisfied with the way things were going in their own lives; nearly 70 percent said things were going well in their own communities' (1994: A21).

In spite of the extensive attention the media have paid to certain news stories, Harwood said that only a small portion of the population cares about or is aware of these stories:

> Every few weeks the Times-Mirror Center for the People & the Press takes soundings of popular reaction to major news stories. In May, the centre reported that only a third of us 'knew that a presidential candidate in Mexico was recently assassinated; 80 percent of us didn't know that North Korea was threatening to withdraw from the nuclear non-proliferation agreement, which has again raised the specter of war on the Korean peninsula.' About 80 percent of us couldn't identify Vince Foster, the White House aide who committed suicide last year, only 14 percent were following events in Haiti, and only 12 percent were following the brutal events in Rwanda. Nearly two-thirds paid little attention to Richard Nixon's death. The same huge majority paid little attention to the caning in Singapore of an American teenager, to the congressional ban on assault weapons or to the administration's health care proposal. More than 60 percent were unaware that the stock market has been in a slide. . . .
>
> We are told, for example, that crime is the biggest social issue in the country. Yet when people were asked a few months ago to define 'the biggest problem facing you and your family' only 4 percent mentioned fear of crime or violence. Their primary concern was a lack of money to make ends meets. On the list of untended national problems, only 2 percent mentioned welfare abuse and only one percent (whites and blacks combined) mentioned gun control, racism, or taxes.
>
> (1994: A 21)

Harwood concluded: 'It is fair to say that "public opinion" exists very spottily in this country – if it exists at all – and that "well-informed" public opinion is even scarcer' (1994: A21). Scholars, public relations practitioners, and the lay person typically react to such a conclusion by saying, 'What a pity!', or by blaming the people for their passivity, ignorance, or lack of interest. However, if we return to the classic theories of publics, such results are to be expected and can be explained easily. Human beings simply do not have the time or the ability to be concerned about every problem in the world. They devote their time and energy to the problems that involve them and for which they can make a difference. What appears to be a small portion of the 'general public' concerned about a problem like gun control or racism actually is a large public. And when those publics engage actively in discussion and behaviour related to the issues, they can interfere with or support the missions of organizations who create the problems or whose mission is to solve the problems.

What is an opinion?

In the same way that the concept of a public has been confused or lost in the last 100 years, so too has there been confusion about the meaning of 'opinion'. In the middle of this century, theorists typically conceptualized opinion as the expression of an underlying attitude or the application of attitudes to specific situations or issues (Price 1992: 45–71). Over time, however, opinions came to be seen more as cognitive and superficial responses to specific issues rather than an expression of an underlying attitude. Researchers also began to apply other psychological concepts such as schema, values and group identification to the concept of public opinion.

The 'opinions' held by publics, then, can be any psychological or sociological construct held by publics that can be affected by communication behaviours. In public relations circles in the United States today, the concept of 'behavioural outcomes' has become more popular than 'changes in public opinion' as a desired outcome of public relations programmes.[4] Loosely constructed, then, the 'opinion' in 'public opinion' could be the perceptions, cognitions, attitudes, or behaviours of publics. In other words, I will use the loose concept of 'opinion' to refer to the 'outcomes' of the communication behaviour of publics. It is important, therefore, to sort out what outcomes are possible before choosing objectives for public relations programs and developing measures of those objectives for evaluation purposes – just as it is to conceptualize the publics with which organizations need to build relationships before developing communication programmes.

A programme of research on publics

For nearly 30 years, I have developed, researched and improved a situational theory of communication behaviour that addresses the questions of 'What is a public?' and 'What are the "opinions" of publics?'. The theory explains why people communicate and when they are most likely to communicate. It explains how predicted communication behaviour can be used to segment the mass population into publics likely to communicate about one or more problems. The theory also explains when cognitive, attitudinal and behavioural effects of communication are most likely to occur, and the publics for which those effects occur most often. Finally, the theory explains when publics develop from loose aggregations of individuals into organized activist groups that apply the pressure of their 'public opinion' to organizations that employ public relations professionals.

The theory that has resulted from the programme of research thus provides answers to the following specific questions, each of which has great relevance for public relations practitioners who need a theory of public opinion on which to base their practice and as a framework for the applied research that is badly needed but seldom conducted in the field:

- What are publics and how do they arise?
- With which publics is it possible to communicate and how can one communicate most effectively with each kind of public?
- When and why do members of active publics join activist groups?
- What communication effects are possible with each kind of public?
- How do activist publics differ from publics that have an intellectual interest in an issue but do not get actively involved with the issue?

As the situational theory has developed over the years, it has become an important component of a general theory of public relations (J. Grunig 1992) – especially of two major components of that general theory, the strategic management of public relations (Grunig and Repper 1992) and the two-way symmetrical model of public relations (J. Grunig and L. Grunig 1992). This chapter, therefore, reviews the intellectual history of the situational theory, recent research on the theory and resulting improvements in it, and remaining unanswered research questions related to the theory.

THE SITUATIONAL THEORY OF PUBLICS

At its current level of development, the situational theory provides a means of segmenting a general population into groups relevant to public relations practitioners. Thus, it is similar to theories of market segmentation. Marketing theorists provide several criteria for choosing a concept for segmentation: segments must be mutually exclusive, measurable, accessible, pertinent to an organization's mission, and large enough to be substantial. Most importantly, however, the market segments must have a 'differential response' to market strategies (Kotler and Andreasen 1987: 124). The situational theory of publics has been designed to predict the differential responses most important to public relations professionals: responsiveness to issues; amount of and nature of communication behaviour; effects of communication on cognitions, attitudes, and behaviour; and the likelihood of participating in collective behaviour to pressure organizations.

Development of the theory began with the assumption that two of the classic theorists of public opinion, John Dewey (1927, 1938, 1939) and Herbert Blumer (1946), first made about publics: Publics arise around issues or problems that affect them (see also J. Grunig and Hunt 1984: 143–5). Dewey also recognized the crucial role that publics play in American democracy: after recognizing that problems affect them, publics organize into issue groups to pressure organizations that cause the problems or to pressure government to constrain or regulate those organizations. The situational theory improves upon the classical conceptions of publics, then, by formalizing those theories and providing means for identifying and measuring publics and their opinions.[5]

Publics, therefore, begin as disconnected systems of individuals experiencing common problems; but they can evolve into organized and powerful activist groups. The concept of a public is extremely useful for public relations practitioners. Organizations need public relations because their behaviours create problems that create publics, which may evolve into activist groups that create issues and threaten the autonomy of organizations. Activist groups themselves use public relations to make publics aware of the effects that issues have on them and to organize coalitions of publics to work with the activist group.

In its present state, the situational theory consists of two dependent variables (active and passive communication behaviour) and three independent variables (problem recognition, constraint recognition and level of involvement). Recent research has added cognitive, attitudinal and behavioural effects to the list of dependent variables. The two dependent variables, active and passive communication behaviour, also can be called information seeking and processing. Information seeking describes what Clarke and Kline (1974) called 'premeditated information seeking' – the 'planned scanning of the environment for messages about a specified topic'. Information processing describes what Clarke and Kline called 'message discovery' – 'the unplanned discovery of a message followed by continued processing of it'.

The independent variables are situational variables in the sense that they describe the perceptions that people have of specific situations, especially situations that are problematic or that produce conflicts or issues. The situational definition provides a logical connection between these concepts and the idea of classical theorists that issues, problems, or situations create publics that change over time. The three independent variables, therefore, can be defined as follows:

1 Problem recognition – people detect that something should be done about a situation and stop to think about what to do.
2 Constraint recognition – people perceive that there are obstacles in a situation that limit their ability to do anything about the situation.
3 Level of involvement – the extent to which people connect themselves with a situation.

The theory states, and previous research has confirmed, that high problem recognition and low constraint recognition increase both active information seeking and passive information processing. Level of involvement increases information seeking, but it has less effect on information processing. Stated differently, people seldom seek information about situations that do not involve them. Yet, they will randomly process information about low-involvement situations, especially if they also recognize the situation as problematic. Because people participate more actively in information seeking than in information processing, information seeking and the independent variables that precede it produce communication effects more often than information processing. In particular, people communicating actively develop more organized cognitions, are more likely to have attitudes about a situation and more often engage in a behaviour to do something about the situation (J. Grunig and Ipes 1983; J. Grunig 1982a).

This, then, is a basic statement of the theory. To understand how the theory developed to its present state, however, it is useful to look briefly at its intellectual history.

Intellectual history of the theory

I published the first version of what is now the situational theory in a monograph (Grunig 1968) on the relationship between communication and economic decision making. Based on theories of decision making from economics and psychology, I theorized that individuals seek information actively when they make genuine rather than habitual decisions. I used Dewey's (1938) concept of a problematic situation to predict that people would seek information actively when they recognize that a situation presents a problem and that they would seek reinforcing information – as predicted by theories of cognitive dissonance – when they do not recognize a problem and behave habitually. Already, the theory was situational: problem recognition was not a trait that people took from situation to situation; it was a perception of a person that a specific situation is problematic.

I developed a second independent variable, constraint recognition, while studying decision and communication behaviours of large landowners (J. Grunig 1969) and peasants (J. Grunig 1971) in Colombia. These studies showed that people have little need to communicate in situations where constraints prevent people from making choices – which especially are prevalent in a developing country but also are common for people everywhere.

At this point, I conceptualized communication behaviour as purposive and active: a tool for solving problems. Thus, the theory fitted into the tradition of uses and gratifications theories, which are based on the assumption that people seek information actively. In J. Grunig (1976), I added Krugman's (1965) concept of level of involvement to the theory to explain passive communication behaviour (which I called information processing) as well as active communication behaviour (which I called information seeking).[6] I defined level of involvement as a perception that people have of a situation, whereas Krugman had defined it as a characteristic of a medium and Ray (1973) and Rothschild and Ray (1974) as a characteristic of a product. When people perceive that they have a personal connection with a situation (an involvement), I predicted, they search actively for information as well as process it passively. When involvement is low, they process information passively that is available without a premeditated search; but they do not search for it actively.

At this stage of his research, I also included a fourth independent variable in the situational theory, the presence of a referent criterion – using Carter's (1965) term. The referent criterion was defined as a solution carried from previous situations to a new situation. Thus the referent criterion reduced the need for a person to seek additional information in the new situation. Several studies, however (e.g. J. Grunig and Disbrow 1977), found that the referent criterion had little effect on communication behaviour. It was more of an effect of communication than a cause, and it was treated as a dependent variable in some studies (e.g. J. Grunig 1983a). The referent criterion now has been dropped in favour of two other cognitive and attitudinal variables. I had defined 'referent criterion' at times to be what now appears to a 'schema' and at other times to be what now appears to be a 'cross-situational attitude'.

Throughout its development, the situational theory could be specified as two regression equations. The following two equations, for example, are taken from J. Grunig and Disbrow (1977) at a point when involvement had been added to the theory and referent criterion was still included. The standardized Beta weights were calculated from data on environmental issues. They fitted the theoretical predictions almost perfectly but did show the weak effect of the referent criterion:[7]

AC = .20PR + .11LI − .16CR − .01RC
PC = .26PR + .03LI − .13CR − .03RC
where:
    AC = active communication behaviour
    PC = passive communication behaviour
    PR = problem recognition
    LI = level of involvement
    CR = constraint recognition
    RC = presence of a referent criterion

J. Grunig and Disbrow (1977) and J. Grunig (1979b, 1982a, 1983a) also used combinations of the four variables, after they were dichotomized, to segment publics for different situational issues. In these studies, we then calculated conditional probabilities to predict the likelihood that each public for each issue would engage in the two communication behaviours − probabilities that could be used to plan communication programmes for each public (see J. Grunig and Hunt 1984, Chapters 7 and 8). In addition, J. Grunig (1982a, 1983a) calculated probabilities of several communication effects for the different combinations of variables. The effects included retention of a message, holding of cognitions and attitudes and the occurrence of individual behaviours. The probabilities for the most active public, for example, (high problem recognition and involvement, low constraint recognition and referent criterion present) as compared with the least active public were 99 per cent vs. 63 per cent for passive communication behaviour, 77 per cent vs. 20 per cent for active communication behaviour, 48 per cent vs. 34 per cent for message retention, 99 per cent vs. 65 per cent for holding of a cognition, 98 per cent vs. 74 per cent for holding of an attitude, and 52 per cent vs. 65 per cent for behaviour (J. Grunig 1982a: 189).

Next, I developed a methodology over several studies to identify publics arising around particular situational issues, publics that public relations practitioners can use to target communication programmes (J. Grunig, 1975, 1977b, 1978, 1979b, 1982a, 1982b, 1983a, 1983b;

J. Grunig *et al*, 1988). A typical study began by identifying several related problems about which an organization might need to communicate with its stakeholders. For example, J. Grunig (1983a) used eight problems (such as air pollution, extinction of whales, and strip mining) in two studies of environmental publics. I then used canonical correlation to simultaneously correlate the independent variables (problem recognition, involvement, constraint recognition) with the dependent variables (active and passive communication behaviour) for all of the situations – thus testing the basic theory. I then used the canonical variates as profiles of the active and passive publics arising from the set of situations studied. Canonical correlation makes it possible to simultaneously correlate the independent and dependent variables of the situational theory – thus testing the basic theory. At the same time, canonical correlation produces one or more canonical variates that are much like the factors that result from factor analysis. The canonical variates can be used to identify publics arising from the set of situations studied – thus providing a segmented profile of actively and passively communicating publics that public relations and other communication professionals can use to target and plan their programmes.

Originally I believed this profile of publics would be unique to each set of situations studied. These sets of situations have included environmental, public affairs, consumer, social responsibility, and employee issues (see Part III of J. Grunig and Hunt 1984, for summaries of most of these studies). However, the canonical variates produced by this research have defined four kinds of publics consistently enough to assume they have theoretical regularity:

1 All-issue publics – publics active on all of the problems.
2 Apathetic publics – publics inattentive to all of the problems.
3 Single-issue publics – publics active on one or a small subset of the problems that concerns only a small part of the population. Such problems have included the slaughter of whales or the controversy over the sale of infant formula in third-world countries.
4 Hot-issue publics – publics active only on a single problem that involves nearly everyone in the population and that has received extensive media coverage (such as the gasoline shortage, drunken driving, or toxic waste disposal).[8]

Examples of applied studies using the theory

The situational theory has been applied widely in academic research on public relations. It has been used to identify employee publics of an electric utility and a telephone company (J. Grunig 1975), scientific organizations (J. Grunig 1977b; Pelham 1977; Schneider [aka L. Grunig] 1978; L. Grunig 1985), educational systems (J. Grunig 1985, 1987; J. Grunig and Theus 1986), a community college (Waddell 1979), and a municipal government (Jeffers 1989a); members of an association (J. Grunig 1979c); consumer publics of a supermarket chain (J. Grunig 1974a); community publics of a hospital (J. Grunig 1978; J. Grunig and Disbrow 1977), a local government (Conley 1977), and a prison (Jenkins 1976); environmental publics (J. Grunig 1983a, 1989b; J. Grunig and Disbrow 1977; Essich 1984; Major 1993a; Abugov 1985); agricultural publics (J. Grunig, Nelson, Richburg and White 1988; Turner 1981; Myers 1985); readers of a specialized agricultural magazine (Jeffers 1989b); student publics for an economic education programme (J. Grunig 1982b); reporter publics for business issues (J. Grunig 1983b); corporate publics for social responsibility issues (J. Grunig 1979b, 1982a); publics for campaigns on drunk driving (J. Grunig and Ipes 1983), AIDS (J. Grunig and Childers 1988), and fire safety (Spicer 1985); users of an information service for the disabled (Al-Doory [aka Ramsey] 1974); publics of the Federal Reserve System (Baldwin 1989); readers of science news (Bishop 1983), an issues newsletter (Davis-Belcher 1990), and a university magazine (Gibbs 1986); donor publics of a fund-raising programme (Kelly 1979); publics for the election of a governor (Hamilton 1992); publics in Hong Kong related to the return of the colony to China in 1997 (Atwood and Cheng 1986); and publics arising from a natural disaster (Major 1993b).

It is likely that the theory has been used in far more studies because graduate students at universities other than the University of Maryland frequently have consulted me about using the theory and to get a copy of a questionnaire to apply it to their thesis research. Professionals also frequently ask about the theory, and it is cited frequently in the newsletter *pr reporter*. It is impossible in this chapter, therefore, to review all of these studies. Instead, I will review a few of my own studies to provide examples of the research and the results it produces.

Two major studies of environmental publics were reported in J. Grunig (1983a) from research that was funded in part by the US National Wildlife Federation. The first study was conducted in 1976 on an urban sample from four major cities: Washington, Baltimore, Chicago and Cleveland. The second study was done in 1977 with a sample from nine rural communities in Maryland, Missouri and Washington State. Eight environmental issues were included in each study: air pollution, the extinction of whales, the energy shortage, and strip mining in both studies; superhighways in urban areas, disposable cans and bottles, water pollution, and oil spills in the urban study; and dams and flood control projects, effect of pesticides on wildlife, fertilizer run-off in lakes and streams, and nuclear power plants in the rural study.

These two studies were among the first studies using the situational theory to identify the four kinds of publics described above: all-issue, special- or single-issue, hot-issue, and apathetic publics. Factor analysis of the eight produced one set of general environmental issues in each study and three special issues that did not load highly on the single factor produced. The special issues were air pollution, superhighways, and the energy shortage in the urban study and air pollution, energy, and whales in the rural sample. At the time, energy, air pollution, and superhighways were hot issues, and whales were a special-interest issue.

The study also showed that the all-issue, general environmentalist public had the same upper social-economic characteristics that other studies of environmentalists had shown: well-educated, liberal, and upper income. People who normally would not be in environmental publics became members of hot-issue publics when issues such as the energy shortage and air pollution affected them directly. Other publics emerged strictly around special issues that did not affect everyone, producing single-issue publics: whales and superhighways. Demographic variables alone could not identify these publics, but they did help locate them and connect these publics to previous research on environmental communication. These studies also measured the extent to which each of the different publics were knowledgeable about the environment and the extent to which each held cognitions about the issues. Most of the publics held an 'idea', a cognition about the issues that brought about the public. And the all-issues public showed the most knowledge about the environment on a set of multiple-choice questions. Effects variables, however, will be addressed in more detail in the next section of this chapter.

A study of issues related to corporate social responsibility included 11 problems about which corporations could be expected to exercise social responsibility (J. Grunig 1979b). That study used Q factor analysis, rather than canonical correlation, to identify publics. It identified three publics (1979: 755):

1 a large public that is aware of and interested in all of the 11 possible areas of corporate social responsibility but primarily in

responsibilities that are indirect consequences of a firm's basic economic functions;
2 an active public concerned about all of the issues except for making contributions to charities;
3 a public latent in many distant social issues but actively concerned about those issues that affect it directly.

Again, these publics can be considered as an all-issue public (number 2), a special-issue public (number 1) and a hot-issue public (number 3).

A second study of corporate issues (J. Grunig 1982a) identified publics that formed around the four issues of nuclear power, the safety of the Ford Pinto (whose gas tanks allegedly caught fire easily in a rear-end collision), steel import policy, and the Nestlé infant formula controversy. This study identified an all-issue public, a hot-issue public, and a special-issue public. The special-issue public arose around the steel and Pinto issues. Nuclear power, however, was the hot issue, the one that brought about publics that were unconcerned until an issue affected them directly. The activist publics consisted of younger, better educated people who tended to be female.

J. Grunig (1983b) reported a study of publics among Washington reporters on issues of corporate public policy. These issues included deregulation of natural gas, break-up of the Bell system, chemical disposal sites and acid rain. The study differed from others, however, in that the reporters were asked to respond to measures of the situational variables both for themselves and for their readers. As a result, canonical correlation identified publics that were publics of reporters, perceived publics of readers and a combination of the two.

This study again identified the four kinds of publics found in previous studies. The self and reader measures of the situational variables produced two publics motivated mostly by individual information needs of the reporters themselves. One type, in particular, was motivated by the environmental situations. The other was personally motivated by the environmental issues but also by its perception that a reader public would be interested in the Bell system issue. Both of these last two reporter publics were activists, especially on the environmental issues. The public motivated only by self-perceptions of environmental issues also held antibusiness cognitions and attitudes. It consisted of younger and, more often, female reporters who covered the science or environmental beat in Washington.

One other reporter public, however, perceived that readers would include an active environmental public; although the reporters themselves were not such a public. An apathetic public consisted of reporters who did not actively communicate about any of these issues themselves but who did write articles about the environment, based on information that came to them passively, because they perceived that their readers would seek or process environmental information. The hot-issue public in this study formed around the issue of deregulation of natural gas, which at the time would have affected the cost of home heating for large numbers of people.

In summary, then, this research showed that there is a general, all-issues environmental public, even among reporters. There is also a public, even among reporters, that is apathetic about the environment. Other publics arise around special issues like whales or acid rain – people interested in that issue even though it does not involve them personally to any great extent. Most people, no matter how apathetic, however, will form into a hot-issue public for such all-involving issues as a shortage of energy, deregulation of natural gas, disposal of toxic waste, or nuclear power.

Extension of the theory to activist groups

In the next extension of the situational theory I studied members of the activist environmental group, the Sierra Club in the Washington-Baltimore area to determine if the theory could predict which publics would organize into an activist group (J. Grunig 1989). Activist groups are especially important to public relations practitioners because they most limit the autonomy of organizations to pursue their goals.

First, the study determined whether all four kinds of publics – all-issues, single- or special issue-, hot-issue, or apathetic – would be found among members of an activist group. The study was based on four issues: disposal of toxic wastes, acid rain, slaughter of whales and pollution of the Chesapeake Bay. Canonical correlation was used in the same way as in previous studies to identify publics. Three of the four publics were identified. As might be expected, there was no apathetic public. There was an all-issues public, a special-interest public (for the whale issue), and a hot-issue public (for toxic waste and acid rain). The all-issues public, however, was most active in the Sierra Club and belonged to the largest number of environmental organizations. As in the other studies, members of the all-issues public also were most likely to communicate actively about the issues, to construct organized cognitions about the issues, and to engage in individual behaviours related to the issues. Membership and activity in the Sierra Club added participation in collective behaviour to this list of effects.

The second major purpose of the Sierra Club study, then, was to determine the reasons why members of active publics join activist groups. That question had great practical relevance to public relations – to determine whether activist groups really represent their members. Many of the targets of activist groups argue that the leaders of these groups do not represent their members. The question also had theoretical relevance because the literature contains several theoretical explanations for why people join such groups. Pluralists, for example, believed that people join interest groups to pursue common individual interests and that they participate in the group to secure these benefits. According to Moe (1980:2), this 'loosely structured theory of interest groups' served well until economist Olson (1971) published his *Logic of Collective Action* in 1965 (a revised edition was published in 1971).

Olson (1971) upset the conventional wisdom by arguing that participation in interest groups is not in the rational self-interest of individuals unless the group is small or unless members are coerced to join or enticed to join by selective incentives. Olson based his theory on the concept of the collective good. Interest groups seek collective rather than individual goods, Olson argued. Once a collective good is made available to one person it must also be available to all. Examples include a clean environment, tax policy, or national defence. Rational individuals, therefore, realize that they do not have to participate in the group to secure a collective good if someone else will do it for them. Sandman (1982:19) explained Olson's theory well for environmental groups when he said that 'rational self-interest dictates that (people) should pass the buck . . . Everyone is best off if someone else saves the environment'.

In small groups, however, members realize that they must do their share or no one else will. Thus, small groups usually are more effective than large ones. Large groups, such as labour unions, often must coerce members to join, as in the closed union shop. Other large groups seek members by providing selective incentives that are only marginally related to group goals. For example, the American Automobile Association provides insurance and towing; and many professional groups provide insurance, discounts on travel, or publications. The two largest US environmental organizations, the National Wildlife Federation and the Audubon Society, provide members with a magazine.

Olson's theory revolutionized thinking about interest groups, although other theories have been proposed to supplement it. Moe (1980), for example, argued that Olson's theory applies only to economic interest groups. In economic groups, he said, economic motivations supercede political motivations. Tesh (1984:30) added that 'whether contested laws and policies will personally benefit group members or not remains for them an insignificant considera-tion'. According to Moe (1980:6), people may join issue groups, to gain a sense of political efficacy, which is the belief that their con-tributions 'make a difference' in providing some of the collective good. Olson could respond, however, that members make a greater difference in small groups.

Clarke and Wilson (1961) and Wilson (1973) published a widely cited theory of incentives for people to join voluntary organizations. These included:

- Material incentives–such as money or things and services that can be priced in monetary terms.
- Solidary incentives–intangible rewards enjoyed by being a mem-ber of a group, such as 'conviviability of coming together', pres-tige of membership, or collective status.
- Purposive incentives–satisfaction from having contributed to a worthwhile cause even if the member 'contributes nothing but his name'.

When Moe (1980) studied several voluntary organizations, he found that all of these incentives provide people with reasons to join volun-tary organizations, although material incentives predominated in eco-nomic interest groups and purposive and solidary incentives in non-economic groups.

The J. Grunig (1989) study, therefore, determined whether mem-bers of the Sierra Club joined because of one or more of Clarke and Wilson's material, solidary, or purposive or Olson's selective incen-tives. The results showed that members of the active, all-issues public joined an activist group for purposive, political reasons. I coined the term 'delegation of activism' to explain their reasoning. Members of this environmental activist group, at least, seemed to want to delegate their activism to affect policy, even though they might not benefit themselves. The results suggested, then, that an activist group such as the Sierra Club does appear to truly represent its membership; those members do not join for selective or solidary incentives.

'OPINIONS': WHAT COMMUNICATION OUTCOMES ARE POSSIBLE FOR EACH PUBLIC?

As mentioned above, public opinion researchers have debated extensively about the meaning of the concept of 'opinion' and its relationship to such standard psychological variables such as cognitions, attitudes, and behaviours. They also have learned that most members of the 'mass public' do not seem to have organized cognitions or attitudes and have debated extensively about the meaning to that result. Converse (1964), for example, learned that members of the 'mass public' are less likely to have a consistent liberal or conservative ideology than are members of the political elite – their thinking is less likely to be **constrained** by ideology, as Converse expressed it. Non-elites, it seems, are more likely to think about problems in terms of their self-interest than in ideological terms. Nearly 30 years later, Jennings (1992) conducted essentially the same research as Converse and reached the same conclusion. Cantrill (1993), similarly, reviewed the literature on environmental advocacy and concluded that few people are consistent environmentalists. Instead, they think about environmental problems most when their self-interest is at stake. Public opinion theorists have debated over the years whether people **should be expected** to think in ideological terms and about whether thinking about policy problems only when one's self-interest is at stake represents narrow, selfish thinking that provides reason for concern.

If one thinks in terms of the situational theory, of course, such results are not surprising at all. As explained by the theory, people are more likely to be motivated to think, evaluate, and act in situations that involve them, which they view as problematic, and in which they feel unconstrained. People less often are motivated by cross-situational concepts such as ideologies, attitudes, and values – although these concepts may frame how they make decisions once they recognize a problem. Research on the situational theory has consistently looked at the cognitions, attitudes, and behaviours of different kinds of publics as well as at their information seeking and processing behaviours. Consistently, research has shown that the more active a public, the more active its communication behaviour, and the more likely it is that members of the public will constuct cognitions and attitudes and participate in behaviours.

Importantly, however, I have predicted that the theory would explain only the presence of cognitions, attitudes and behaviours and not their content or valence. People **construct** cognitions, attitudes and behaviours. Thus, they actively control their own thinking and behaviour and cannot easily be persuaded by others. The situational theory, in other words, is a teleological theory. It predicts when people will think and communicate purposively about situations. Logically, then, it also should be able to predict when they will develop cognitions and attitudes about situations. It cannot predict the nature and direction of cognitions or the valence of attitudes because people control those personally. They are not the product of deterministic forces outside the individual.

In J. Grunig (1983a), I reviewed the literature on environmental communication, which I said had been preoccupied with finding empirical support for a cross-situational attitude paradigm. That literature essentially took a deterministic view of attitudes, assuming that attitudes govern behaviour. If communication could change attitudes, the paradigm maintained, then communication could indirectly change behaviours. In the case of environmental communication and education, pro-environmental messages could create or maintain favourable attitudes that would, in turn, programme people to behave in a way that would protect the environment in many different situations. That kind of theory, it should be obvious, is the one that many client organizations hope is true for public relations programmes in general and that many public relations people are reluctanct to challenge. Unfortunately, years of research on attitude change have not supported that deterministic assumption.

Research on communication and attitudes reviewed in J. Grunig (1983a), however, showed that theorists now conceptualize attitudes to be more situational and teleological than cross-situational and deterministic (see Fishbein and Ajzen 1975; Petty and Cacioppo 1986). Attitudes are situational when people form different evaluations of solutions to issues as situations change. People may have a cross-situational attitude, which I previously called a referent criterion. Situational attitudes, however, predict actual behaviour much better than do cross-situational attitudes. Attitudes also are teleological – purposive – rather than deterministic in that people have the ability to control their attitudes and that attitudes do not necessarily control their behaviour.

As a teleological theory, the situational theory predicts when people will think and communicate purposively about situations. Logically, then, it should also be able to predict when they will develop cognitions and attitudes about issues. It cannot predict the nature and direction of cognitions or the valence of attitudes: People control those personally; messages do not control them deterministically.

Consistent with this reasoning, several studies have shown that active publics, as identified by the situational variables, are more likely to hold both attitudes and cognitions (e.g., J. Grunig 1982a) and to hold **organized** cognitions (J. Grunig and Ipes 1983) than are apathetic publics. Other studies have looked for the kinds of attitudes held by the different kinds of publics and have tried to explain how these cognitions and attitudes vary with situations.

In environmental studies, the most common attitudinal and cognitive variables utilized have been the cognitive strategies formulated by Stamm and Bowes (1972). Stamm and Bowes identified two basic orientations toward scarcity that they defined as attitudes about the environment: **reversal of the trend** toward scarcity and using a **functional substitute** to replace a scarce resource. Originally, Stamm and Bowes believed that people would use these attitudes cross situationally, that an individual would apply one of them consistently in different environmental situations. Their data, however, showed that people often advocated different solutions for different situations and that they sometimes chose both. To explain those data, Stamm defined two 'cognitive strategies', **hedging** and **wedging**. Hedging occurs when a person believes that both reversal of trends and functional substitutes should be used to resolve an environmental problem. Wedging occurs when an individual believes only one of the solutions should be applied.

My studies of environmental publics have shown that people do not consistently apply reversal of trends, functional substitutes, hedging and wedging across situations (J. Grunig 1983a; Stamm and J. Grunig 1977; J. Grunig and Stamm 1979). As the theory predicted, these are situational strategies. There was some regularity, however. In most situations, people tended to apply the solution that made the most sense in a given situation (J. Grunig and Stamm 1979: 719). In general, however, the studies showed that environmental publics applied the reversal of trends solution across situations as a referent criterion. For most environmental situations, members of these publics used the reversal of trends strategy to wedge out functional substitutes. When a situation involved people personally, however, they hedged the reversal of trends solution and used the functional substitutes solution as well. When they had to give up something personally in an environmental situation, that is, they were more willing to find a substitute resource at the same time they believed that people should stop using up a resource.

In three studies of publics forming around corporate policy issues, the concepts of hedging and wedging were used in a slightly different way. In two studies (J. Grunig 1982a; 1983b), respondents were asked the extent to which they believed several statements describing pro- and anti-business cognitions. Scores then were computed for the extent to which respondents wedged pro- or anti-business cognitions or held the two jointly (hedged). In the third study (J. Grunig 1979b), respondents were asked the extent to which four groups (government, business, interest groups and individuals) should be responsible for solving several social problems. A high hedging score meant that a respondent thought all four groups should be responsible. A low score meant that the respondent thought only one group should be responsible.

In the two studies of pro- and anti-business cognitions, the respondents who wedged – both the general respondents in the first study and Washington reporters in the second – generally did so with anti-business cognitions. Most members of both samples held anti-business cognitions across situations; when they held pro-business cognitions they wedged them by keeping the anti-business cognition. Also, both studies showed that respondents held the strongest anti-business cognitions on environmental issues and that the more active the public the stronger the anti-business cognitions, especially on the environmental issues. In the study of corporate social responsibility, the one environmental issue was pollution. For this issue, all publics hedged. They assigned the responsibility for solving the problem jointly to government and business. However, the most active public assigned more responsibility to government, suggesting that active publics may become more activist in pressuring government.

Two studies, J. Grunig (1982a) and J. Grunig and Ipes (1983), showed that passive publics are more likely to hold attitudes than cognitions. Active publics are equally likely to hold both cognitions and attitudes. These results are consistent with the theory that cognitive responses generally precede attitudes, but only for actively communicating publics. Less active publics, however, express attitudes – at least in a survey – even when they have no cognitions. That conclusion would suggest that attitudes can be manipulated more easily for passive publics – often using manipulative communication devices – than for active publics. The attitudes would be changed more easily than those held by active publics, however.[9]

Two other groups of researchers also have done experimental research to determine if active publics have more cognitive responses than passive publics. Cameron (1992) found that active publics remembered experimental messages about investor relations more than did passive publics (memory was measured as cued recall and recognition memory). Slater *et al.* (1992) found that subjects with high problem recognition and involvement were more likely to have thoughts (cognitive responses) when exposed to messages about the use of agricultural chemicals than were subjects with low problem recognition and involvement. The active publics were especially likely to have negative cognitive responses – suggesting that for this issue, at least, active publics are more likely to develop cognitions that produce negative attitudes than positive attitudes.

Finally, some of the studies of publics also have determined the extent to which different kinds of publics engage in individual behaviours. In general, behaviours are infrequent effects of communication programmes for all publics (see J. Grunig and Ipes 1983: 49). Nevertheless, active publics are considerably more likely to engage in behaviours than passive publics and, therefore, more likely to use the information coming from a communication programme as the basis for a behaviour. In the study of corporate issues (J. Grunig 1982a), for example, the most active public had a probability of 52 per cent of engaging in a behaviour related to the issues, the least active public a probability of 6 per cent. In addition, the probability of behaviour was less than 20 per cent for all but the most active publics.

One behaviour that has been studied with great frequency by communication researchers has been the adoption of innovations (see Rogers 1983). Myers (1985) used the situational theory to explain the adoption of innovations that Maryland farmers could use to help reduce pollution of the Chesapeake Bay. In a canonical correlation, he used the three situational variables as independent variables and adoption of the anti-pollution innovations and several communication, media, and knowledge variables as dependent variables. One canonical variate resulted. Problem recognition, level of involvement, and constraint recognition correlated .74, .66 and .80, respectively, with this variate. Adoption of innovations correlated .45, showing again that the more active the publics the more likely is behaviour.

These studies, in summary, show conclusively that not only is communication with active publics more likely than it is with passive publics but that active publics are also more likely to hold cognitions and attitudes and to engage in behaviours than are passive publics. Passive publics may hold attitudes more often than cognitions, but these attitudes usually are weakly held and supported only by disorganized cognitions. Communication, therefore, is more likely to produce each of these effects with active publics. It does not follow, however, that a given communication programme will usually be effective in producing a change desired by the organization sponsoring the programme. Active publics communicate with many sources of information; and their cognitions, attitudes, and behaviours will be formed from the composite of all information they receive, not from the information from a single programme or campaign.

Thus far, therefore, this chapter has reported research on and theoretical development of the situational theory from 1968 until appoximately 1988. Since that time, I have conducted additional work on the theory that as yet has not been published. In addition, the theory has become popular with researchers in many universities, and several articles using the theory recently have been published in scholarly journals – especially in the *Journal of Public Relations Research*. This research has in some cases extended the reach of the theory and in other cases provided new challenges. The next section, then, discusses the new research and the following section the new challenges.

NEW RESEARCH

The new research falls into the two categories discussed throughout this chapter: The nature of publics and the nature of the 'opinions' of publics (outcomes of communication behaviour).

The nature of publics: do 'intellectual' publics differ from activist publics?

As conceptualized to this point, the situational theory has not distinguished between what might be called internal and external components of the three independent variables (problem recognition, level of involvement and constraint recognition). Are the problems that are recognized in the person's mind only or are they problems perceived in the environment? Is involvement perceived or actual? Are constraints 'real' or only perceived? These questions have been raised by reviewers for several journals over the years and particularly by rhetorical scholars who see the three concepts as strictly cognitive (internal) (or 'communicative' in their terms[10]) rather than as perceptions of real (external) situations. If the concepts are strictly internal, they could be changed by communication; if they are external, real changes must be made in a person's environment before his or her perceptions of the situation and, therefore, communication behaviour will change. In past research, I have not believed that a distinction between the internal and the external components of the three concepts would be useful. A retrospective look at my research and at other concepts in the literature suggested, however, that the distinction might resolve the theoretical questions raised by rhetoricians as well as some practical public relations problems – especially those related to communication about science, health and the environment, which are of more intellectual than practical interest to many publics.

In J. Grunig (1974b), for example, I examined the effects of several science writing devices on different publics, as identified by the concepts of problem recognition and constraint recognition. The measures of problem recognition and constraint recognition were external: 'Is the problem discussed in this article important to you?' (problem recognition) and 'Do you think ordinary citizens like you could use information like that presented here to have an impact on government policy?' (constraint recognition). Bartholomew (1973) did a similar study in which the measures were internal: 'Are you interested in understanding physics?' (problem recognition) and 'Do you feel you could understand physics if you wanted to?' (constraint recognition). Both studies produced similar results. The active publics, which were high in problem recognition and low in constraint recognition, read science stories more actively and learned more. The question that was not answered was whether different publics would have been identified if both the internal and external concepts had been measured for the same subjects and whether different writing techniques would have been more effective on the different publics.

Applied to environmental publics, the internal situational concepts would seem to identify the 'intellectual' publics suggested in the literature (J. Grunig 1977a) – publics that are concerned about the environment but not active in doing something about it. The external concepts, on the other hand, would identify the publics actually engaged in individual or collective behaviours to do something about environmental problems.

A closer look at the differences in conceptualization of internal and external concepts makes the distinction clearer. For problem recognition, the distinction lies in the fact that problems recognized could be in a person's environment or strictly in his or her mind. Internal problems reflect curiosity or intellectual interests. External problems are problems with which an individual conceivably would have to deal in the real world. The distinction between internal and external constraint recognition can be seen in Weick's (1979) cognitive theory of organizations. Weick emphasized that the environment of an organization exists partly in the mind of the people in an organization who observe it and partly 'out there.' Thus constraints could be either internal or external. Similarly, Bandura (1977) used the concept of 'self-efficacy' to explain why some information campaigns are effective and others are not.[11] If people believe they can do something about a problem, they are more likely to use information related to that problem. However, Bandura also theorized that communication campaigns can increase self-efficacy by providing a model of how a change can be made. If self-efficacy can be changed without making actual changes in constraints, then it must be based at least in part on an internal conception of constraints. Salmon's (1986) extensive review of the literature on involvement finally identified what appears to be internal and external involvement. Internal involvement essentially is ego involvement, as described by Sheriff, Sheriff and Nebergall (1965). External involvement is actual involvement in the situation.

Thus far, I have completed three studies using new indicators of the internal and external concepts.[12] The first study was completed on the issue of AIDS, which has been published only as a paper (J. Grunig and Childers [aka Hon] 1988). The other studies were conducted on risk situations and on the health-care situation in the United States. Neither of the studies have yet been published. In the AIDS study, two indicators were used for each of the independent concepts. Previously, I had used only a single indicator for each variable because of the large number of problems to which respondents had to respond for each indicator. The use of a single indicator has been of concern to a number of journal reviewers over the years, however, because of the difficulty of determining reliability. Thus, these new measures also were developed to overcome that criticism. The two indicators for external constraint recognition did not correlate, however, and were kept separate. One indicator seemed to measure individual constraint and the second group efficacy.[13] The lack of correlation, therefore, seemed to show that people may feel constrained as individuals from doing anything about an issue such as AIDS, but that they also may feel they can do something collectively. In the risk and health studies, the constraint items were rewritten and a higher correlation was attained between both indicators. Both the original single-indicator questions and the new double-indicator questions are included as an appendix for those who might want to use them in research. It is important to recognize, though, that the single indicators have performed well in research for many years and that it may be necessary to use them rather than the double indicators to reduce the length of questionnaires when multiple problems are studied.

In all three studies, the internal and external concepts did not identify separate publics. That result suggests that people do not become intellectual publics unless they also believe a problem actually affects them at least to some extent. In other words, externally involved publics also are more likely to take an internal, intellectual interest in issues than are publics that do not perceive an actual involvement.

In spite of this failure to find separate internal and external publics, the two dimensions did add information to the understanding of each public – thus suggesting that the distinction has practical as well as theoretical value. For example, in all three studies, the variate that identified an active, all-issue public had a moderate-sized positive correlation with internal constraint recognition – suggesting that even the most active publics felt somewhat constrained in their ability to understand these science- and health- related issues. Although the AIDS study did not identify a separate 'intellectual' public, a second canonical variate identified a public that was characterized most highly by correlations with internal constraint recognition: the inability to understand the AIDS issues. It also was interesting that this public held the strongest negative attitudes about AIDS on valenced scales of both situational and cross-situational attitudes – even though members of this public held fewer cognitions about AIDS and had a negative correlation with holding an attitude (i.e. many gave no response to the attitude scale). In short, as I have found before, the AIDS study showed that people will give responses to attitude questions in a survey even if they have not thought about an issue or previously held attitudes about it.

In the risk study, we applied the internal and external concepts to three different risks: global warming, heart disease, and drug-related violence. Three publics resulted. The first essentially was an all-issues public, although the global-warming issue was of more concern to this public than the other two issues. The second public mostly was a single-issue public, concerned with heart disease, although drug-related violence was of secondary concern. The third public, also a single-issue public, was concerned mostly about drug-related violence. In this study, the new information added by the internal-external distinction was the revelation that even though both internal and external problem recognition and involvement were high for the problems of concern to each public, the internal concepts correlated with the canonical variates more highly than the external concepts.

Those results suggested, therefore, that these risk issues are more intellectual issues to these publics even though they perceived them to be real problems that affected them to some extent.

The health care study was conducted in spring 1993, just as the Clinton administration was introducing the health care issue and had a task force at work studying it. Thus, health care was covered extensively in the media at the time. In the study, the situational variables were applied to four problems being discussed about health care: the quality of health care, people with no health insurance, unhealthy lifestyles and the health-insurance industry. As might be expected from the heavy media coverage, these four issues produced one major public – a hot-issue public – with high correlations on all of the variables for all of the issues. Again, though, the internal-external distinction contributed new information – information that shed new light on the nature of a hot-issue public. The highest correlating set of variables for this hot-issue public was internal problem recognition. In addition, both the internal and external level of involvement correlated lower than either internal or external problem recognition; and internal level of involvement correlated higher than external involvement. In short, the results suggested that when media coverage creates a hot-issue public, that public is characterized more by the internal than the external variables and by problem recognition more than involvement. In short, hot-issue publics are more intellectual publics than actively behaving publics – although, again, they perceive a real connection to the issue to some extent.

The health care study also produced a second, minor public characterized mostly by high internal constraint recognition on all four problems – much like the second public in the AIDS study. The canonical variate that produced this public, therefore, tells us something about what is probably an apathetic public. Just as in the AIDS study, this public is apathetic because of internal constraint recognition – the belief that it cannot understand the issue. Thus, the internal-external distinction seems to help understand better both hot-issue and apathetic publics – publics whose nature was not clear in studies where the internal and external concerns were not separated.

Are the independent variables of the study independent or correlated?

In the original formulation of the situational theory, I maintained that problem recognition, level of involvement and constraint recognition were independent of each other. Thus, it would be possible, for example, for problem recognition to be high even though level of involvement is low. In J. Grunig and Hunt (1984), therefore, I constructed a typology of 16 kinds of publics based on the combinations of high and low values on the three variables – called, for example, the high-involvement problem-facing public and the low-involvement fatalistic public. The probabilities of information seeking and processing and of the presence of cognitions, attitudes, and behaviours discussed in the section on the intellectual history of the theory, were calculated for each of these 16 types of publics. Several researchers, including Atwood and Cheng (1986), Major (1993a and 1993b) used these categories to identify publics and to analyse their communication behaviour.

In most of my research, however, the three variables have been correlated with each other – especially problem recognition and level of involvement. In addition, the canonical variates used to identify publics repeatedly have correlated highly with all three variables – albeit for different problems on different variates. It would seem appropriate, therefore, to explore theoretically and empirically the meaning of these correlations. J. Grunig and Childers [aka Hon] (1988) reported a causal analysis using the LISREL computer program to explore the interrelationships among both the independent and dependent variables of the theory. The results reported in that chapter were problematic, however, because several of the correlations between the situational variables were very high; and the result was LISREL estimates of path coefficients greater than 1.0, which is impossible.[14] Hon and I since have simplifed the LISREL model by combining the internal and external dimensions of the variables and running separate causal models for information seeking and processing. We also have allowed for causal paths among the independent variables rather than assuming they are independent – thus allowing us to examine the theoretical meaning of correlated rather than independent predictor variables.

The results suggested one especially important theoretical insight. The two causal models that we calculated suggested that a path runs from the combined variable of internal and external level of involvement to a combined variable of internal and external problem recognition. The path coefficients were very high – .885 when information processing was in the model and .927 when information seeking was in the model. Theoretically, then, these coefficients suggested that problem recogition is key to the occurrence of communication but that it is to a large extent a function of level of involvement – i.e. that people are more likely to recognize problems in a situation they believe involves them. Of course, the cause and effect relationship could run the other way – which is suggested, for example, by the results for the hot-issue public in the health-care study. Internal problem recognition could produce involvement. We have not yet done a LISREL analysis on the health care data, though, to be able to answer this question.

Extension of the theory to new outcomes of communication

Cognitive structures

As discussed in the section on opinions, several studies have shown that active publics, as identified by the situational variables, are more likely to construct both attitudes and cognitions (J. Grunig 1982a) and to hold organized cognitions (J. Grunig and Ipes 1983) than are apathetic publics. Other studies (Stamm and J. Grunig 1977; J. Grunig and Stamm 1979) have looked for the kinds of cognitions and attitudes held by different kinds of publics and have tried to explain how they vary with situations.

Also as discussed in that section, many attitude theorists now conceptualize attitudes in ways that make the concept more compatible with the situational theory – as situational and teleological rather than cross-situational and deterministic. Attitudes are situational when people construct new solutions to problems as situations change. Nevertheless, people also may have a cross-situational attitude, a solution which they apply across situations – which is one of the definitions I previously used for referent criterion. Attitude research has shown, however, that situational attitudes predict actual behaviour better than do cross-situational attitudes (see Fishbein and Ajzen 1975).

In addition, attitude research now is dominated by cognitive-response theories such as the elaboration likelihood model discussed above (Petty 1981: 225–52; Petty and Cacioppo 1986; Markus and Zajonc 1985). Those theories state that people are most likely to form or change attitudes from messages that produce thoughts, especially in highly involving situations. Finally, research based on cognitive response theories has shown that attitudes formed from elaborated cognitions are most likely to produce lasting effects on behaviour (Petty and Cacioppo 1986: 21). Changes in cognitions produced by communication programmes also can produce short-term changes in behaviour if the behaviours are specific and easy to implement (Winett 1986; O'Keefe 1985).

These trends in theory building, therefore, reinforce the importance of elaborated cognitions as effects of communication, both as ends in themselves and for the mediating effects they have on attitudes and behaviour. Cognitive variables especially have value as objectives for public relations programmes because they can be changed in the short term, whereas attitudes and behaviours are more long-term effects of changes in cognition. Thus, cognitive changes can be measured in the short term and used to evaluate the outcomes of a communication programme in time to make midcourse corrections in that programme. The situational theory has become even more useful in light of these trends because its variables predict when people will communicate actively. Active communication, like cognition, is valuable in itself; but it too is an important mediating variable because it produces elaborated cognitions, which produce attitudes and behaviours.

Given the importance of cognitions to understanding the outcomes of communication research, we have turned to theories of cognitive psychology to help understand the nature of elaborated cognitions more precisely. Craik and Lockhart (1972) introduced the concept of depth of processing to describe what cognitive psychologists previously had called long-term memory. To Craik and Lockhart, 'depth of processing' means that people apply 'a greater degree of semantic or cognitive analysis' to incoming information. Cognitive researchers concluded later that Craik and Lockhart's original concept of **depth** should, more accurately, be described as **breadth** of processing, where breadth meant 'number of elaborations' (J. Anderson and Reder 1979: 391) Both J. Anderson and Reder (1979: 390) and Craik (1979: 449) distinguished breadth from depth. Breadth represented **quantity** of elaborations, depth **quality** of elaboration. Depth, according to Craik, meant that a cognition has 'abstract, symbolic properties' (1979: 457).

An increase in breadth of processing can be defined as an increase in the number of 'cognitive units' held in memory (J. Anderson 1983: 76, developed the term 'cognitive unit'). Depth of processing, in turn, can be defined as organizing these cognitive units into a 'schema', a large, complex unit of knowledge (J. Anderson 1985: 103).[15] Psychologists have defined schemas in somewhat the same way that I defined referent criterion in some studies. In those studies, I defined referent criterion as a decision rule based on prior knowledge. Since I have used the term referent criterion to refer both to a schema and a cross-situational attitude, I now use those terms in its place.

Markus and Zajonc (1985) concluded that 'schema' has not been a well-defined concept; and, as a result, the term has taken on diverse meanings for both cognitive and social psychologists. Markus and Zajonc captured the essence of its meaning for our theory, however, when they said:

> For the most part social psychologists who have used the term *schemas* have viewed them as subjective 'theories' about how the social world operates.
>
> (1985: 145)

Theories are abstract; schemas are abstract. Deep cognitive processing, therefore, means that a person develops and uses a semantic abstraction to organize and explain the cognitive units that he or she accrues by increasing cognitive breadth.

Pavlik (1983) developed similar concepts of breadth and depth from the literature on cognitive style and information processing. In a study of the effects of two health information campaigns, he defined breadth of cognition as 'dimensional complexity', the number of strategies or suggestions mentioned in response to an open-end question as solutions for a health problem such as smoking (1983: 84). Pavlik defined depth as hierarchical complexity, 'the levels of abstractness reflected in a response' (1983: 84). His results, then, showed that the information campaign produced greater increases in breadth than in depth and that this increase was higher for people with a high level of involvement.

Results of the AIDS study

The AIDS study, then, provided the first test of the relationship of the new concepts of cognitive breadth and depth and situational and cross-situational attitudes. Results of the study provided moderate to strong support for the theoretical predictions that active publics are more likely to have cognitive structures of breadth and depth and to hold situational attitudes more than cross-situational attitudes. Cognition was measured with an open-ended question that asked respondents to tell whatever they knew about AIDS. Two additional probe questions, 'Anything else?' followed. Breadth was coded by counting the number of different ideas mentioned. Depth was coded by the extent to which respondents were able to use a theory – the viral cause of AIDS – to connect their ideas.

Breadth of cognition correlated moderately with the canonical variate that identified the active public (.21), but depth of cognition had a low and non-significant correlation (.05). Similar results occurred in the LISREL path model where there was a small but significant coefficient for the path between information processing and breadth (.139) and a similar but non-significant coefficient between information seeking and breadth (.113). (Both information seeking and processing were preceded by the three situational variables in the model.) The coefficients for depth were approximately zero. We included education in this causal model, however, and it had significant coefficients for a path to both breath (.409) and depth (.384). In the canonical correlation, however, education did not correlate with the variate identifying the active public (.06). Together, then, these results suggested that the situational variables motivate people to communicate about a problem such as AIDS regardless of education. The success that actively communicating publics achieve in organizing information into cognitive structures, however, depends on their level of education. Those results also suggested that practitioners might want to segment an active public further by education for a complicated scientific or medical problem such as AIDS because different communication strategies would be needed for the more- and less-educated segments of that public.

The results for attitudes in the AIDS study also were similar to past research. The variate for the active public correlated with holding both a situational and cross-situational attitude.[16] Active publics were just as likely to hold the cross-situational attitude as the situational attitude, however – in contrast to our expectations. For the direction of the attitude, the active public agreed with attitude statements that AIDS experts suggest are reasonable solutions to the problem ('Limiting oneself to a single sexual partner makes it possible to avoid getting AIDS' and 'Educating people about AIDS will solve the problem') and not to an inadequate solution ('AIDS patients should be isolated from other people'). The active public also agreed with the cross-situational attitude statement that 'More money should be spent on AIDS research even though AIDS has been limited mostly to homosexuals so far' and to disagree with the statements that 'AIDS is God's way of punishing homosexuals and drug users' and 'Good people are unlikely to get AIDS'. As stated previously, a second public characterized by a high level of internal problem recognition agreed or disagreed with these statements in exactly the opposite way.

Although Petty and Cacioppo's (1986) research showed that positive or negative cognitions produced positive or negative attitudes,[17] the cognitions mentioned by respondents in this study generally were factual and neutral and their direction could not be coded (statements such as 'AIDS is common among homosexuals', 'AIDS is passed through the blood and other body fluids', or 'AIDS can be passed through blood transfusion'. Thus, in this study the complexity of the cognitive structure predicted the direction of attitudes better than the valence of the cognitions – i.e. the more people knew about AIDS the more reasonable their attitudes were.

Results of the risk study

Researchers studying risk communication (for example, Sandman 1985; Covello 1992) have learned that lay publics think of risks such as radon, nuclear power, or toxic wastes more often in terms of what the researchers have called outrage factors than in terms of the statistical probability of death or harm from a risk as risk experts do. The outrage factors mean that lay publics are more concerned about risks they believe to be involuntary, immoral, out of their control, dreaded, undetected and not understood by science or experts. In this study, we correlated these cognitions (outrage factors) about the three risk problems studied and a general assessment of the risk of the each problem with the variates that identified three different publics. We also correlated an index of behaviours (such as joining an activist group, contacting a government official, or changing one's personal behaviour) with each variate.

The results consistently showed that the three active, special-issue, publics identified were more outraged, perceived a greater risk and were more likely to engage in a behaviour related to the risk problem that produced each public. In this study, therefore, the valence of cognitions seemed to have a greater effect on attitudes and behaviour than it did for AIDS. People who believed they might be affected adversely by a risk factor opposed that factor and engaged in behaviour to get rid of it – the clear profile of an activist group that has appeared previously in research using the situational theory.

Conflict resolution variables

The major purpose of the health care study was to extend the concept of 'opinion' (outcomes of communication behaviour) to an area of theory (conflict resolution) we thought to be especially relevant to the two-way symmetrical model of public relations – one of the major characteristics of our model of excellence in public relations (J. Grunig and L. Grunig 1992). Thus, we took a set of variables developed by researchers in the Harvard Negotiation Project (Fisher and Ury 1981; Fisher and Brown, 1988; and Ury 1991) and applied them to the conflict-ridden discussion of the health issue in the United States that began in 1993 and continues as this chapter is written.

These conflict-resolution concepts included underlying interests, which the Fisher, Ury and Brown writings suggested conflicting people should discuss rather than their positions on issues; and the 'best alternative to a negotiated agreement' (BATNA), which the writings suggested a conflicting party should keep in mind as a bottom line for determining how much to give up during a negotiation.

In this study, then, we wanted to combine the situational variables with these cognitive variables to see if survey research could be used to segment publics, identify their interests, and search for means of managing conflict about a contentious issue. Thus, after asking questions to measure the situational variables for the four problems studied, we asked a series of open-ended questions to measure the perceived self-interests of each public, what they perceived to be the interests of groups they felt in conflict with, and their BATNAs. As stated previously, a single hot-issue public resulted. After responses to the open-end questions were content analysed, the results for these conflict-resolution variables clearly identified the nature of the conflict. Members of the hot-issue public saw their underlying interests largely as controlling the rising costs of medical care – in general and in terms of the costs of malpractice suits, insurance regulations, drugs and the cost of medicare (for the elderly) and medicaid (for the poor) to the government. Nearly half of the respondents also saw the problem as lack of access by many people to health care and about 12 per cent as poor quality of health care.

Respondents also saw their opponents interests as financial: They stated that groups they disagreed with – such as conservatives/Republicans, the American Medical Association, doctors, hospitals, special interests, lawyers, pharmaceutical companies and insurance companies – were interested only in their own financial gains. Some also stated that politicians were looking for ways to raise taxes. Thus, the research showed the conflict to be a financial one. The BATNAs, however, showed some reason for optimism. Some respondents thought they would be better off if no health-care programme could be passed because they already had good coverage. Most, however, believed that they would be worse off if nothing is done to change the system because they thought that costs would keep rising. Some also expressed concern about people who now are not covered by health insurance. The study, therefore, successfully clarified the financial interests involved in the conflict over health care. We did not ask respondents for solutions to the conflict, so the study could not suggest them. At the time this chapter is written, the conflict in Congress reflects our survey: People want universal access to health care at stable prices, but no one wants or knows how to pay for it. Negotiation is underway in Congress and a solution might be achieved. The major lesson of the study, though, is that public relations practitioners can use the situational theory and the conflict variables in survey research to better understand conflicts with their publics – or in focus groups or other forms of qualitative research. Then, however, they will have to communicate with those publics to find symmetrical, win-win solutions to the conflict. Finding solutions to conflicts will not be easy, however, especially when, as Springston *et al.* (1992) have theorized, there are multiple publics with conflicting interests. When multiple publics conflict with an organization in different ways, asymmetrical public relations cannot work because different asymmetrical messages cannot be given to different publics without the deception eventually being revealed. With multiple publics, therefore, only symmetrical public relations can resolve the multi-party conflict.

RESEARCH CHALLENGES

The programme of research reported in this chapter has developed a picture that portrays publics as groups of people who are most likely to be motivated to communicate about problems that involve them, that they recognize and that they feel they can do something about. People are less likely to be motivated to communicate by attitudes or values that programme them to seek reinforcement of what they already believe or favour. According to the situational theory, people make judgements, but they are relatively open-minded in making those judgements even though their prior knowledge (cognitive structures) and attitudes affect those judgements. At the same time, people seldom take an interest in problems or situations that do not involve them and seldom communicate about these problems or situations. The theory suggests, therefore, that the efforts of legions of public relations practitioners often are wasted because they try to communicate with publics who are unlikely to communicate with them. These practitioners hope they can, in essence, change the level of problem recognition, involvement and constraint recognition through communication so that the publics communicate more actively and eventually behave as the practitioners hope. In particular, these practitioners hope that media exposure will produce such an effect. In the logic of the situational theory, however, that hope is close to impossible: People cannot be affected by messages that they do not seek or even process.

In spite of an extensive body of research supporting this picture of publics, some theorists, researchers and practitioners still refuse to accept it and call for research they hope will provide a different picture. Three such challenges to the situational theory have been made most often. Fortunately, the most recent research summarized in this chapter seems to provide answers to the challenges.

Challenge 1: the theory should include or predict attitudes

Cameron and Yang (1990) and Slater *et al.* (1992) have suggested that 'valence of support' should be added to the situational theory because they believe that whether publics see a problem positively or negatively determines the effect of messages on them. Slater *et al.*, for example, suggested that a valence can be attached to problem recognition and level of involvement. Other researchers have suggested informally that since activists in particular usually oppose an organization, it is important for public relations people to understand their attitudes so they can prepare messages that reinforce those attitudes.

On the one hand, I reject these suggestions for two reasons. The first is philsophical because of the presuppositions these suggestions impose on the resulting theory.[18] They presuppose a deterministic theory that assumes attitudes control behaviour – including communication behaviour. Philosophically, also, the suggestions seem to presuppose an asymmetrical rather than symmetrical approach to public relations – i.e. that messages should be tailored to make the behaviour of a client organization appear to be what the public wants to hear. My second objection is pragmatic: extensive research reviewed in this chapter shows that attitudes do not explain communication behaviour as well as the variables in the situational theory. The research shows that people usually do not have cognitions or attitudes – or that they are weakly organized – until after they communicate. Instead, people seek or process information because it is relevant to them and not because it reinforces their attitudes. Cognitions, attitudes and behaviour, therefore, result from communication behaviour – as the history of my research on the referent criterion shows. On the other hand, though, these critics have a valid point. We need to know how publics think, feel about and behave towards our client organizations so that we can understand the publics and communicate more effectively with them. However, I believe the programme of research discussed in this chapter already has resolved the challenge. Research with the situational theory has always included measures of cognitions, attitudes and behaviours of the publics identified. And we have done a great deal of conceptual work to clarify the nature of these communication outcomes. Our research shows that these outcomes differ greatly from situation to situation and that the situational variables cannot predict their valence. Sometimes, as in the risk study, most members of a public oppose an organization. At other times, as in the AIDS study, a public is more neutral; and the complexity of their cognitions is more important than their attitudes. The solution provided to this challenge by our research, therefore, is a simple one: Include cognitions, attitudes and behaviours in the theory as an outcome of communication behaviour and not as a cause. In that way, research can help us to understand our publics, but we are not drawn into the asymmetrical presupposition that the research will allow us to control the behaviour of publics.

Challenge 2: can messages, especially in the mass media, create publics?

This challenge, as well as the third one, centres on the question of whether messages can cause communication behaviour, or whether people ignore messages unless they are communicating actively or, at least, passively. Public relations campaigns for or against many causes are based on the assumption that exposure to information in the media or elsewhere can make non-publics into publics – i.e. that media exposure can create publics.[19] Public opinion researchers also assign a large role to the media in the process of developing public opinions (e.g., Van Leuven and Slater 1991; Price 1992: 78–83). From a rhetorical perspective, Vasquez (1993, 1994) also has theorized that messages cause the situational variables. Within the framework of the situational theory, the only way such an effect could occur would be through random, and passive, information processing. The theory would be falsified completely if people were found to seek information actively when problem recognition and involvement are low and constraint recognition is high.

Our research has shown consistently that such an effect, if any, is small. In the LISREL model of the AIDS data, for example, we included a path from information processing to problem recognition as well as a path from problem recognition to information processing. The idea was that passive processing of information about AIDS could trigger problem recognition, which could in turn produce further information processing and information seeking. The path coefficient from information processing to problem recognition was positive but small and insignificant (.076). The coefficient from problem recognition to information processing was large (.652).

Those results are discouraging to public relations practitioners who base their work on information campaigns. The results especially are discouraging to communicators who want to want to change behaviours related to health or the environment through the media. People who most need health information or who most often suffer from environmental risks typically are unlikely – based on the situational variables – to communicate about those risks.[20] Most public relations people are unwilling to give up on these vulnerable non-publics even though the situational theory suggests that is the most realistic option. I suspect that the answer to the challenge of creating publics out of non-publics lies not in the mass media but in creating publics by other means. Health communication studies suggest that interpersonal support of people at risk can make them more active (e.g. Flora, Maccoby and Farquhar 1989) i.e. support provided by family members or such groups as Alcoholics Anonymous. Thus, I think public relations researchers who are concerned about vulnerable people should turn their attention to interpersonal, grass roots means of creating publics. When such publics are developed, they will in turn process and seek information from the media.[21]

Challenge 3: explain hot-issue publics, which the media can create

Many public relations practitioners who hear this assessment of the limited power of the mass media point to the obvious effect media attention has had in arousing attention to crises and scandals. In research with the situational theory, Major (1993b) also found that media attention to a predicted earthquake increased problem recognition and involvement. Many organizations and politicians have been destroyed or severely injured by media coverage, and people pay great attention to media coverage of disasters and scandals. Thus, practitioners should ask rightly whether that widely known fact does not negate the conclusion stated to Challenge 2. The research on the situational theory suggests an interesting solution to the dilemma: media coverage seems to be much more likely to produce a public when the information is negative than when it is positive. Extensive coverage of problems that affect or interest most people can create a hot-issue public. But the converse does not seem to be true. Campaigns to communicate information that supports the mission of an organization do not create hot-issue publics; instead, only publics who already are active and attentive pay attention to the campaign. The difference in the effects of media coverage, therefore, lies in the difference between hot-issue and active publics.

Nevertheless, the research on hot-issue publics suggests that practitioners should not throw up their hands in despair. In early research (e.g. J. Grunig and Ipes 1983), we found that hot-issue publics have high levels of constraint recognition and that they do not have well-organized cognitions, even though they often express spontaneous but transitory attitudes. In addition, the research suggests that hot-issue publics dissipate when the media coverage ends. Our new research now clarifies this picture more by showing that the situational variables that create hot-issue publics are internal rather than external. Internal problem recognition means that hot-issue publics are more curious than active, their involvement is more ego-related than actual and they often do not believe they can understand the issues. It is important to note, though, that the external variables are moderately high for hot-issue publics – that is, they can see some connection to their real lives. That means that organizations who blunder in their public relations during a crisis can turn the relatively harmless hot-issue public into a dangerous active one.

Our research, therefore, suggests that the two-way symmetrical model, applied to media relations (see Hunt and J. Grunig 1994, Chapter 3) is especially important for hot-issue publics. For crises, scandals, disasters and major national problems, an organization has little alternative other than to be open, express candor and take blame when necessary. Anything else will produce cynicism and distrust in the hot-issue public and the media. And cynicism and distrust can be irreparable and destroy the ability of an organization to accomplish its mission.

CONCLUSION

Thirty years of research on the situational theory has produced a theory that, I believe, provides nearly complete understanding of the nature and behaviour of publics. Research has resolved most of the challenges to the theory, although the challenge of reaching vulnerable non-publics still requires additional research. Most of the research on the theory has been done by academic researchers, however. Public relations practitioners who use research, in contrast, generally use the services of marketing research or polling firms who know how to segment markets but not publics or who continue to view publics as one large 'general public'. The greatest remaining challenge, therefore, may be the task of transferring the situational theory from academia to professional practice.

ACKNOWLEDGEMENT

Portions of this chapter have been adapted from J. Grunig (1989a) and J. Grunig and Childers (aka Hon) (1988).

APPENDIX 1.A
QUESTIONS TO MEASURE VARIABLES OF THE SITUATIONAL THEORY

The first set of questions are those used in the most recent study, of the health-care issue in the United States. They use a fractionation scale – a scale with a zero bottom point and an open top point. A Likert-type scale, like that used for the original single indicators below, can be substituted for the fractionation scale. The indicators of information seeking and processing have been used for many previous studies. The indicators of problem recognition, level of involvement, and constraint recognition are new, multiple indicators.

Information processing

First, I am going to ask several questions about the kinds of stories you would pay attention to on television. Let me take a minute to explain how to answer.

1 I will read you the opening lines from some possible stories that you might hear on a television news programme. In answering, please think of 100 as the average extent to which people pay attention to these kinds of stories. Please give me any number above or below the normal score of 100 that tells me how likely you would be to pay attention to each of these stories after hearing the opening lines. Zero is the lowest possible score, but you can go as much above 100 as you like.

(a) In a study published in today's *New England Journal of Medicine*, researchers reported that adults and children with good health habits and healthy lifestyles have significantly fewer illnesses than those who don't. ____

(b) The Consumer Federation of America released the results of a survey showing that more than 50 per cent of Americans do not believe they are getting high-quality medical care from physicians or hospitals. ____

(c) An estimated 35 million Americans today do not have health insurance. People who want the government to guarantee care for the needy or unemployed are deciding on what means can be found to provide them health care. ____

(d) The Clinton Administration is considering managed competition and the Canadian plan of government health insurance as it examines the structure of the health insurance system in the United States. ____

Information seeking

Now I would like to switch to a question about printed information.

2 Many organizations offer informational materials about health care and other public problems. If you were to see an announcement offering each of the following free booklets, how likely would you be to call or send for it. Just as in the previous question, give a number above or below 100, which is the average likelihood that people would call or send for a brochure like these.

(a) How to determine if you are getting quality health care. ____

(b) Providing health insurance to the uninsured 13 per cent. ____

(c) Ten easy steps you can choose to reduce the likelihood of getting sick. ____

(d) Restructuring the health insurance industry: Four options. ____

Problem recognition, level of involvement, and constraint recognition

(EPR = External problem recognition, IPR = Internal problem recognition, ELI = External level of involvement, ILI = Internal level of

involvement, ECR = External constraint recognition, ICR = Internal constraint recognition)
For the next questions, I would like you to continue using the scale you have been using. I will ask several questions about four problems related to health care. For each question about the four problems, please give me an answer above or below 100, which is the average response for people on a typical problem like these.

3 On this scale, please give me a number that indicates how much you would like to understand each of these problems better. The first problem is: (IPR1)
   (a) The quality of health care.   _____
   (b) People with no health insurance.   _____
   (c) Unhealthy lifestyles.   _____
   (d) The health insurance industry.   _____

4 To what extent do you believe this issue is a serious national problem? (EPR1)
   (a) The quality of health care.   _____
   (b) People with no health insurance.   _____
   (c) Unhealthy lifestyles.   _____
   (d) The health insurance industry.   _____

5 How strong would you say your opinions are about this problem? (ILI1)
   (a) The quality of health care.   _____
   (b) People with no health insurance.   _____
   (c) Unhealthy lifestyles.   _____
   (d) The health insurance industry.   _____

6 To what extent do you believe this issue is a problem that you can do something about? (ECR1)
   (a) The quality of health care.   _____
   (b) People with no health insurance.   _____
   (c) Unhealthy lifestyles.   _____
   (d) The health insurance industry.   _____

7 To what extent do you think this problem is too complicated for you to do anything about? (ICR1)
   (a) The quality of health care.   _____
   (b) People with no health insurance.   _____
   (c) Unhealthy lifestyles.   _____
   (d) The health insurance industry.   _____

8 To what extent do you believe this problem could involve you or someone close to you at some point? (ELI1)
   (a) The quality of health care. ____
   (b) People with no health insurance. ____
   (c) Unhealthy lifestyles. ____
   (d) The health insurance industry. ____

9 To what extent would you say you are curious about this problem? (IPR2)
   (a) The quality of health care. ____
   (b) People with no health insurance. ____
   (c) Unhealthy lifestyles. ____
   (d) The health insurance industry. ____

10 To what extent would you say that this problem is more difficult for you to understand than other problems? (ICR2)
   (a) The quality of health care. ____
   (b) People with no health insurance. ____
   (c) Unhealthy lifestyles. ____
   (d) The health insurance industry. ____

11 How often do you stop to think about people who are affected by this problem? (EPR2)
   (a) The quality of health care. ____
   (b) People with no health insurance. ____
   (c) Unhealthy lifestyles. ____
   (d) The health insurance industry. ____

12 In your mind, how much of a connection do you see between yourself and this problem? (ILI2)
   (a) The quality of health care. ____
   (b) People with no health insurance. ____
   (c) Unhealthy lifestyles. ____
   (d) The health insurance industry. ____

13 To what extent do you believe that you could affect the way this problem is eventually solved if you wanted to? (ECR2)
   (a) The quality of health care. ____
   (b) People with no health insurance. ____
   (c) Unhealthy lifestyles. ____
   (d) The health insurance industry. ____

14 How much do you believe this problem affects or could affect you personally? (ELI2)
   (a) The quality of health care. ____
   (b) People with no health insurance. ____

    (c) Unhealthy lifestyles.   ____

    (d) The health insurance industry.   ____

The second set of questions are the original, single indicators of problem recognition, level of involvement, and constraint recognition. They use a Likert-type scale. The fractionation scale also can be used with these single indicators. The measures of information seeking and processing used with these indicators are the same as those above; thus, are not repeated. These questions were used in the study of Washington reporters (J. Grunig 1983b) and were reproduced in J. Grunig & Hunt (1984:).

Problem recognition

1 First, I would like you to consider how often you *stop to think* about each of four issues. After I name each of these issues, please tell me whether you stop to think about the situation often, sometimes, rarely, or never.

	Often	*Sometimes*	*Rarely*	*Never*
Deregulation of natural gas	4	3	2	1
Breaking up the Bell telephone system	4	3	2	1
Chemical disposal sites	4	3	2	1
Acid rain from air pollution	4	3	2	1

Constraint recognition

2 Now, would you think of whether you could do anything personally that would *make a difference* in the way these issues are handled. If you wanted to do something, would your efforts make a great deal of difference, some difference, very little difference or no difference?

	Great deal	*Some*	*Very little*	*None*
Deregulation of natural gas	4	3	2	1
Breaking up the Bell telephone system	4	3	2	1
Chemical disposal sites	4	3	2	1
Acid rain from air pollution	4	3	2	1

Level of involvement

3 Now, I have a third question about the same issues. For each situation, tell me to what extent you *see a connection* between yourself, personally, and each of these situations. There would be a connection if you believe the issue has affected or could affect you. Tell me if the connection is strong, moderate, weak, or no connection.

	Strong	Moderate	Weak	None
Deregulation of natural gas	4	3	2	1
Breaking up the Bell telephone system	4	3	2	1
Chemical disposal sites	4	3	2	1
Acid rain from air pollution	4	3	2	1

NOTES

1 Even the public relations departments that L. Grunig, Dozier and J. Grunig (1994) identified as most excellent in a major study for the IABC Research Foundation were found to do little research in the qualitative phase of the project.
2 In Price's words: 'But the 'general public,' when equated with the general population, is clearly not a public in the more traditional sense of the term. Fifty years of survey research has pretty much overwhelmingly confirmed . . . that the bulk of the general population is both uninterested and uninformed on most matters that could be construed as public affairs . . . ' (1992: 36).
3 Converse's (1964) concept.
4 This argument has been made, especially, by Patrick Jackson, a principal in the public relations firm of Jackson, Jackson & Wagner and editor of *pr reporter*, in the pages of *pr reporter* (e.g., July 30, 1990). See also J. Grunig (1993).
5 Van Leuven and Slater (1991) have used the situational theory as a way of conceptualizing how publics, public relations people, and the media interact in the process by which public opinion forms and is articulated.
6 Grunig (1979a) showed how the concepts of involvement, information processing, and information seeking could extend uses and gratifications theory to explain passive as well as active communication behaviour.
7 Similar regressions are reported in Grunig (1983a).
8 Graber (1984, pp. 105–107) called these 'hot issues' 'obtrusive issues.' Lang and Lang (1981: 35) called them 'low-threshold issues'.
9 This explanation is consistent with what Petty and Cacioppo (1981, pp. 225–252) described as the 'peripheral route' to attitude change, as compared with the 'direct route'.
10 The term used by Vasquez (1993).
11 See R. Anderson (1989) for further application of Bandura's social learning theory to communication problems.

12 All three studies were conducted by telephone on random samples of residents of the Baltimore and Washington metropolitan areas. Graduate students enrolled in the seminar on Public Relations Publics at the University of Maryland helped design the studies, write the questionnaires and conduct the interviews.

13 The question that seems to measure individual constraint read: 'To what extent do you believe AIDS is a problem that you can do little about?' The questions that seems to measure group efficacy read: 'To what extent do you believe people like you could affect public policy toward AIDS if they wanted to?'

14 Essentially, this is a problem of multicollinearity.

15 For reviews of literature on schemas and their application to communication, see J. Grunig, Ramsey and Schneider (1985) and Schneider [aka L. Grunig] (1985).

16 We measured the presence of both kinds of attitudes with a dichotomous variable distinguishing between respondents who completed six attitude statements versus those who gave a 'no opinion' response. We also correlated the direction of the attitude responses for those who gave them with the canonical variates.

17 Slater *et al.* (1992) did the same in research using the situational theory.

18 For a discussion of the effect of presuppositions on theory building, see J. Grunig (1989c).

19 There is an extensive body of literature on the effects of information campaigns. See Rice and Atkin (1989). In health communication, an approach called media advocacy has become popular (Wallack 1993).

20 In risk communication, a concern with environmental justice now is attracting a great deal of research attention (see Vaugan 1994).

21 A doctoral student at the University of Maryland, John McGrath, is beginning work on a dissertation on creating publics. He is responsible for most of the ideas expressed in this paragraph.

2 Requisite variety in public relations research

Larissa A. Grunig

INTRODUCTION

In 1986, the Foundation of the International Association of Business Communicators (IABC) began to fund the most extensive programme of research on public relations ever undertaken. 'Excellence in Public Relations and Communication Management' is a multi-year, cross-cultural analysis of how public relations is conceptualized, valued, supported, managed and carried out. The second key stage in the study began in Spring 1992. The research team began to develop a plan for probing in greater depth a few of the 300-plus organizations surveyed in the initial phase.

This qualitative phase of the research, completed in spring 1994, helps determine the economic value of excellent public relations departments to their organizations. A smaller number of less-than-excellent organizations were studied as well, in an attempt to measure the cost of **not** having effective public relations. The team also tried to fill gaps of understanding left by the survey research. In particular, the team investigated the roles and status of practitioners of different races and ethnicities, the seeming inconsistency between what top management reports as the value of public relations and the support it accords it, and the historical factors that led to the development of programmes deemed 'excellent'. In this chapter, I will describe some of the findings of the qualitative research only as the context for my larger purpose: exploring the consequences of heterogeneity in public relations research.

As we on the IABC research team went about testing the interaction among the variables included in the qualitative phase, in particular, we learned at least as much about our methodological approach as we did about the organizations we studied. We came to acknowledge that aspects of our own cultural and individual identities intruded on our research. The team process complicated our data collection and subsequent search for commonalities in the data. So, too, did the decision to interview several people within each of the organizations singled out for scrutiny. However, exploring this variety of perceptions became critically important in understanding the organizational context. Through our experience on this project, we came to affirm the validity of Weick's (1979b) notion of requisite variety. His principle holds that there must be as much diversity inside the organization as outside for the organization to build effective relationships with all of its strategic publics.

This notion generally has been used to support the argument for diversity in public relations – that employing minority practitioners, for example, enhances the effectiveness of their organizations because they may enact critical parts of the environment that majority practitioners would not recognize or consider legitimate. This chapter applies requisite variety in a different context: comparative research. It argues that the diversity inherent in the IABC research team of 16 and in the two or three interviewees within a single organization is critically important. It concludes with a discussion of the implications of requisite variety for conducting any research, basic or applied, in public relations.

THE COMPARATIVE STUDY

Several characteristics help set the 'Excellence Project', as it has come to be called, apart from previous, less comprehensive studies. It is international in scope. It combines a quantitative, statistical analysis of a large number of different types and sizes of organizations with qualitative study of a carefully selected handful of both outstanding and more average organizations. Data came from top management as well as from public relations practitioners and rank-and-file employees. The study is, in a word, **comparative**.

One of the most important hallmarks of the Excellence Project is its cross-cultural nature. The original six-member grant team surveyed public relations practitioners, top management of their organizations and a purposive sample of at least a dozen employees in organizations in three countries: the United States, the United Kingdom and Canada. Time, co-operation, cost and language constrained us to study just these three English-speaking nations. However, other scholars working under the direction of members of the research team have gone on to apply the survey instrument (or a modification of that questionnaire) in additional contexts. For example, graduate students from the University of Maryland have investigated the practice of excellence in public relations in southern India (Sriramesh 1991), Greece (Lyra 1991) and Taiwan (Huang, 1990). Scholar/practitioners in Slovenia (Gruban, Verčič and Zavrl 1994) and France (Laufenburger, forthcoming) have conducted similar studies.

Analysis of this body of research led the Excellence team to agree that the cross-cultural nature of the research would be denied if we relied solely on quantitative methods. Across countries, researchers tended to rely on a face-to-face, qualitative approach. They modified the survey instrument as necessary to convey the **sense** of the questions to the practitioners whose language, customs, beliefs, values and norms all differed from those of us who developed the questionnaire.

Thus the second stage of the Excellence project became qualitative. It was designed to add context to the picture first painted through the survey data. One complication, of course, was that the context could have changed significantly in the two to three years between our initial data collection and this second wave of qualitative research. If that were the case, then building in 'longitudinality' or tracking change over time becomes critically important. Certain issues, such as cultural diversity, may have assumed more prominence today than they enjoyed, say, in 1990.

Purposes of the qualitative stage of the research

Our main purpose in this field study was to solve any anomalies in the quantitative data. In addition, we could explore questions we did not think to pose in that initial stage. For instance, we have been queried by audiences hearing the preliminary report about why we did not include issues of race and ethnicity when we **did** focus on questions about gender.

With this second major step, then, we could deal with questions that we heard from IABC members around the world where we presented our initial findings – questions that those results did not address adequately. Together, members of the research team, the IABC Foundation board and chapters around the world developed a long list of items that we could address in the qualitative stage of the project. We on the research team pared the 'ideal' list rather brutally to four major areas.

Our first group of questions dealt with perceptions of the chief executive officers, in large part because of their role as cultural leaders within the organization and also because the power-control perspective suggests that members of the dominant coalition tend to determine the approach to public relations practised. We were especially interested in learning how a close relationship of credibility and trust developed between members of the power elite and their top communicators. Next, we posed a group of questions that speaks to the growing diversity of the field of public relations and of the workforce in general. One of our goals here was to elicit helpful suggestions or remedies for the discrimination that disadvantaged groups often encounter at work. The third group of questions dealt specifically with public relations: the history of the function within the organization, strategic management, career planning, relationships with the dominant coalition and counterparts throughout the organization and ways of transcending the technician's role into management. The final group of questions dealt with the perceived monetary value of public relations to the organization.

Our study used a multiple-case design. That is, we conducted a series of case studies using multiple sources of data (primarily long interviews) within each case. This design offers the advantage of more compelling evidence than either the single-case study or the survey (Yin 1989). Despite its strength, however, it is rarely feasible. Only with an ample team of researchers underwritten with sufficient funding can such a robust study be undertaken.

Standards for evaluating qualitative research

A recent article (Eadie 1994) in the newsletter of the Speech Communication Association spoke of the need for adequate financial and human resources to conduct research its author deemed 'credible'. The article reviewed two major, multi-year studies in communication. The first, directed by the University of Arizona's David Buller, involved a four-person team that received $1.3 million from the US National Cancer Institute for designing curricular materials to persuade families to adopt skin cancer prevention methods. Buller and other colleagues (including scholars from communication, sociology, nursing, and family and community medicine) are working on two additional funded projects. The cancer institute also has funded a proposal from a team headed by Vicki Freimuth of the University of Maryland. In his interviews with both Buller and Freimuth, Eadie learned that 'participation on interdisciplinary teams is essential to the credibility of such a large-scale project' (1994: 5).

Qualitative research typically is held to different standards than its quantitative counterpart. In qualitative studies, we hear much about credibility, for example, and little about validity and reliability.

Criteria such as credibility are no less rigorous than the latter; they simply are better suited to the purpose and the methods used. The naturalistic work of Lincoln and Guba (1985) uses the term 'credibility' in a somewhat different way than Eadie (1994), however. To Lincoln and Guba, credibility is the standard that speaks to subjects' adequate portrayal so that the final portrait seems to have 'truth value'. They emphasized the importance of credibility to the constructors of the original reality – the participants themselves. We took this to mean that interviewees should be able to recognize themselves and their situation in our analysis of the data.

Lincoln and Guba offered qualitative researchers three additional standards as alternatives to the reliability and validity so familiar to their quantitative counterparts. These criteria include dependability, or the assurance that appropriate adaptations to the situation under investigation have been made, and transferability, or the ability to transpose the set of findings to a relevant new situation. The burden of transferability lies with the person who would do the transferring, rather than with the initial researcher. However, that researcher is obliged to make the context clear to other scholars.

Lincoln and Guba's (1985) final standard for judging the merit of qualitative research has special significance for this chapter on teamwork in the research process. They termed it 'confirmability', or having enough objectivity in the data analysis that a second researcher would be likely to come to the same conclusions. 'Objectivity' here refers to intersubjective agreement. As this chapter will go on to demonstrate, our research team in the second phase of the Excellence Project did indeed achieve confirmability.

However, we made no inappropriate claims about generalizability, in particular, for this second phase of data collection. We continue to believe that the value of our work lies in its potential to discover patterns or commonalities that could be extrapolated from the organizations sampled to other organizations striving for effectiveness and to develop the theory of excellence in public relations first set forth in the conceptualization for the quantitative phase (J. Grunig 1992).

Likewise, we made no claims of objectivity in the classical logical-positivist sense. We, as human beings, substituted for the survey instrument in the quantitative study. We on the research team – not the questionnaire or the computer – were both the mechanisms for collecting and for reducing and analysing our data.

Instead, through our scientific, systematic method we could and did make the claim of closeness to our participants – a concept consistent with Lincoln and Guba's (1985) notion of credibility. Through our research design we sought to discover participants' perspectives rather than merely reflect our own inherent subjectivities or cultural biases. Like the poststructuralists, we questioned constantly whether we were invested in our own power at the expense of paying close attention to what our participants were trying to tell us.

Like much qualitative research, then, ours relied on people's words as the primary data (Marshall and Rossman 1989). We considered it incumbent upon us to value those people and those words. One typical way in which qualitative information (and thus the people who provide that information) is **devalued** is through questioning the validity of self-reports. (In much the same way, we as the qualitative scholars can be devalued when our colleagues of a more quantitative bent question whether we can deal adequately with our own biases.)

We were acutely aware that our field study rested heavily on verbal reports from the participants. Observing directly all the relevant variables in our study was impractical, if not impossible. Of course, our exhaustive conceptualization (J. Grunig 1992) and the survey data helped validate the self reports we gathered. Standardization of the interview protocol further allowed for valid comparisons among responses of the participants. Also, embedded in the research questions were multiple measures of key concepts.

VARIETY IN INTERVIEWEES' PERSPECTIVES

Perhaps more important for the purposes of this chapter, we attempted to interview more than a single member of each organization in our sample. In large part through the pilot test of the qualitative stage of the Excellence Project, we learned how vitally important it was to include the perspectives of chief executive officers. We conducted a single case study as a pretest of our research design. In this exploratory work with a chemical association, we interviewed both the CEO and his vice president of public relations.

That CEO provided several insights that ended up figuring prominently in our results. Lest readers dismiss the importance of including the perceptions of top management in a study of public relations, consider the understandings we gleaned from our interview with a single chief executive officer:

• The monetary value of public relations far exceeds what we might have imagined.

- If we are not comfortable with two-way, dialogic communication then we have no business being in public relations.
- Collaborating with activist groups – rather than fighting them – may lead to learning and thus greater effectiveness as an organization.
- Directors of public relations should enjoy what the CEO called a 'peer professional' relationship with the heads of other functional areas of the organization.
- Public relations people should have 'grazing rights' in all departments, rather than being territorial and sticking strictly to their own department or to issues narrowly defined as communication.
- The head of public relations must therefore be included in the dominant coalition and that person must be empowered to take risks.

Enlightened by these notions, we went on to conduct long personal interviews with several dozen organizational elites: the top public relations people who agreed to participate from selected organizations and the CEOs or other members of senior management with whom these practitioners work. Finally, we interviewed a few other members of the public relations department in selected organizations because we believe that these lower-level employees may have a more critical perspective on communication and less of a vested interest in their organization.

Largely because of limitations of time and travel, some of these interviews with members of the dominant coalition and with others in public relations were conducted over the telephone. However, we deemed it **vital** when studying organizational processes that more than a single individual be queried. Our understanding of the process was bound to increase if we were able to draw on several perceptions of the same process.

Qualitative research design typically represents a compromise between the ideal and the realistic. Our desire to be comprehensive was tempered with the understanding that time and financial resources were limited. As a result, we investigated in depth approximately twice as many excellent organizations as average or mediocre (or worse) ones (on the assumption that we had more to learn from the outstanding operations). We ended up studying two dozen organizations in depth.

A second decision about sampling,[1] apart from the characteristics of excellence or mediocrity, involved which specific organizations to approach. Beyond the organization's willingness to co-operate was a consideration of the appropriate cultural mix. Here again, we had to temper our enthusiasm for gathering data in Canada and the United Kingdom with the realization that only two of our team members were working outside the United States. Thus, we decided to include three British organizations – two excellent and one less-than-excellent. We studied one Canadian organization as well. These non-US organizations added the important cross-cultural dimension to our analysis of the American cases.

Most organizations came from the United States. All sections of the country were represented. Analysis of the survey data indicated few significant differences among the three countries in terms of excellence in public relations, so we did not feel compelled to balance the numbers proportionally across countries in this qualitative phase. Mere representation of each societal culture was adequate for our purposes.

Organizations included small, medium and large size. Interestingly, the cases chosen for this qualitative analysis because of their level of excellence represented a variety of size as well as type: associations, governmental agencies, not-for-profits and corporations. They were as different as the chemical industry, a blood bank and a cosmetics company.

Other organizations analysed in the qualitative research include a Canadian medical association, an oil company affiliate in the United Kingdom and an oil company based in the United States. We looked also at a US state lottery, a metal manufacturer, two public utilities, arts and health organizations, a medical products manufacturer, a financial services company, a hotel chain, two insurance companies, the aerospace industry, an engineering experiment station, a real estate developer, an economic development agency and a disabled services organization.

In each of these cases, we spoke at length with a top communicator. We were both gratified and somewhat surprised to find that we were able to interview a member of the dominant coalition as well. And when our interviews included two or even three public relations practitioners in the same department, the variety of their perspectives proved invaluable. For example, early on we learned that strategic management in public relations may be the key to moving from the technician's role to the management team. We also discovered, however, that this concept means different things to different people. To some, such as the oil company affiliate, strategic management is sophisticated media relations. To others, it means managing the entire public relations department. To still others – such as the top communicators in the utility company, the industry association, the medical association and the chemical corporation – strategic management is not limited to communication with the media or supervision of one's own department. Instead, it extends throughout the organization. As a result of these understandings, we never again will refer to 'strategic management' without first defining exactly what we mean by the term.

Similarly, we sought a variety of viewpoints on the financial value of public relations. We reasoned that interviewing only public relations practitioners might result in answers that sounded self-serving. Would consumers of our research be surprised to learn that communicators consider the communication function vitally important, important enough to justify big budgets because of its impressive return on investment? More than worrying about inflated senses of self-worth, we questioned whether public relations practitioners – even those at the managerial level – would be able to attach a real dollar amount to the effects of the work. After all, we in public relations reputedly are wordsmiths rather than number crunchers. We did find that few of our interviewees in communication were able to assess the monetary contribution made by public relations. Instead, most of our data on this contribution came from the CEOs we talked with. However 'soft' readers of our research report may consider these figures to be, we urged them to keep in mind that we were addressing our questions related to financial value to the people with the greatest expertise: CEOs or other members of the dominant coalition in addition to their managers of public relations.

Of all the questions we posed that elicited wide-ranging responses among our participants, none provided more of a mixed picture than what we came to consider the 'chicken or egg' question: 'Which came first – good communication or value and support for communication that led, in turn, to the hiring of an expert practitioner?' Typically, we heard that having a skilful communication manager on board led to increasing value and support for the function. However, some interviewees even seemed to contradict themselves, as in the case of an industry association CEO. He told us first that he had gone looking for an expert communicator and hired one. He went on to explain that because he was not expert in public relations himself, he could not judge precisely who would fit the bill.

A striking example of diverse perspectives in a single organizational context came from the medical association we studied. In answer to the question of how public relations practitioners are involved in strategic planning, we heard first from the assistant executive director for public affairs. He considered himself a participant in setting the 'strategic agenda' for the organization, despite what he deemed the president's 'lukewarm support' for public affairs. He described his own role as advisory to the board of directors. A second communicator in the same association saw the interplay between the communication function and strategic planning quite differently. She considered her counterpart in public affairs **too** involved in strategy. She believed the public affairs function had taken over the strategic agenda of the entire organization. As a consequence, she predicted a power struggle between the president, whom she believed values participation, and the head of public affairs, whom she characterized as a 'one-person kingdom'.

A second instance of strikingly divergent viewpoints within a single organization came from the cosmetics company. There, the manager of public relations credited Total Quality Management (TQM), or what her office called 'creative action', with helping motivate its promotion and sales forces. As a result, she valued TQM wholeheartedly. The top communicator in that company espoused a more cynical view of TQM and the action teams it recommends. Although he acknowledged that the programme does provide these groups of employees with a sense of ownership in various initiatives, he told us that it 'leads to programmes coming down the pike as partially presold.'

This kind of variance of viewpoints caused some vexation among members of the research team. How, we found ourselves questioning, could two people working in the same department of the same organization have such different perceptions of that organization? In the end, this question served more to validate our methodological approach than to call it into question (unless, of course, we are to question the legitimacy of **all** research). We came to understand through our own immersion in this project that the environment of the organization and even its inner workings truly are enacted. 'Enacted' means that the organization or its environment will not be perceived as the same by different people in the same organization or by people outside the organization. So, exploring a variety of perceptions became critically important in understanding the organizational context.

Through our long interviews, we listened to what happens in the organizational context as a way of understanding the reasons for excellence in public relations. We reasoned that by studying internal dynamics in this way, we could help public relations practitioners improve their own effectiveness. This reflective process also led to our own development and empowerment as researchers. The chapter turns now to a description of the research team and its process.

THE VARIETY INHERENT IN TEAM RESEARCH

The research team for this qualitative project included four of the six permanent members of the IABC Research Foundation grant team,[2] one former graduate research assistant, several current graduate students and one former graduate student. We were 16 in all. Two of us are based in the United Kingdom. The rest are split between San Diego State University and the University of Maryland at College Park. As mentioned earlier, trustees of the Foundation and individual IABC chapter members helped develop ideas for the research questions. The synergism inherent in such a group process undoubtedly enhanced the quality of the research design and its execution. At the same time, teamwork complicated the process.

Despite the flexibility inherent in qualitative research design, we tried to standardize our process as much as possible. Our intent was **comparability** – so that data collected by different investigators would be comparable, rather than apples and oranges. At the same time, we did not foresee perfect overlap in the outcomes and understandings that resulted from the work of different members of the team. As Clifford (1986: 14) warned, suspect 'any overly confident and consistent ethnographic voice' because of the inevitability of incomplete knowledge.

The procedures necessary for sending the team into the field may have seemed overly detailed and elementary to senior members of the research group. Further, the length of the research plan we ultimately developed seemed to violate some or all of the traditional standards of writing such a plan – simplicity, clarity and parsimony (Locke, Spirduso and Silverman 1987). However, a comprehensive research design reduced the onerous task of preparing the final report of the study's findings and conclusions. And, given the team's training primarily as quantitative scholars, we considered such a thorough set of guidelines both appropriate and helpful.

More specifically, the blueprint for the design of the qualitative phase of the Excellence Project served four purposes. First, it provided for communication among the members of the research team and between the team, its graduate assistants and members of the IABC Research Foundation. Second, it set forth our plan of action as we went into the field. Third, it could be considered a contract between the research team and the sponsoring Foundation. Finally, the design provided a framework for interpreting the results with dispatch.

That said, however, we did not feel shackled by the procedures developed for this study. Like Kauffman (1992), we believe that to stand on protocol when the situation suggests flexibility would be to invalidate ourselves as qualitative researchers, our participants, our relationship with them and the entire project.

Going into the field with this philosophy and having personal contact with our participants brought us close to many of the people being studied. In our systematic effort to understand the realities of their workplace, we became collaborators with them as well as with each other on the research team. In other words, the public relations practitioners and the CEOs we interviewed became co-researchers. And when people study themselves, the research becomes more readily understandable and accessible to all potential consumers of that research.

We also believe that collaboration between researcher and participant helped crack the code of the organizational culture that determines certain actions and outcomes. In this qualitative stage, we tried to discover what respondents meant when they marked a certain number on the survey questionnaire two or three years earlier. This search for meanings seems especially important in cross-cultural research.

The **flexibility** inherent in qualitative research proved both frustrating and rewarding. Researchers discovered they had to be detectives, probing for answers to key questions and, in some cases, even going to extraordinary lengths to obtain the documentation they needed to complete their individual analyses. Many initial plans for gaining access to key sources were scrapped. Alternative approaches were tried – alternatives that depended on the resourcefulness and self-confidence of members of the research team. Thus our method of data collection became almost idiosyncratic despite our lengthy and detailed research design.

So, too, were the research questions posed. Recall that we began with an initial set of questions that focused on CEOs, culture and gender diversity, the public relations function and its contribution to organizational effectiveness. We found, though, that because the researcher in qualitative studies is the instrument of the research (rather than, say, the questionnaire as the survey instrument), questions actually asked or emphasized reflected in part the underlying interests of the researchers. For example, one graduate student was preparing to write a doctoral dissertation about the role of conflict resolution in public relations. Thus his questions in the Excellence Project tended to emphasize negotiation and 'getting to yes' strategies. A second example was a former graduate assistant on the first phase of the project who subsequently had written a doctoral dissertation on women in public relations. She contributed a sensitivity about cultural and gender diversity that few others on the team could boast.

Rather than decrying this heterogeneity of emphases, we celebrated the breadth of perspective and new insights it provided. At the same time, each researcher made a real effort to stick to the interview protocol for the sake of the ultimate comparative analysis – the look for commonalities across cases. If time ran short, we either skipped some questions (marked as less crucial on the interview guide) or asked several in tandem. We also modified our interview protocol as a result of each organization's unique situation as we understood it from the quantitative data we reviewed before going into the field. Thus each researcher added 'special research questions' pertinent to his or her assigned organization.[3] These questions typically addressed any wide discrepancies between responses in the original surveys of CEOs and their public relations heads. So, for example, in the case of a real estate company we were determined to find out why the dominant coalition seemed to devalue communication even when the top communicator's skills were top-notch.

To these questions, the 16 of us brought a broad, rich base of experience from which to approach our analysis of the answers. This value of diversity in work groups increasingly is being established through research in fields such as organizational behaviour and human resource management. The work of Nemeth (1985), for example, helps support this contention. Through an extensive series of investigations, she found that including heterogeneous viewpoints raises the level of critical analysis in the decision process. Consideration of minority perspectives improves the quality of that process regardless of whether the minority view ultimately prevails. Like Nemeth, we found that our mixed groups allowed for consideration of a number of alternative explanations. The assumptions and implications of these alternative scenarios were subjected to exceptionally thorough examination. However, this understanding alone fails to explain **why** diversity and especially dissent in the group process is linked with creativity and more adequate decisions (Nemeth 1985).

Without considering Weick's (1979b) concept of requisite variety, we are left with 'duelling cliches'. On the one hand, we could reason that 'many hands make light work' and that 'two heads are better than one'. On the other hand, we might think that 'too many cooks spoil the broth'. A closer examination of our process of data analysis, in particular, should lead us to the depth of understanding that may benefit future scholars embarking on a team project in public relations.

Teamwork in qualitative data analysis

Analysis consists of two main processes: data reduction and interpretation. Data reduction is one of the greatest challenges facing the qualitative scholar. Woolf (1929) questioned how one ever should find the grains of truth embedded in all this 'mass of paper'. Indeed, Yin (1989: 105) considered data analysis one of the 'least developed and most difficult aspects' of case studies.

So, before tackling the difficult process of interpretation, we had to reduce the massive amount of information we had gathered. Our data **reduction** began with the tape recordings of interviews. Rather than transcribing the entire tapes, most members of the research team listened carefully to the recordings – probably several times – and made notes of where the key quotes were. Handwritten notes taken during the interviews helped with this.

Key quotes were passages that we most wanted to include verbatim in our final report. They also included statements so telling that they actually answered our research questions, either because they represented a typical response or because they were strikingly idiosyncratic.[4]

Interpretation of the data began with individual interviewers. We each tried to make sense, first, of what each individual participant was telling us. Then, we tried to describe the situation within each organization by integrating the responses of each interviewee from that organization with each other and with the written materials we had reviewed about that organization. We factored in the original survey data collected from the organization, as well. When we put the cases together, talking in small groups with other members of the team,[5] we were able to synthesize the patterns that emerged.

Throughout this interpretive process, we took care not to force consistent patterns or to ignore information that was interesting or important but did not seem to 'fit'. We continuously asked ourselves how the insights we gained through our interviews were consistent with, contradicted or otherwise elucidated the survey data. So, on the one hand we were after commonalities in the conversations and on the other hand, we accepted responses that indicated differences.

Finally, we found that the best way to analyse the reams of data that resulted was to return to the theoretical concepts and propositions that guided the survey research. In other words, theory served as the best device for integrating our findings across the 24 cases. We grouped our results not by country, type or size of organization or degree of excellence but by concepts such as symmetry of communication, role of the top communicator, his or her potential for public relations, relationship with the dominant coalition, the history of that relationship, organizational culture, cultural diversity and social responsibility.

Our method of analysis became 'analyse as we go'. In other words, we did not wait until all cases were complete or even until each case was concluded. Instead, we used the first interview in a given organization as a basis for asking questions and interpreting responses in the subsequent interviews there. The more we learned about a public relations department or its top management, the better we were able to fine-tune what we asked and what we made of the answers. Thus the research that was compressed into a single spring season was more intensive than the typical process of collecting all the data and then starting to analyse those findings.

Teamwork in writing up the results

The process of writing up the findings began with fieldnotes and tapes. From these recordings, each member of the team wrote a 'mini report' of each case. We based the writing of these case reports on a 'template' developed by David Dozier and his seminar students at San Diego State University. Although this format seemed to introduce disconcerting redundancies of phrasing, it did allow for the crucial comparability among all cases. Ultimately, as director of this phase of the qualitative research, I assumed responsibility for integrating all of these data into the results of the quantitative phase for the two books of findings that will follow. Miles and Huberman (1984) talked about the importance of seeing emergent links across different parts of the data and then achieving a successful integration of the findings.

Because context – including the background of each organization – was so important, each member of the research team began his or her 'mini-report' of an individual case with an executive summary that described the organization and reiterated its excellence score. These backgrounders were deliberately vague so that no organization (with the exception of the association involved in the pilot study) could be identified.

We went on to review briefly the most important elements of the quantitative data for each case. These findings led, in many cases, to 'special research questions' for that case. We spelled out the number, length and location (on site? over the telephone? in person but away from the office?) of each interview conducted along with the job titles of the people we spoke with.

At that point in our mini-reports, we departed from the Dozier template to deal with whatever major concepts were especially relevant to the organization in question. We included in our detailed description of what we heard during the interview some direct quotation – but, once again, nothing so characteristic of either the participant nor the organization as to identify that person or company. Each mini-report included conclusions. The conclusions drawn from a single instance, of course, mean little. Only when aggregated with all of the other cases and with the results of the survey research will we be able to draw true conclusions from them about our sample of nearly 300 organizations and extrapolate from those cases to other organizations.

One important disclaimer here: we acknowledged that aspects of our own cultural and individual identities undoubtedly intruded into the writing process. The ultimate test of adequacy for the resultant text will be readers' determination of whether we have bridged the gap (even imperfectly) between our own and the cultures we are exploring. The bridge, of course, is a shaky one. Geertz (1988: 10) explained its tenuousness as 'at one and the same time an intimate view and a cool assessment'. In other words, through our qualitative research we hoped to get close to our participants and the context in which they work. At the same time, as scientists we hoped to maintain our own standpoint somewhat apart from that context as we assessed and ultimately reported on that situation.

Published research on teamwork in communication studies

Despite adequate funding and the human resources of our research team, throughout this study we wrestled with a constellation of frustrations. Many of them speak specifically to teamwork in research. These included:

- the long-distance relationship of members of the research team;
- the different values and experiences those scholars have of qualitative methodology;

- cross-cultural complications inherent in a three-nation project;
- the ambiguous procedures and standards for qualitative research;
- the flexibility and creativity qualitative research requires; and
- the ubiquitous constraints of time, money and energy.

Thus what may have come to seem like a tidy, linear process when described in the final research report actually reflects the fits and starts, sidesteps and backtracking that characterize the development of most qualitative research and, perhaps, most research designs *per se* – whether executed by individual scholars or by teams such as ours.

Perhaps, because little has been written about teamwork in communication research. I consider this a real problem in moving research forward, since students of public relations theory and research rely especially on the literature in our field for their understanding of how to conduct their own investigations. An admittedly cursory review of several US textbooks dealing with research design and methodology in the disciplines of public relations, communication and the social sciences showed no direct references to the team process. I read carefully the tables of contents and indices of those texts, looking for references to such terms as 'teamwork', 'collegiality' and 'collaboration'. I also scanned, albeit quickly, the pages of each of the texts for similar allusions.

Contemporary Communication Research Methods (M. Smith, 1988) is one of only two texts among the two dozen on my shelf that even mentions these concepts. In her subsection dealing with 'Researcher effects', she alludes to the potential for the researcher's personal characteristics to compromise a study's internal validity. Her suggestions for overcoming this bias are (a) to use a double-blind paradigm to achieve what she called 'a neutral psychosocial posture' (1988: 187) and (b) to bring in men and women of different racial backgrounds to conduct different aspects of the project if these demographic variables are deemed likely to affect participants' responses. In her subsection on 'Personal and professional aspirations', Smith also discussed the problems inherent in individual subjectivity. She acknowledged that scholars' professional aspirations may dictate their choice of problems and methods. Ambition also may compromise scholarly integrity. Her resolution here rests on the *post hoc* vigilance of colleagues: 'In the final analysis, the health of scholarship, like most other human endeavors, depends on the integrity of individual researchers *coupled with a research community's willingness to exact swift and severe sanctions on all who violate intellectual bonds of trust*' (1988: 291, emphasis added).

Similarly, Babbie's (1992) *The Practice of Social Research* alluded to the 'watchdog' role of other researchers in helping overcome what he considered two common errors in human inquiry: overgeneralization and selective observation. He, too, concluded that colleagues working independently but on the same problems, later on, would expose these inadequacies. He alluded to the 'totally independent replications by other researchers' (1992: 22) as a safeguard against assuming that a few similar events are evidence of a general pattern. In the case of overlooking something that contradicts one's conclusions, he noted that 'your colleagues will notice it and bring it to your attention. That's a service scientists provide to one another and to the enterprise of science itself' (1992: 24).

Maybe so, but I would prefer this 'service' to be an inherent part of the research process – built into research designs from their inception to the writing of the final report of results. It not only should preclude the embarrassment of public disclosure of distortions, but it should keep those distortions from being published and thus added to the so-called 'body of knowledge' in the first place. Working as a team, as we did on the Excellence Project, also should help overcome several of the other typical problems Babbie catalogued: *ex post facto* hypothesizing, illogical reasoning, ego involvement in understanding, the premature closure of inquiry and mystification (the fact that 'none of us can hope to understand everything' [1992: 26]). Published works take on a certain legitimacy, especially with students, so maintaining the integrity of the journals and texts in the field is paramount.

One notable example to the dearth of information about team research comes from the work of Bantz (1993). Unlike the direction of this chapter, his analysis explored group process. I am more interested in focusing on the **outcomes** than the **process** of teamwork. However, Bantz contributed several valuable insights that have relevance to this work.

Bantz (1993) began by delineating the advantages and what he considered the serious disadvantages of team research. On the pro side, the minds and hands of a group limit the amount of work any one person must do. Team process also allows for a convergence of concepts, theories and methods. On the negative side, teamwork presents the challenges of co-ordinating the work, balancing task and social dimensions and what Bantz described as 'working across time, space, and culture' (1993: 1).

Throughout his analysis, Bantz equated team research with cross-cultural research because that was his experience of the process. In particular, he reflected on his ten years of involvement on an eight- to ten-person team conducting a comparative study of social conflict (Cohen, Adoni and Bantz 1990). This group of scholars went beyond the Anglo (American, Canadian and British) to include Yugoslavian-born and American-born Israelis, an Austrian-born Berliner and an English South African. In all, the team was influenced by eight national cultures.

Bantz' (1993) purpose was to illustrate the potential impact of cultural diversity on group process. He was careful to point out that his analysis is only illustrative rather than a literal representation of the members' cultures because the individual – his level of analysis – is not the culture. He began unpacking the group dynamics of his team using Hofstede's (1984) theoretical dimensions. He found that all four major dimensions – power distance, uncertainty avoidance, masculinity and individualism – affected the development of group leadership, norms, conflict and roles. He concluded that 'working together necessitates an intensity and continuity of interaction that highlights cultural diversity' (1984: 18). He suggested that members of a research team must use an array of tactics to manage diversity if the project is to succeed.

We on the Excellence team believe that we succeeded in the qualitative phase of our research. Despite the complications inherent in a diverse team – disadvantages that Bantz' (1993) analysis seems to dwell on at the expense of the many advantages we experienced – the research report that resulted exceeded our expectations. On the one hand, we could use a cultural-analytic perspective to try to explain what led to the credible, dependable, transferable and confirmable report we believe we generated. On the other hand, the cultural composition of our team would suggest the opposite outcome. A brief review of Hofstede's (1984) cultural dimensions should explain why.

In terms of Hofstede's (1984) dimension of **individualism**, in particular, we would be in trouble. Members of our research group all came from societies that score close to the top of the range from individualism to collectivism (91 for the United States and 89 for the United Kingdom). In fact, America and Great Britain are ranked number 1 and number 3, respectively, on the Individualism Index (IDV). This suggests that our primarily Anglo team would be likely to experience difficulty in agreeing on roles and norms and that our work would be confounded with trying to balance group versus individual needs. This is exactly what happened on Bantz' (1993) team. It was characterized more by individualist than collectivist expectations. For just one relevant instance, Bantz explained that 'it cost us two years . . . before accepting that ten people couldn't write a book' (1993: 9).

Bantz described a shifting life pattern over the years that characterized our research as well: 'As time passed, it became clear that mix of individual involvement and collective commitment shifted, reflecting the members' participation in other projects and changes in their lives (one member retired completely during the project, another retired from one institution as we completed the project)' (1993: 9). So, too, with our initial grant team. We all took on other projects in the ten-year course of the Excellence research. One team member became seriously ill, another retired from teaching, one switched from university teaching to consulting and back to teaching at a different university, and one merely changed universities. Research assistants graduated and other students took their place. I only can account for the team's continuing to work for the collective good despite our individualistic heritage by speculating that we discussed each phase of the project extensively and came to agreement before proceeding. We also accepted different levels of involvement for each member during the multi-year project.

Fortunately for the IABC team, we tended to come from societal cultures ranked in the mid range on **power-distance**. That meant that we as Americans (40 on the Power Distance Index) and British (35 on the PDI) did not attach so much importance to human inequality in terms of the relative power of superiors and subordinates as, say, the scholar of Yugoslavian descent (76 on the PDI) on Bantz' (1993) team.

Nevertheless, we did have to grapple with at least two levels of hierarchy involved in this research. First, there was a project director and the other team members. However, the potential power of the team leader was tempered by a number of factors. First, I was not the overall project leader. Then, too, the group working from the West Coast was headed by another member of the team. Thus the three of us – the project director, the West Coast team leader and the director of the qualitative phase of the research – had to work together to ensure a co-ordinated effort. Unwittingly, we adopted one of Bantz' (1993) suggestions for teamwork that accommodates the power differential: we expected that different people on the team would take the leadership at different points, usually reflecting different expertise.

A second power differential involved the fact that some team members were faculty and others were graduate students or former students. One would expect students to defer to faculty. Fortunately, what students lacked in perceived power they seemed to make up for in numbers. Quite simply, there were three times more of them (12) than us (4). I observed during team meetings on the East Coast that as soon as one graduate assistant spoke up, others tended to chime in – often agreeing, supporting the point, or bravely volunteering their own experiences even when they contradicted those of the senior faculty.

Only in this way could the vitally important insights of the students and former students become incorporated into the data collection and subsequent analysis. One major instance in which this happened was our discussion of the potential contribution of public relations to the organization's 'bottom line'. Believing we understood the agenda of the Research Foundation sponsoring the study, we leaders of the project stressed to our student assistants the vital importance of gathering information about monetary value. We had been concerned that Foundation board members faulted our survey research for failing to establish the connection between excellent public relations and its financial contribution. We intended to remedy this perceived shortcoming in the qualitative study. By the time students on the East Coast team had completed their half-dozen case analyses, however, they helped us realize that IABC members at large may not echo the concern of IABC Research Foundation trustees for attaching a dollar value to public relations.[6] Students on the team offered the following explanation, which is reproduced here verbatim from the report of research results:

> Practitioners of public relations and their CEOs alike were reluctant or unable to attach a monetary value to the contribution of public relations. There are several reasons for this.
> Professional associations such as IABC and the Public Relations Society of America (PRSA) all tend to emphasize the need to attach a financial value to public relations. The people we talked with, however, were not thinking in this way. Instead, CEOs and their top communicators alike were thinking about how public relations fits into the big picture of the organization. That picture includes, but is not limited to, bottom-line profitability. Long-term relationships with strategic publics and a sense of responsibility to those stakeholders seemed equally important. Credible, positive relationships may serve as a buffer between the organization and its key constituencies in times of crisis.

Our participants questioned how such dimensions could be measured. They believed that the integration of responsibility and profitability makes such a determination nearly impossible. Public relations practitioners in the most excellent operations did not see a compelling *need* to measure their contributions. They had what we determined was a confidence borne of a history of success. They knew they added value . . . and so they did not perceive a need to justify their existence in monetary terms. At least one top communicator was reluctant to link dollar figures to public relations efforts because of fear that the numbers would seem almost unbelievably high.

Uncertainty avoidance, a third Hofstede (1984) concept, refers to a person's lack of tolerance for ambiguity. Individuals low on the Uncertainty Avoidance Index (UAI) chafe under rules, are open to change, are highly motivated and tend to reject hierarchy. Both cultures represented on our research team, American and British, rank low in uncertainty avoidance (in the 32nd and 35th percentiles, respectively). Perhaps because we did not vary widely on the UAI, we did not find it difficult to work together within a research design that had to remain adaptable. Undoubtedly some members of the team found flexibility more of a challenge than others. However, agreement on the project's goals, once again, seemed to supersede the stress of facing uncertainties in the process of data collection and interpretation.

Finally, Hofstede described the dimension of **masculinity**, based on the understanding that societies socialize individuals in gendered directions. Bantz (1993) equated masculinity with the instrumental dimension: instrumental cultures socialize people to be assertive, seek advancement and strive for wages. He equated femininity with the expressive dimension: expressive cultures socialize people to be nurturing, be oriented toward providing service, emphasize interpersonal needs and be concerned about the physical environment. Key to this discussion is the understanding that cultures low on instrumentalism or masculinity are more likely to value co-operation, certainly a useful ingredient for teamwork. Anglo cultures tend to rank higher than average on the masculinity index (66 and 62 for Great Britain and the United States, respectively). At the same time, however, half of the team involved in the qualitative phase of the Excellence Project was female. If values such as nurturance and co-operation are indeed associated with femininity, then perhaps these eight women balanced the more stereotypically masculine characteristics of assertiveness, need for recognition and independence in decision-making found within the group as well.

This brief discussion correlating the Hofstede (1984) cultural dimensions with the composition and the process of the Excellence team is inadequate for any conclusions about the efficacy of our team. Earlier on in the chapter, I made the claim that our qualitative research was a successful team effort. The **explanation** for our achievement lies in more in the work of Karl Weick on requisite variety.

THE CONCEPT OF REQUISITE VARIETY APPLIED TO PUBLIC RELATIONS RESEARCH

Through personal experiences on this project, we came to affirm the wisdom of Weick's (1979b) notion of requisite variety. His principle suggests that there must be as much diversity inside the organization as outside for the organization to build effective relationships with all of its strategic publics – both internal and external. More specifically, Weick maintained that what he called the 'enactment pool' or the perspectives of those (such as public relations practitioners or marketers) who do the enacting should be matched to the degree of variation present in the market-place.

Bantz (1990) credited Weick's programme of research (1969, 1977a, 1977b, 1979a, 1979b, 1983, 1984) with influencing theorizing in organizational communication throughout the last two decades. Weick, a social psychologist, conceptualized organizations as a series of linked processes that run from enactment to selection to retention. His is an information-processing model. Taken together, the processes increase shared meaning among members of an organization. Weick considered the processes akin to organizations talking to themselves 'over and over to find out what they are thinking (1979b: 133–4). Although he acknowledged that enactment operates at the level of individual psychology, selection is a group process. Everett considered selection, or the determination of which enactments are acceptable to the organization, 'diagnostic of the collective' (1994: 101). Effective selection requires what Dobzhansky *et al.* called a 'large pool of raw material' (1977: 125). Selection tells us more about the organization's culture than about its individual members. Retention, or continuing to operate based on the same enactments, limits the organization's ability to adapt or evolve.

In public relations this notion of requisite variety generally has been used to support the argument for diversity – that employing minority practitioners, for example, enhances the effectiveness of their organizations because they may enact critical parts of the environment that white practitioners would not recognize or consider legitimate (L. Grunig, J. Grunig and Ehling, 1992). Indeed, our research showed that top management values public relations precisely for this reason. **The greatest contribution that CEOs acknowledged for public relations was help in providing a perspective** or broad picture of both the internal and external landscape of the organization.

'Broad' is a critical qualifier because obviously the perspective of public relations is only one of many provided for top management. Several of our interviewees told us that advice coming from the communication department balances counsel emanating from other quarters. One top communicator said: 'You're going to find people in the organization – some of them at pretty senior levels – who are going to say, "Don't talk; don't say a word. We might be sued or we're going to damage our market."' He saw his role as countering that closed attitude. However, he reminded us that communicators must be at a level of responsibility and respect within their organizations to guarantee that their opinion carries equal weight. Many of our participants in the qualitative study alluded to the necessity of working well with others in the organization. We concluded that the most excellent communicators are more likely to be team players than independent operators. They cultivate relationships not only with members of their external publics but with their counterparts inside the organization. They promote teamwork within their own departments as well, empowering middle managers there to develop and work toward achieving a vision.

This breadth of perspective becomes critically important as the organization faces pressure from activist groups, in particular. In fact, our findings led us to assert that activism or other crises for the organization push it toward excellence in communication.

A vice president of strategic planning in the chemical company we studied described this broad perspective that public relations can provide both inside and outside of the organization as 'the sharing of thoughts from all directions'. His comments captured the essence of requisite variety:

If you have a communication function that represents the points of view of only parts of the employee population, then you have a hell of a time making sure we're addressing the sensitivities of all the people in the employee population. If I have a communication department that is made up of all white, male Pulitzer Prize-winning people off the *New York Times*, I might have some great writers but I'll probably have a tough time making sure all points of view are reflected.

His colleague, another top manager, explained that diversity *per se* – rather than any proportional representation – is what matters: 'We don't worry as much about the numbers we have of women, Blacks and Hispanics. The main thing is in the process of making decisions, that we get the opinion of people and staff with different backgrounds'. The pay-off? 'That way we come up with better solutions'. In some cases, the requisite variety only comes from outside. We interviewed one agency head about his value to a client:

> I believe he trusts my opinion and judgement; and he knows above all that I won't bullshit him, that I'll tell him what the truth is . . . I still maintain that the PR guy has got to bring to the table the outside perspective that is by definition lacking by those inside the organization. Otherwise, the outside perspective is not going to be at the table when decisions are made . . . My CEO is smart enough to know that I'm not telling him that out of any vested self-interest, that I'm looking out for his interest and the company's interest.

Despite his three decades in the association business, the CEO of another organization explained that his vice president of public relations contributes the viewpoints of both employees and clients that he himself, even as head of the association, may not have. Public relations is an essential function because, in his words:

> Those of us who think lawyer-like, those of us who think CEO-like, those of us who think technical-like don't always take the big picture. And that's what the public relations/communication expert's forte is: to take that big picture, to place it in the instant context and to make sure that the system responds to what the real issues are in a real-world kind of way.

Interestingly, this CEO seemed to equate enactment of the environment with reality. Taking the 'big picture' provides for adaptation to 'real issues' in 'a real-world' way.

Weick's (1979b) model defines a reciprocal relationship between enactment and adaptation. As such, it is an ideal framework for understanding how and when to intervene in organizational processes. Only with an appropriate enactment of an organization's environment can the scholar suggest appropriate transformations of organizational dynamics. Interpretists, according to Everett (1994), believe that organizational processes merit study for their own sake, not necessarily because such study can affect organizational outcomes. However, we believe conducting a research project funded by a professional association such as IABC assumes such an applied purpose.[7] **Enactment** may be the key concept in Weick's (1979b) theorizing. As such, it warrants an elaborated discussion here. Weick himself emphasized its centrality to the theory: 'It is this enacted environment and nothing else that is worked upon by the processes of organizing' (1979b: 64). Enacting the environment takes place at the boundary between the organization and the external groups that matter to it – groups public relations scholars would call 'strategic publics'. Public relations practitioners are boundary-spanners. They assume primary responsibility for defining, characterizing and then responding to those environmental elements that have the most potential to help or hinder the organization.

Thus the environment is, as Smircich (1981) contended, one form of social construction. Its very existence is consensually determined within organizations. The importance of this understanding cannot be overstated. As Putnam (1983: 53) described those who embrace the interpretist perspective, '[They] have a critical role in shaping the environment and organizational realities'. They both create and maintain meaning in the context of the organization and its external constituencies. And they try to account for that context holistically.

Weick believed that this kind of enactment is complicated by what he considered ambiguous externalities or 'flows of experience' (1979: 103). He went on to call the environment the organization's 'puzzling surroundings' (1979: 312). In the course of our qualitative study for the Excellence Project, we on the research team often found ourselves puzzled indeed.

Weick cautioned that diverse perspectives may cause 'contradictions and ambivalence' (1979: 231). Despite these uncertainties and incongruities, requisite variety is just that – **necessary** for an organization to enact strategic parts of its environment that it might have overlooked otherwise. So, too, with our research. The discrepancies we heard when interviewing more than a single source in an organization made for complex analyses and interpretation. Without those different perceptions, however, we would lose much of the richness and depth of understanding that characterize this part of the comparative study. I simply point out to other researchers how mightily we struggled to sort out the often-contradictory information we received.

An earlier section of this chapter discussed the significance of drawing on multiple perspectives within the same organization when using long interviews to conduct qualitative research. This notion is not unique to qualitative methodology, of course. It is akin to the concept of representativeness inherent in most sampling for quantitative research. Our approach was more purposive than random sampling, but it accomplished much the same objective: ensuring that a single viewpoint would not determine our own view as researchers of what was going on within an organization made up of an entire constellation of people.

Even before going into the field, however, our enactment of the organizational context had begun. In a sense, conducting an exhaustive review of relevant literature and having undertaken one's own programme of research in a related area both add a variety of perspectives to the new research. The conceptualization of any solid piece of research that builds on previous work represents one's own evolution of thought as well as other scholars' theories and models. In the Excellence Project, the conceptualization was so comprehensive it had to be published in book form (J. Grunig 1992).

Despite the advantages inherent reviewing such a massive body of theoretical literature, we also risked the problem Weick identified as 'adaptation precludes adaptability' (1979b: 134). That is, we on the research team had been successful in publishing a great deal of that literature ourselves. With the exception of our practitioner member, we each had established a programme of research and were associated throughout the field of public relations research with theories explaining such concepts as publics, social and gender roles, models of public relations, feminization of the field and organizational response to activism. Weick might contend, then, that we would find it difficult to overcome our retained enactments during the process of any new enactment – such as the qualitative phase of the project.

Once again, we were helped by the interaction of our group. For example, most of the senior scholars on the team were steeped in theories of organizational sociology. Thus we clung to the notion that the collective – rather than any individual – is the determinant of organizational processes and outcomes. In several of the cases we conducted, however, we came to acknowledge that a single CEO or even an exceptionally capable public relations professional can make a real difference.[8]

Recall that even inadvertently, we had the opportunity to build in a longitudinal component to our comparative study. By waiting for more than two years between its first and second stages of data collection, this research tracked organizations over time. We could see what difference a new leader makes to the practice of public relations. Thus our comparisons went beyond societal culture, the perception of communicators versus others in the organization and methodological approach. We could compare across **time** as well. But without discussing these issues in our team meetings, we team leaders might not have been willing to forsake our initial assumption about groups versus individuals in organizations, for just one example.

CONCLUSIONS

In this chapter, I apply requisite variety in a non-traditional context: comparative research. We found that the diversity inherent in our IABC research group and in the two or three interviewees within a single organization was critically important. Triangulation of method also was important.

Our combination of qualitative and quantitative approaches allowed for both breadth and depth in this study of organizations. Only survey research could provide the picture of CEOs, their heads of public relations and at least a dozen employees in nearly 300 organizations. Only subsequent interviews with top management and top communicators in two dozen carefully selected organizations could have provided the rich explanations of **why** participants answered as they did in the survey.

Determination to publish even the preliminary findings of this multi-year, multi-country study (e.g. IABC 1991) made the results accessible to practitioners and scholars alike. In this way, the study's applied purpose was fulfilled early on. Dissemination of the survey results, for example, served as an intervention in a number of the organizations that received their individual reports and modified their communication practices in response. Willingness to share the survey instrument led to the inclusion of scholars who were not part of the original IABC research team. These researchers subsequently conducted similar studies in their own countries and thus contributed to the data base and, especially, to our depth of understanding about public relations in additional contexts.

The gap between the initial survey and the long interviews allowed for tapping into changes over time. We could assess the impact of the quantitative research through the qualitative research. In some cases, the dynamism could be explained by a shifting cast of organizational characters – a new CEO, a new head of public relations or an increasingly multicultural work-force throughout the organization.

In other cases, a specific programme such as Total Quality Management or one of its variants led to organizational transformation. In still other instances, the Excellence Project itself made a difference. Public relations practitioners who read the theory book, studied the report of their own organization or attended an IABC workshop on Excellence were likely to move toward a more symmetrical and strategic approach.

Such factors as triangulation of method, longitudinal research and cross-cultural study may require more extensive funding than has characterized most public relations research to date. Granting agencies can underwrite such significant studies. However, they typically choose to fund research proposed by a team. The credible team will be headed by a well-known scholar and composed of researchers representing the diverse qualities (disciplinary? gender? ethnicity? race?) relevant to the grantor. The human resources represented on such teams of researchers can overcome one significant limitation of qualitative research in general and case study method in particular. That limitation is the inability to generalize from a handful of cases. With a team of 16, we managed to conduct robust studies of two dozen organizations. The patterns that emerged actually became clear to us even before the last few cases were analysed. Thus the commonalities were striking enough to allow us to extrapolate to other, similar contexts. And we did all of this without exceeding the energy of any one team member, because no one was responsible for more than two cases.

As early as the preliminary design stage of the qualitative study, we on the Excellence team worked with members of the IABC Foundation board and chapters around the world to determine the focus of our research questions. We discussed the 'laundry list' of queries that resulted among all members of the expanded team, students and faculty alike, to arrive at the core questions. In this way, we hoped to avoid the almost inevitable bias of scholars in selecting problems worthy of study (M. Smith 1988; L. Grunig 1988).

We avoided much bias in responses from our participants by interviewing more than a single person in each of a variety of organizations. CEOs spoke for themselves about the value they attach to the public relations function. Communicators at different levels in the organization offered their perspectives not only on why the CEO felt as he or she did, but on a host of issues related to strategic management, diversity, professionalism, ethics and effectiveness. At times these viewpoints were in stark contrast with their colleagues' views. We included in our research report both the commonalities and the divergences in what we heard. Within the team, we also managed to sort out what we were hearing and come to at least tentative conclusions about each case. The patterns we described were so complex within and across cases that we concluded only team analysis could have led to this understanding of the organizational context.

Each of us, senior scholars and our more junior colleagues, was stretched – especially in the data analysis phase of the qualitative research. We learned from each other. In the end, we felt empowered by the process because we grew in our understanding both of the method and of the substance of the study.

Earlier on this chapter described four main standards to which research of this type is held. We believe that the array of data-collection and interpretive techniques we used succeeded in meeting or exceeding these criteria. Throughout our flexible process, we made the adaptations necessary to guarantee **dependability**. We achieved **confirmability** largely through sharing findings and conclusions between the two parts of our research team, one based on the West Coast and the other in the East. Through that process, we reached a high level of agreement on the meaning of our results. **Transferability**, or the ability to apply those findings to other organizations, is the third standard for qualitative research. Because the patterns that emerged from our data are highly consistent with what the literature suggests and what we found in the survey research as well, we believe that we also have met this standard. However, only the participants in the study can gauge whether it meets the final standard of **credibility** – whether we have managed to portray their perceptions adequately.

If we have achieved all of this, then the study should have the quality L. Smith (1978) called 'undeniability'. We considered the patterns in results compelling. No longer can we equivocate on such questions as whether the CEO makes a difference in how public relations is practised . . . or whether dialogue with abrasive activist groups is a good use of our time . . . or whether strategic management falls within the purview of public relations.

Throughout the process of arriving at the answers to those queries, the rewards of this massive group project far outweighed its complications and frustrations. Just as organizations have to learn to manage diversity, so too do research directors. Co-ordination alone was a challenge. A team of 16 researchers from California to London, exploring organizations in three countries qualitatively but basing our explorations on a quantitative survey, is highly unusual in the scholarship of public relations. Thus we considered ourselves trailblazers. Our complex trail, with all its twists and turns, led us to a destination – a set of common insights.

By looking for commonalities in our qualitative data, we may extrapolate beyond the 24 organizations studied in depth to the larger universe of organizations. Even these patterns, however, present a more unidimensional portrait of the relationship between public relations and organizational effectiveness than will these results when combined with the survey research that came before. We grounded the case study research in the same theoretical concepts and propositions that had framed our survey research. Those propositions, once again, were strikingly supported through the long interviews we conducted.

One major proposition held that two-way, symmetrical communication is a vital component of effective public relations. In fact, we long have argued that excellence in communication is characterized by two-way, balanced relationships with strategic publics – especially activist groups and employees (J. Grunig 1992). Open communication – explaining one's position, listening to others and making adjustments in response to what one is hearing – helps improve the functioning of the organization overall. The practitioners and CEOs alike whom we interviewed in this qualitative phase of the project considered this kind of interactive communication not preferable but essential for survival in this dynamic era. This chapter hopes to establish that the same process of open, dialogic communication is essential to credible, significant research in public relations.

Like much applied research, our purpose was to help provide interpretations for the experiences of the many practitioners who helped support this study since its inception almost a decade ago. We further hoped that the report of our research and the models included therein will help impose order on the dynamic world of public relations work they face – a world ever more diverse and, thus, more challenging.

The growing importance of the **international** arena suggests a corresponding escalation in the expertise of communication managers. Decentralization of operations within the multinational corporations we studied and contention with competitors and suppliers from other countries both presage a need for two-way public relations. The globalization of business and an increasingly multicultural work-force are just two of the factors we found to be complicating the lives of the top managers we interviewed. In fact, the first pattern we identified from our analysis of our two dozen cases alluded to the ubiquitousness of change. Turbulence, rather than stability, is the norm in today's organizational environments. Undoubtedly, the new technologies of communication can help practitioners stay in touch with their publics globally. We still have to ask, however, how a single public relations practitioner could be expected to enact that environment – especially when it includes diverse cultures?

Jack Bergen (1994), president and chief executive of GCI Group that is based in New York but boasts offices in 25 cities around the world, recently spoke of the impossibility of doing just that:

> While technology can facilitate a borderless constituency, it can never replace the quality of counsel produced by fertile minds of several professionals engaged in a dialectical process of problem solving. Nor can it replace practitioners on the ground in each market, practitioners who know well both the media and their audiences.
>
> (1994: 47)

Bergen suggested that agency managers create international forums where practitioners could meet to discuss issues. There they would learn of the talents of their colleagues in other locations . . . and in so doing, 'They will discover a resource that goes far beyond the limits of their own intelligence and experience, a resource that cannot be duplicated by any data base or expert system' (1994: 47). The future he envisioned was one of a 'collegial environment unhampered by geographical separation' (ibid.), wherein wireless interactive technology is a necessary but insufficient condition for success in global public relations.

Similarly, today's heterogeneous and dynamic context seems to require more than a lone researcher if the goal is to enact adequately that research context. Just as public relations firms will need to develop teams of practitioners to address the array of issues their multinational clients face, so too will scholars need to work together to gather and – especially – to interpret the quantity and quality of data necessary to understand those complex issues.

Experience alone cannot guarantee a faithful portrayal of the situation. In fact, successful enactments in the past may hinder the researcher's ability to portray a new, although comparable, situation. If, indeed, adaptation precludes adaptability (Weick 1979b), then the scholar with a track record may be a liability. I came away from the qualitative phase of the IABC study convinced that the student members of our team were valuable in large part because they were not wedded to or invested in any particular paradigm from which to interpret the findings. As novice theoreticians, they were more of a *tabula rasa* than any of the project leaders.

The question becomes how to take advantage of the wisdom of the senior scholar without ignoring the lessons of requisite variety learned in the course of conducting Phase 2 of the Excellence Project? The final section of this chapter explores several implications of Weick's (1979b) concept for future research in public relations.

IMPLICATIONS OF REQUISITE VARIETY FOR RESEARCH IN PUBLIC RELATIONS

The qualitative phase of the IABC Excellence Project offers fertile ground for exploring the team process in research. Mining that process yields the factors that most contribute to planning and implementing practices likely to capitalize on its potential advantages while minimizing its potential drawbacks. Just as scholars of diversity (e.g. Cox 1994) hold that when properly managed, diversity in work groups adds value to organizational performance, I believe that the diverse membership of our Excellence team contributed significantly to the quality of the research report we ultimately generated.

In the final analysis, our team process hinged on three significant factors: equal information, opportunity and motivation to contribute. Deconstructing the process throughout this chapter leads to the following, more specific implications for public relations research.

● 'Learning by doing' seems to be the chief avenue available to scholars interested in the team process. Methodology and design textbooks in our field do not deal with this approach. With few exceptions (such as Bantz 1993), published works ignore both the process and the outcome of group research. Thus teamwork in public relations or communication research represents a viable direction for future investigation and subsequent publication. As it is now, the committee serves as an initial group to guide the graduate student. However, the typical student ultimately must work independently on the dissertation or thesis.[9] From that point in the academic career, he or she is expected to labour virtually autonomously. Promotion decisions are based primarily on one's individual achievement rather than a demonstrated ability to work together. So, for example, single-authored articles, papers or books are given substantially heavier weight in most universities' tenure deliberations than are co-authored works.[10] This project suggests that we should re-visit the decision to value autonomous over collaborative work in the academy. Curricula and supporting materials should be developed to teach team process to graduate students intending to pursue a career in research.

- Just as we need to question traditional approaches to teaching and evaluating research and perhaps to develop alternative worldviews about them, we need to conduct more research akin to the Bantz (1993) study of cross-cultural teams. This research should look more at the effect of such pluralism than merely the process. Our IABC team was overwhelmingly Anglo. This led to a relatively smooth process because we did not have to accommodate radically different attitudes toward ambiguity and power differentials despite the masculine bias and individualism inherent in our group. As the Excellence Project extends into more non-Anglo societies, we need to consider how, if at all, the ethnicity of the researcher will influence the outcome.

- For us, overcoming the disadvantages of team research Bantz (1993) underscored in his analysis seemed to hinge on nine main factors. First, including a critical mass of junior scholars (graduate students, former grad students and an assistant professor) rather than merely a research assistant or two helped mute the effect of the inevitable hierarchy. Second, an appropriate mix of women and men seemed to balance the latter's instrumental values with the former's emphasis on co-operation. Third, the sheer size of the team contributed to its success. No one person had to do too much. In actuality, of course, the group size exceeded its 16 formal members. We collaborated, in the best sense of that word, with IABC members at large, with trustees of the Research Foundation and with our interviewees.

Fourth, we allowed for different levels of responsibility and leadership at different points of the project – capitalizing on each person's expertise and availability at the moment. This helped reduce the power distance within our team. At the same time, it accommodated what Bantz (1993) described as the 'life pattern' within any team. Fifth, we discussed the project extensively before going into the field and throughout the data collection and analysis. Sixth, we came to a resolution of each point of potential disagreement before proceeding. Seventh, we developed an extensive research design, a blueprint full of detail and contingency plans. This scheme served us well; it provided the efficiency that helped account for completing the extensive data collection and interpretation phases of the qualitative research in a single spring season. Eighth, we took advantage of the individual interests of our team members – not shackling them to the plan but allowing for the exploitation of those interests. This flexibility during the interview process did not compromise the ultimate comparability of the cases compiled.

Finally, and perhaps most important, the team leaders truly listened to what our colleagues were telling us they heard during their interviews. We were willing to set aside many of our dearly held notions, such as the importance we assumed practitioners place on attaching a dollar figure to the value of public relations, in favour of the evidence the other team members presented. Their commitment to the project, their resourcefulness and their underlying interests in particular aspects of the research (such as conflict resolution or gender) undoubtedly contributed to the compelling arguments they marshalled. In the process, they helped us avoid the common pitfalls of overgeneralization and selective observation and interpretation.

• The explanation for why all of these strategies seemed to lead to an extraordinarily satisfying result lies in Weick's programme of research (e.g. 1979b) on requisite variety. As he theorized, enactment for us began as an individual process. Each team member took responsibility for contacting an organization, arranging for interviews there, conducting the interviews, analysing them and writing up case reports. Selection, though, became a group process. Through extensive conversations, we on the team determined which individual enactments mirrored the collective or population of organizations of interest to us. Because the large number on the team allowed for an inordinately large pool of raw material, we consider the patterns resulting from the selection process to be both credible and undeniable. Once again, including a diversity of perspectives on the team overcame the problem Weick identified as adaptation precluding adaptability. We could not retain only the theories or models that we brought to the project. Instead, through the group's extensive and pluralistic interaction, even we senior scholars came to consider and ultimately adopt new, more adequate enactments of the organizational context we were studying.

When pressed, such a man almost universally acknowledged as the leading theorist in public relations described 'the researcher' in this way: 'I see myself sitting at my computer'. His quarter-century of research and publication in the field have made him visible world-wide. His *modus operandi*, however, and thus the image he conjures up of the researcher may change over the years. The scholar musing about theory and crunching numbers in the solitary splendour of his office may give way to a lively give-and-take among a disparate group of researchers in a room more reminiscent of the graduate seminar. Teamwork in public relations research may well become the norm. Given this chapter's analysis of qualitative research conducted for the IABC Research Foundation, that may be most appropriate.

None of this is revolutionary. We long have acknowledged the value of triangulation of method, counterbalancing the weakness of, say, survey research with the strengths of, say, ethnography. We also have appreciated the need for an adequate number of participants in any research project – participants who, in many cases, are chosen to represent a variety of relevant characteristics. In this chapter, I merely extend the notion of paradigmatic research, in particular, from its traditional notion of scholars working independently but within a common paradigm to a concept of scholars working jointly on a common project. Both have the potential of overcoming piecemeal research – a problem that may doom any scientific field to immaturity.

Piecemeal research is more commonly associated with **monism**, or the belief that a single set of paradigmatic assumptions is appropriate in a given discipline (Smith 1988). However, scientific revolution as Kuhn (1962) described it simply represents the substitution of one monistic paradigm for another. If public relations is to mature as a scholarly domain, the **pluralism** inherent in teamwork may remove the conceptual, methodological and even personal blinders that would hold us back. Requisite variety – so critical to contemporary public relations practice – fosters the healthy respect for alternative explanations that I believe will characterize postmodern research in our field as well.

NOTES

1 'Sampling' may be a misnomer here. Yin (1989), the acknowledged expert on case study methodology, said that 'replication logic' is more appropriate than 'sampling logic' in relation to multiple-case design. That is, we did not sample in the classic systematic way. Rather, we repeated the procedure of interviewing, observing and reviewing relevant documents in a sufficient number of cases to feel secure that our research questions had been answered adequately.

2 The permanent team was smaller and more homogeneous than its successor, despite an attempt to diversify its make-up. The project director deliberately included a woman, a practitioner and a non-US scholar on the team. Of the six members, five were men. Five of the six also were

university professors; the sixth was a retired vice-president of public relations. Five came from the United States. The sixth was British – a man who had worked in Canada as well. All were Caucasian and of European extraction. During the first (quantitative) phase of the project, four graduate students assisted these researchers, primarily in determining the sample and collecting the data. The assistants' role in data analysis was minimal and in developing the report of findings, non-existent.

3 Each researcher investigated only one or two cases to avoid the 'burnout' that can accompany the exhaustive process of collecting and sorting through massive amounts of qualitative data.

4 Tapes and transcripts were archived at the University of Maryland, in large part to preserve the confidentiality of participants over time but also as a data base that could be re-mined in future.

5 The West Coast team, composed of a graduate seminar led by David Dozier, met weekly. The East Coast team met less frequently but more intensively toward the end of spring 1994. These two groups communicated with each other and with the two-person British team frequently by telephone, by fax and by internet. We only rarely relied on express mail.

6 I need to add this note of clarification to the explanation: when participants in the qualitative research did attempt to talk about the value of public relations in dollar amounts, the numbers were high (such as millions of dollars saved in fending off a law suit, the entire company salvaged by the successful handling of a crisis and crediting public relations efforts with saving human lives, at a cost savings of $100,000 per life).

7 We were gratified to learn that even the early stages of our research seem to be affecting organizational practice. Through our long interviews, we heard that publication of the Excellence theory book (J. Grunig 1992), circulation of the initial quantitative data report (IABC 1991) and distribution of individual reports to the organizations that participated in the survey all made a difference. So, too, did the seminars and workshops sponsored by IABC and its Research Foundation and conducted by members of the research team along with local chapter members and Foundation trustees.

8 One of the most undeniable instances came from the industry association we studied. There, the head of public relations was credited with developing a programme of citizen advisory panels that has changed his entire industry's way of operating and, concomitantly, its reputation. A second case supports this argument for the potential influence of a second person. After our initial survey research, the communication department in this chemical corporation began to report to a new vice-president whose background was in strategic planning. He recognized and made use of the knowledge of two senior communicators, one in corporate communication and the other in marketing communication. Today, the public relations function is part of strategic management and the organization is moving closer to excellence as measured on our index.

9 The University of Roskilde in Denmark represents an important exception. It has developed a programme wherein public relations students

work in teams. Even theses are group projects. The *International Public Relations Review* recently published the results of one such work by two young Danish women (Biker and Hovgaard 1994). The thesis, which won an honorary mention in the CERP programme of educational awards, 'is regarded as a valuable contribution to the theoretical basis of public relations' (IABC Research Foundation 1991: 16). Most US universities, however, reject out of hand any consideration of such collaboration on theses and dissertations.

10 The rule of thumb at the University of Maryland seems to be that dual-authored publications are accorded half the credit of a single-authored piece.

Part II

German-Austrian perspectives of public relations

This section of the book contains three chapters by authors from Germany and Austria. The two German contributions have in common a concern with the social context of public relations which they approach from different directions. In the first chapter Gunter Bentele examines the relationship between public relations practice and reality, beginning by establishing an historical background account of public communication and emerging notions about its influence on social reality. Subsequently he assesses the treatment of public relations and reality in the literature, noting that, with a few exceptions, it is dealt with only implicitly in the main American texts through discussions of professional ethics, and the identification of norms of truth and accuracy for public relations practice.

Gunter Bentele suggests that the current handling of the relationship between public relations and reality is too simple. However he does recognize attempts to discuss the problem of reality through the application of a constructivist approach to public relations theory, but argues against Mertenís proposition that public relations is a process of constructing desirable realities, for and about an organization, in the mind of publics.

Given these limitations he seeks to bring greater theoretical clarity to the relationship between public relations and reality by adopting a reconstructivist approach. In the ensuing explanation it is suggested that a model for the social flow of information may also be applied as a model for the social construction and reconstruction of facts and events in a public relations context. Through the proposition of rules governing the relationship to reality, and a clearer delineation of the nature of natural, social, and media events, the discussion presents a fresh perspective on public relations and reality.

In Barbara Baerns' contribution the discussion is equally absorbing, but differs by addressing some of the theoretical issues discussed earlier through an empirical investigation into perceptions and practice of community public relations in Germany. This is approached by setting out the socio-political context for transparency in the public sector and counter poising this with a detailed critique of the theoretical weaknesses of public relations in a marketing context.

The study showed a marketing orientation to be in the ascendance in community public relations in Germany, with the concept of participation low on the list of communication priorities. Interestingly, little difference is found between the old and new German Lander. The study is of additional value because it provides a basis for comparative research in to public sector public relations in other countries.

The final chapter in this section is a challenging and thoughtful reflection on the organization of public relations research. Benno Signitzer's initial premise is that the infrastructure supporting systematic public relations research remains rather weak. For some time to come the majority of public relations research will be undertaken by students doing MA or PhD theses. Therefore it makes sense to develop systematic programmes for student public relations research. By way of a contribution to this process he proposes a typology of the subject matter of these theses.

The typology is a presentation of ideal types that Benno Signitzer suggests may be useful in helping students to more clearly focus on their research questions, and additionally help theses supervisors to plan programmes of student research. The strength of the chapter is that it provides a practical, carefully constructed tool for educators and students, which may be modified to suit their own views on the elements of a research typology, and sets out a strong argument for the adoption of some form of a systematic plan for student research within public relations education programmes.

3 Public relations and reality: a contribution to a theory of public relations

Gunter Bentele

INTRODUCTION

A nationally renowned hotel is confronted with the publicly circulating rumour that it would close down in the near future; a department store is said to be going to open on the premises of the hotel. Hotel bookings drop at an alarming rate. The committed public relations counsellor recommends a simple course of action: the hotel manager's contract should be extended on a long-term basis, and his salary should be raised considerably. The information about this action is published, bookings rise again considerably, and the rumour disappears.

Another hotel wants to consolidate and enhance its outstanding prestige. Its PR counsellor recommends celebrating the hotel's thirtieth anniversary in a festive way and setting up an anniversary committee to be composed of the city's most distinguished citizens. The celebration takes place, the media report extensively about this social event, and the goal of PR has been reached.

These two (and many other) examples from the early period of PR counselling are reported by Edward L. Bernays in 1923 in the world's first book to subject public relations to what was at that time a systematic analysis. Both cases relate to the same subject matter as is dealt with here: the relationship between public relations activities and reality. In the first case, a communicative impulse (the prolongation of the contract) given in the form of an organizational action, which is reported by the media, is actively used in order to counter a development that threatens the hotel's existence and is caused by obviously false communication. It is not a – perhaps plausible, but not credible – denial of the rumour that is resorted to, but an organizational action, which is in flagrant contradiction to the rumour. Since the public is, in addition to this, informed about this action in a purposeful way, this approach may be called 'indirect counterinformation'. The hotel's image – in a broader sense – improves, and subsequently people's attitude toward the hotel changes, too.

In the second case, a social event (the anniversary celebration) is actively shaped or staged in order to stabilize and improve the reputation of the hotel. Here an event is 'constructed' and the – intended – public information about this event is used to improve its image.

In both cases it is not only the image of the hotel concerned, but also the attitude of segments of the public toward the hotel that changes, due to information relating to actions or events, respectively.

Actions and events planned and carried out by organizations are part of the social reality we perceive. In most cases, we do not perceive those institutions directly (by participating in the organizational actions or events), but as mediated through media reality. The information contained in the media reality may influence our perception and our images of social reality, thus it is, in principle, capable of influencing our attitudes and actions with respect to those institutions. In the two cases cited, Bernays's PR counsellor was able to contribute – with obvious success – to bringing about a change in the public's perception of institutions (the hotels) in favour of these institutions. The institutions themselves did not change in their structures. What was necessary was only a certain effort of action and information: in the first case, the hotel manager got a prolonged contract; in the second case, an organizational effort was required in order to organize the celebration and the presumably concomitant press conference.

Although public relations can also contribute to changing the social reality of social organizations (enterprises, parties, public institutions, associations, etc.) structurally, it will contribute more frequently to effecting a changed perception of the organizations by different segments of the public outside these organizations. What is essential here is often a comparison of the different perceptions 'from the inside' and 'from the outside' as well as an attempt to co-ordinate an intraorganizational perspective with the organization's perception from the outside and to approximate the latter to the former. In practical PR activities too, the central issue is the relationship between PR information and PR communication and underlying reality, which is made the subject matter of the PR activities; furthermore, what matters is the relationship between PR information and communication and – to use the trade term – the 'events' created or staged within these processes.

If, in agreement with Ronneberger and (1992) Ruhl, (communication) science is seen as having the task of investigating the PR reality of practice, and if it is furthermore assumed that PR theories have the task of developing systematic reconstructions of conceptually differentiated and empirically tested PR knowledge, which may also serve as blueprints for further research processes, then the problem fields mentioned above (i. e. the relationships between PR information and communication and their relationship to reality) may be considered as problems not only of PR practice, but also as problems of PR theories.

PUBLIC RELATIONS, ITS CONCEPT OF REALITY AND RELATIONSHIP TO REALITY – SOME HISTORICAL REMARKS

Members of various professions, who may be considered as belonging to the field of public communication (journalists, practitioners of PR, marketing and advertising), were writing early on in professional journals about the relationship between public communication and its media on the one hand, and social reality on the other. And through the application of their profession, norms have developed – presumably due to certain communicative necessities – which have sought to impose a degree of regulation on this relationship. For journalism, the basic norms have been those of truthfulness and objectivity: both were supposed to guarantee a direct, accurate and adequate relationship to reality, guarding against any tendencies toward distortion by the media. The problem of the media's relationship to reality itself became recognized by the time of the rise of the periodical press; the professional norms mentioned, however, originated as late as in the mid-19th century.

Communication science has, since the 1950s, produced several attempts to explain the relationship between the communicative product and the extratextual reality portrayed within its subject matter. But these theoretical reflections and attempts at reconstruction were primarily related to journalistic norms. In PR practice, this discussion has obviously been not quite as easy as in journalism. On the one hand, PR communicators were generally obliged to orient themselves more strictly to the interests of individual social systems such as businesses or governments, than was the case with at least part of the (suprapartisan) press. As a consequence, there has been a greater tendency to distort those social realities. On the other hand, it appeared – from a critical journalistic point of view – that PR practitioners had the task of 'constructing' a communicative reality for the public, i.e. at first for the journalists, which they were then supposed to help disseminate and mediate. In the case of the construction of social realities, from the point of view of professional theory, it is considered less easy for PR practitioners than, for example, journalists with regard to news, to utilize a simple (naive) relationship to reality.

It must be assumed that, until the start of this century, a naive concept of reality – steeped in everyday theory – and, moreover, a belief in facts were predominant in all the professions involved in public communication. The idea was that, on the one hand, events and occurrences 'happen', which were to be portrayed journalistically. Although they were frequently violated, the norms of truthful and objective reporting, i.e. the least biased description of those occurrences and events possible, had very early attained validity. But this naive belief in facts as well as the belief in the possibility of providing a portrayal 'true to nature' in reporting was, however, shaken at the beginning of this century at the latest.

It was Walter Lippmann in 1922 who contradicted this belief and advanced the concept of news as a 'mirror of society'. In contrast to naive constructivist views, Lippmann adhered to a clear separation between the outside world, or, as he called it, the 'world outside of range', 'outside of view', 'outside of our minds', on the one hand, and the 'pictures in our head', on the other.

Since 1920s, primarily two factors have emerged that led to a decline of 'naive empiricism'. One of them was the rise and development of public relations, the other the experiences gathered with war reporting. Ivy L. Lee, besides Edward L. Bernays (one of the first influential practitioners and theorists of PR) and other members of this profession, which was developing in the US at that time, self-confidently made subjectivity and the partisanship of information a new value. Ivy L. Lee argued that nobody would be able to describe facts or events completely, that all descriptions were merely interpretations of facts by the journalists. The very concept of 'fact' was called in to doubt. Thus, Lee embraces a relativistic conception, seen from the angle of epistemology. He recognized better than many journalists that a great deal of the so-called facts in the process of public communication were 'created', in the first place, by the PR side.

The experience gathered with war reporting or war propaganda not only showed clearly what power the media could hold, what influence the media could wield, but also what role they could play in the people's perception of world events (reality).

In addition to the rather epistemological dimension of this position adopted early in this century, the reality that many facts are 'made' or 'produced' (today also 'constructed') may be one of the reasons for the still somewhat tense relationship between journalists and PR practitioners. Already at that time, information had become less and less researched by the journalists themselves and increasingly produced by press and PR offices in order to induce journalistic reporting. This development was, and still is, a threat to many journalists' conception of themselves.

In spite of early recognition of the quality of being constructed of many events, in spite of reservations against too naive an understanding of facts, the relationship between reality and PR communication has always played an important role both in professional practice and the literature written by practitioners. Here the relationship to reality is understood as the professional attitude of PR communicators, the goal of which is to inform and communicate about one's own organization with the least distortion possible. Such professional attitudes frequently develop into professional norms, which are laid down in writing at certain times within the professionalization process of the industry or profession.

The often quoted *'Declaration of Principles'* produced by Ivy L. Lee from the first decade of our century is a very early written statement of a professional attitude, which originally referred to only one PR office. Since that chapter was written, thrust, accuracy and a minimum of transparency or openness have become accepted as the PR norms about which a general consensus exists. But attention must also be drawn to the fact that early PR techniques frequently disregarded the norm of truth. In their model of public relations, Grunig and Hunt (1984: 22) point out that the truth often did not play a major role in the early publicity programmes. For instance, the circus director P.T. Barnum is reported to have said that there is no such thing as 'bad publicity'. Thus truthful information does not play a central role in the publicity model, neither historically nor at present.

As early as 1923, Bernays dissociated himself from the widespread practice of the press agents. Advancing a moral point of view, he introduced the concept of the 'PR counsellor'. In 1952, he described the 'ideal PR man' as a human being of character and integrity, who should, among other things, be truthful and cautious, objective, interested in problems as well as trained in the social sciences and PR techniques.

In the first professional code adopted in 1951 by the Public Relations

Society of America (PRSA) which was established in 1948, such norms as 'accuracy' and 'truth' figured prominently. Thus, the notion that public relations should portray reality as accurately as possible was normatively laid down in American practice in the early 1950s. In German public relations literature, which has been written mainly by practitioners, the postulate of truth had already been a topic in the early monographs that appeared after World War II. Gross (1951: 92 ff.), for instance, stressed the importance of such norms as openness and transparency. On the basis of these criteria, the cultivation of public opinion – the synonym for public relations used by Gross – is clearly distinguished from advertising and propaganda. Carl Hundhausen's (1951: 159 ff.) chapter discusses six basic principles of public relations which include, as the first principle, truth, as the second principle complete truth, and, as the third principle, openness. Hundhausen does not, however, decide to what extent public relations should, or could, always comprise the 'complete truth', but this norm is included in the canon of 'basic principles'. Explaining the rough-and-ready formula 'Do good and talk about it', which has often been misunderstood in this country as the 'definition of public relations', Zedtwitz-Arnim (1996) emphasizes that it is of prime importance that something 'good' is seen to be done. This is also the central point in his definition of public relations. Of course, Zedtwitz-Arnim proceeds from a very simple – i.e. naively realistic – comprehension of the relationship of the different images (external and internal image). But at the same time the central relevance of generally acceptable performance by organizations (here: enterprises), which can be directly perceived and verified – e.g. by the employees – is evaluated correctly. Albert Oeckl also stresses the importance of comprehensive and objective information forming the basis of public relations (Oeckl 1960: 3), and emphasizes the importance of professional codes (Oeckl 1976: 349 ff.).

Harry Nitsch (1975: 55) calls the norms of truth, clarity and agreement of word and deed the three supreme commandments of public relations. Truth means the whole truth, which should be verifiable, and also signifies that nothing of importance to the public should be concealed. As to the norm of clarity, it is demanded that simplification strategies must not be distortion strategies, that ambiguities are only apt to foster mistrust. Listing guidelines for public relations, Neske (1977: 37 ff.) cites, among other things, openness, objectivity, honesty and the congruence of information and action. All these guidelines deal with the relationship between the reality of organizations and, mediated through communication norms, PR communication.

In view of this early emphasis on adequacy norms in the practitioner literature, it is somewhat surprising to find that the norm of truth does not figure more prominently in the most important European public relations code – the Code of Athens. The reason for this is perhaps because there have always been certain discrepancies between the declarations issued by the professional associations, which focus on the norm of truth, and at least some segments of professional practice. Ethical principles formulated in writing are, on the one hand, not always taken seriously by individual public relations counsellors or even sometimes by association heads; on the other hand, there are many evaluations in textbooks and practitioners' literature that clearly qualify the requirement for truth, even claiming that lies are necessary on occasions for the exercise of the profession.

In more recent public relations literature in Germany, the moral dimension has already become an established feature – a moral orientation of public relations work is normatively demanded wherever complex problems are discussed.

In the German-language area, an initial empirical study by Martina Becher (1993) contains the results of a representative survey on ethical problems conducted among members of the DPRG. According to this study, nearly 90 per cent of those surveyed agreed with the view that one should not lie to journalists, but respondents also agreed that practitioners must not necessarily say something that would have negative consequences for their organization. On a scale ranging from 1 to 5, used to determine which values/norms should be observed in public relations practice, the norm of truth and objectivity was given the very high value of 1.4. At the same time, the norm of 'disclosing one's interests', the norm of transparency, received the lowest average value of all, namely 2.3. Half of those surveyed thought that in training for public relations great attention should be devoted to ethics; but only slightly more than one third of those questioned claim to know the Code of Athens well.

In summary, it may be concluded that:

- A naive concept of reality has dominated the everyday theories of journalism and public relations well into the early decades of this century.
- The quality of events being socially constructed, events about which journalists and the media report, was, however, recognized

early in public relations practitioners' literature, resulting in a relatively naive concept of reality.

● Nevertheless, the relationship to reality was soon emphasized normatively in professional attitudes – public relations codes and public relations definitions. The relationship to reality is established by both the positive and the negative relationship to the norm of truth (the alleged necessity of not telling the whole truth or even lying).

THE CONCEPT OF REALITY IN THE MORE RECENT LITERATURE ON PR THEORY

During the first decades of our century, it can be argued that too simple a concept of reality was used as a basis not only for professional theory, but also in the literature on journalism and communication science. This concept was, however, defined more precisely in Germany when – in the early 1960s – journalism science began to change from a normative and liberal-arts discipline into a discipline using empirical social-science approaches. The discipline was dominated by a comprehension of reality that was oriented toward the natural sciences and initially operated with a rather hard-science concept of reality.

What was also important for the way of dealing with 'reality' in communication science was the introduction of the concept of the 'pseudoevent', literally, 'false', 'phoney' or 'non-real' events, and their systematic description by Daniel Boorstin (1963). Boorstin explains what he regards as the most important characteristics of 'pseudoevents' as follows: they do not occur 'spontaneously' (like railroad accidents or earthquakes), but are 'arranged' by somebody; they are more dramatic than real events; they can be disseminated more easily and shaped more vividly; they can be repeated as often as desired; they cost money, and somebody is interested in recouping the money spent on them. Pseudoevents are comprehensible and entertaining; they provide the subject matter for 'public talk', generating, 'in accordance with geometric rules', more pseudoevents. According to Boorstin, interviews, press conferences or anniversary celebrations are perfect examples of such pseudoevents.

Boorstin especially emphasizes the idea of events' quality being made (socially constructed) which renders the naive concept of reality even more obsolete. Subsequent literature focused primarily on this type of event which is believed to play an even more central role in the framework of public communication today than in the 1960s.

Boorstin did not write about natural events or genuine social events; but these two types of events continue to play an important role both in public relations practice and public communication as a whole. Apart from a few exceptions, the more recent scientific literature on public relations theory deals rather implicitly with the concept of reality as well as the problem of the relationship to reality. This is illustrated by the fact that most American textbooks contain a chapter on ethics in PR, where the norms of truth and accuracy etc. are mentioned as important foundations of PR practice. Only a few authors deal with the problem of the relationship to reality in greater detail. Newsom, Scott, van Slyke Turk (1993: 4), for instance, treat the relationship to reality in a listing of ten fundamental principles of public relations, demanding that, as a first principle, public relations should deal with facts and not with false façades or fiction. Pearson (1989) discusses three different epistemological approaches to the concept of truth: objectivism, relativism and intersubjectivism. Grunig and Grunig (1992: 308) and Grunig (1993: 84) argue that the symmetrical two-way model of public relations as an ethical orienta-tion is already contained in the public relations process itself and that, for this reason, the results or products of this public relations model are highly likely to meet ethical requirements.

The development of newer constructivism in the theory of science and also in communication science has recently given rise to attempts to transfer the constructivist paradigm of thought to the theoretical reconstruction of public relations activities or, to put it differently, to public relations theory.

In addition to voicing a clear and sometimes rather polemical criticism of traditional public relations conceptions in a pamphlet entitled '*What PR ' really' is*', Jarchow (1992: 89 ff.) tries to develop a different comprehension of public relations which refers to con-structivist considerations in the fields of cognition and communica-tion. Apart from the fact that here certain theoretical inconsistencies can be observed – not rare for authors using a constructivist argu-mentation – this pamphlet succeeds only on a very general level in developing suggestions for a public relations theory on a constructi-vist basis.

With similar aim in mind, Merten (1992) sought to develop ideas for a constructivist approach to public relations theory, defining the comprehension of public relations as follows: 'PR is a process of the intentional and contingent construction of desirable realities by producing and consolidating images in the public.' (1992: 44). But two critical comments about Merten's ideas must be made: it may not be possible to deny the use of fictional elements in public relations activities, but in no way should they play the dominant role suggested by Merten. On the contrary, if the relationship to reality were non-existent in public relations communication and if it were substituted by – communicatively possible – fiction, this would necessarily and very quickly lead to such effects as lack of credibility and the loss of trust in the media system and also among the public. This would immediately produce symptoms of a communication crisis for the organizations concerned. Apart from the fact that the establishment of public relations communication is certainly not always 'positively coloured' – i.e. distorted, public relations cannot be reduced to simply fulfilling the role of image construction. Determining these differing theoretical positions would require empirical studies which would have to measure the shares of 'fictitional information' and 'authentical information', respectively. A public relations actor can hardly afford to give an unauthentic, distorted account of statements by the board chairman or association president. And the selection of statements used for public relations communication cannot be made at will, because it is severely restricted by the reality of the social system it is supposed to report about.

In what has so far been one of the most comprehensive attempts to develop the foundations of a modern public relations theory, Ronneberger and Ruhl refer to the concept of reality a number of times. On the one hand, the task of science is regarded as making the 'reality of PR practice the problem to be investigated' (Ronneberger and Ruhl 1992: 23). In this process, public relations reality is seen as an observable and 'experienceable' reality. Elsewhere, the authors, using their equivalence-functionalistic approach, oppose an empirically abridged concept of reality. Communication and interaction are seen as possibilities that may become realities through selectivity in human cognition generally, and in the process of research. Thus, the notion that there is a reality *per se* which exists independently of the researcher is rejected.

It is not previously existing phenomena, but problems that are regarded as objects of research. This seems to characterize a position that is vehemently opposed to a naively empirical concept of reality, but which does not ignore the fact that a social public relations reality will have existed well before any research process begins, and thus, the research task involves attempting to reconstruct this reality in theoretical terms within the framework of theory formation. If this position is adopted not only for the perception of reality by researchers, but also for the perception of reality by professional communicators such as journalists and public relations experts, it comes very close to a reconstructive position. This proposition will be described in the following section.

TYPES OF EVENTS, RELATIONSHIP TO REALITY AND CONSTRUCTION OF REALITY BY PUBLIC RELATIONS

A basic model of information and communication relations within society

The traditional arguments in public relations theory about the relationships between the social reality of social organization and the reality constructed by public relations actors are, nowadays, no longer sufficient because in view of the more recent level of reflection in communication theory, they have become too simple. On the other hand, newer positions of constructivist origin have so far been insufficiently elaborated and, in part, remain too contradictory to constitute a solid position concerning this problem. In the most advanced attempts to date to outline a public relations theory, the reality problem has been treated rather marginally. Therefore, I want to try to outline the reality problem from a reconstructivist perspective with the intention of bringing this problem nearer to a differentiated theoretical solution.

The starting point is a simple – but not naive – model of the social flow of information. At the same time, this approach may be perceived as a model for the social construction and reconstruction of facts and events and may also serve as a starting point for further reflection about the construction of information and media societies as well as about the relationship between partial social systems of the media and public relations. This proposal is based on a 'hypothetically realistic' model of individual human process of cognition and deliberately embraces other traditions of thought than the constructivist cognition models which have been advanced with greater intensity in recent years.

It would certainly be too simple an idea to imagine communicators – i.e. the media – as organizations, and journalists as their actors, as systems that edit objective reports obtained from their colleagues in the agencies or, with regard to local reporting, send out reporters to watch and write down what happens during the day so that their readers may know on the next day what had occurred all over the world. This idyllic picture may sometimes have existed in the minds of readers, listeners, viewers and also journalists, but is not only an over-simplification of the reality of the process, but, in fact, a complete misconception. It would, however, be equally naive and distorted – as suggested by the constructivist paradigm – to impute that, as far as the media, journalists and public relations communicators are concerned, the construction of a reality simply runs its course inside operationally closed systems as an autopoietic process no longer related to a social reality that has existed previously both socially as well as in space and time.

It would seem to be more meaningful to consider reality – understood as everything that has existed, exists or will exist here – on the basis of information theory, and to proceed from the fact that reality contains potentially infinite amounts of different items of information and can, neither at a certain moment nor in a human lifetime, be depicted as representing completely or as a whole, man's cognitive activities.

A certain part of the infinite amount of potential information, which constitutes information offered to the individual human brain, is being actualized within the process of human perception, cognition and communication. This actualization process is, at the same time, a process of construction and reconstruction: new information is produced here, too. This process does not occur at random, but on the patterns of subjective and objective information already available. The production of information and messages, e.g. in the form of texts, as well as the conglomeration of texts into topics, occurs in keeping with certain specifically 'human rules' that have evolved over time. Even these 'rules' do not originate at random, rather they arise subject to the restrictions found in social reality and the very necessities of human coexistence.

Actualizing potential information means selecting from an infinite amount (selection), thus generating new information (construction), at first in the mind, and, in a second step, in a material medium. With its materialization in communicative and technical media (speaking, language, writing, pictures, texts, books, brochures, films), the process of communication and – as soon as the public comes into play – of public communication begins.

'Outside' reality presents itself to professional communicators – be they individuals or social systems – primarily as a complex of facts and events. These events happen either in a natural way (natural events), are socially induced or constructed (social events) or are destined especially for public communication (media events).

Events are perceived, reconstructed and translated into texts in accordance with rules and routines related to professions, media and genres. In the case of media events, not only the texts, but also the events themselves are, within a social process, contructed (social construction) as real in keeping with such or similar rules and professional routines, and translated into texts only through a process involving further steps.

Within the partial social system of 'public communication', two important subsystems may be distinguished: the communicator system of public relations and the communicator system of journalism or the media, respectively. Selection takes place between the two partial systems, and within each there are again several steps of information selection – at the same time steps of actualization, construction or reconstruction. The communicative 'products' resulting from the two partial communicator systems are, as journalistic products of signs or texts (in the broadest sense), identical with what is appropriately called 'media reality'. As already mentioned, texts conglomerate into topics of public communication. The function of topic setting may – on the social macro-level – be regarded as the central function not only of the media, but also of systems of public relations.

'Media reality', which may in many ways be differentiated into the communicative realities of total media, individual media, topics and texts, are certainly a reality communicatively constructed by the communicator systems. But it is frequently a reality modelled or reconstructed on previously existing patterns. The information thus generated – in the form of written, oral, auditive or visual text or topics – in several respects bears relation to the originally, potentially or actually, existing items of information and information structures. In the framework of a reconstructive approach, special emphasis is put on this aspect of the relationship between the text and extratextual information or reality, respectively. In constructivist approaches, these relations are largely negated, denied or regarded as unimportant. The degree of structural congruence between previously existing realities, on the one hand, and the media realities constructed by communicators on the other, is not only controlled as a process by such professional norms as truth or objectivity, but can also be investigated scientifically. The degree of adequacy of media realities is, at the same time, a criterion for the quality of professional communication. In principle, there is an insoluble difference between social realities and media realities.

This difference between facts and events, on the one hand, and the portrayal of facts and events, on the other, still exists in the case of media events: where a piece of social and communicative reality (e.g. a press conference, an anniversary celebration, etc.) was actually created (constructed) socially by public relations actors. In the case of this type of event too, the 'portrayal' of media events in media reality is subject to the same adequacy rules (truth, objectivity) as the 'portrayal' of other types of events. The reconstruction of previously existing facts and events as adequately as possible may be perceived as a fundamental form of the – necessary – relationship to reality.

Another form of the relationship to reality results when media events are constructed socially, then reconstructed communicatively in a second step; this second form primarily results from the restriction of the possibilities of social construction.

The recipients or the audience, who become 'the public' or, as partial publics and target groups, largely perceive the originally existing facts, events and media events only in a mediated way through the construction and reconstruction process of mass communication. Frequently there are segments of the audience who, as the participants or persons involved, are directly affected by the events reported. The individuals are able to compare, within a comparison of realities, the directly and subjectively experienced reality with media reality (similar to the journalists reporting from the spot). But those segments of the audience who did not participate in the events – this is by far the largest segment – have, by using interpersonal sources of information or comparing different media, a perception of reality that is, at least in part, independent of media reporting.

The audience is able to appraise the accuracy or – more general – the adequacy of the information contained in the media reality both when making a comparison of reality and a comparison of the media. This provides indicators for the perceived credibility of reporting, the media as a whole and the professional communicators behind it. The audience's ability to make such appraisals of the credibility of media reality may historically and functionally have been an important reason for the development of adequacy rules (truth, objectivity) on the communicators' side. If communicators or communicator systems disregard these rules, media reality will contain distortions. At the same time, the partial publics may perceive discrepancies between the sections of reality directly perceived and media reality, on the one hand, or between the different media realities, on the other. The perception of distortions by the audience results in declining credibility and trust values for communication.

This mechanism according to which perceived discrepancies and attendant distortions may lead to losses of credibility and trust, does not only exist between the audience and the two communicator systems, but also between the two communicator systems distinguished here. Due to their professional experience with public relations people, journalists also evaluate these sources as being more or less trustworthy. This is also the reason for the 'adequacy rules' which have existed in the professional practice of public relations since the time of Ivy L. Lee. The distortions which media communicators may perceive include, for example, untruth, taboos, errors, but primarily euphemisms, the omission of negative information, etc.

With regard to natural and social facts and events, about which public relations communicators must create a communicative reality *vis-à-vis* media communicators, the following rules governing the relationship to reality may be identified:

- The facts contained in public relations texts must be accurate.
- The public relations texts must not contain any false statements.
- They shall be free of distortions.
- Communicative action and real action (word and deed) shall be consistent.
- Public relations communication shall be objective rather than positively appreciative.
- Information having a negative effect on the organization shall not be concealed.
- The active and symbolic portrayal of images must correspond to the perception of the enterprise by the employees of the enterprise. Discrepancies between the perception from the outside (external image) and the perception of organizations from the inside (internal image) will result in a lack of credibility.

Some empirical studies of public relations research conducted in the 1980s found that it is less the journalistic side, but rather the public relations side that largely controls the topics and the timing of public combination. In order to differentiate here, it must, however, be added that this 'power of public relations' could not arise 'arbitrarily', but can only be explained in terms of the basis of the rules governing the relationship to reality. The power of public relations primarily consists in the possibility of creating media occurrences or – in practitioners' parlance – events. With respect to these types of events, rules governing the relationship to reality also apply, some of which may be reconstructed as follows:

- Relevance must be a feature of the reason for reporting, and this reason must be an 'appropriate' one. Here the criteria of relevance are largely determined by 'media logic'. If discrepancies between the perception of relevance by journalists and by PR communication arise, effects of incredibility may result. This point refers to the reason for press dispatches, press conferences or other instruments of work with the press.

- The timing of the reporting, e.g. of the press conference, event or business report, may be chosen variably within certain limits, but it cannot be scheduled arbitrarily, because it is tied to patterns of social reality.

- In the case of product events, there must be consistency (harmony) between the product or service and the content or form of the event. A festival in which a heavy-metal band performs would be imaginable for a private radio station, but hardly for an exclusive furniture store, for which a string quartet would be more 'appropriate'.

- Sponsoring activities in the fields of sports, culture, etc. cannot be scheduled arbitrarily, because they are linked with the kind of product or the image of the enterprise.

Such rules governing the relationship to reality restrict the possible diversity of organizational communication by establishing certain limits that manifest themselves as a specific 'band width' in public relations practice, only within which communication activities are possible.

Here it needs to be be pointed out that the often demanded quality norm of 'openness' and 'transparency' constitutes some kind of a meta-norm. Openness and transparency of communication enable journalists and segments of the public to better verify the accuracy, adequacy and appropriateness of communication.

Types of reality and public relations

Natural events and public relations

Events, understood as sections of reality that can be delimited in time, location and space, are of infinite diversity. Nevertheless, certain structures of events and, thus, certain types of events may be distinguished analytically. The most important types of events may be differentiated as 'natural events', 'social events' and 'media events'.

Examples of natural events are earthquakes, volcanic eruptions, the weather, landscapes, etc. These facts and events either exist (landscapes) or happen (volcanic eruptions, thunderstorms). As a rule, natural events cannot be produced or influenced by human action, or at least only to a small extent. The process of event constitution occurs largely 'in a natural way', without human intervention. Human effort is, however, required to watch these events, process their latently existing information as well as shape and translate them into texts or pictures. Pictures or – more generally – information about natural events are, for example, supplied by competing camera teams, who film volcanic eruptions or grey whales trapped in the ice, and also by meteorological or other measuring stations, which, with a considerable technical apparatus, monitor natural occurrences for man's benefit. Whereas the event structure is generally not influenced by man, the information about these events is, often by relying on technical devices, constructed and – depending on the structure of the event – reconstructed by man.

Natural facts and events are in many respects relevant for active public relations communication. In the case of accidents in chemical plants, press reporting requires relevant chemical and physical knowledge, or alternatively chemical, biological and technically accurate reports must be written before they are passed on to the media. Especially in the field of environmental communication, such natural facts and events are relevant. Accuracy, exactness and precision are the norms for producing such public relations texts. The objectivity and transparency of such texts is provided by references to methods and test procedures of (natural) sciences. Often difficulties appear when facts are being evaluated: for example, the determination of limiting values, below which specific substances are still regarded as harmless, and above which they are considered to be harmful, mostly requires a period of prolonged examination and consensus finding. Frequently, in cases of risk assessment, it is very difficult to achieve consensus.

Social events/realities and public relations

First, social events differ from natural events in a decisive way because they can be influenced or produced to a greater or lesser extent by human activity. The 'social construction of reality' is essentially the continuous construction of social relations and structures through social actions. Social events are 'constructed' as real through human behaviour or intentional action of different types. Here communicative action, a subtype of social action, plays a central role in differing forms. The 'materialized' forms of communicative action such as texts are also elements of social events. Social events happen or are produced world-wide in infinite numbers every day. Only a small part of all the social events and complexes of occurrences exhibit structures which make them interesting for the media and for public reporting – i.e. have news value. Examples of these types of events are summit meetings, elections, party congresses, olympiads and world championships. Nowadays the structure of these type of events can no longer be described adequately without the existence of the media – and especially television. At least as far as the form, the timing and the content of these types of events is concerned, there is a mutually constitutive relationship between the social systems producing these events and the media system. In spite of this, such events take place in relative independence from the media system's possibilities for intervention: a party congress or an election would take place even if there were no television, but the two events would be structured somewhat differently. In social events, communicative realities in a material form, e.g. spoken comments or written texts, also play a role. As a rule, a meeting of the town council works with written documents, and in the social event of a 'strike', appeals are written and distributed.

It is, however, important to note that meetings of the town council, or of those on strike are 'constructed' in accordance with clearly different social rules than reports in the print or broadcast media on the town-council meeting or the strike committee. Whereas it is the task of reporting not only to construct the social event in keeping with certain adequacy rules, but also to reconstruct it communicatively, the town-council meeting and the strike themselves by no means have the task of 'portraying' a different social reality. This decisive difference between social and communicative 'construction processes' is generally overlooked in the literature with a constructivist orientation.

Media events and public relations

As mentioned above, Boorstin (1963) introduced the concept of the 'pseudo-event' to describe a type of event that is now more appropriately termed a 'media event'. But Boorstin did not explicitly formulate the most important characteristic feature of the structure of media events: namely, that it is the primary goal of this type of event to induce reporting by the media. Press dispatches, press conferences, anniversary celebrations, etc. are produced or staged specifically for the purpose of causing the media to report them.

In addition to this primary goal, which may be regarded as a constitutive characteristic, there are frequently other objectives (e.g. political, economic, technical) or communicative goals. In the political field, these may be the self-portrayal of politicians, the creation of a profile *vis-à-vis* competitors or the regular presence of the politician among the general public.

The timing and structure of media events can only be explained on the basis of the fact that there are media (especially television) that are expected to report these events. The occupation of a tower by the organization Robin Wood or an action by Greenpeace make sense only if the media become aware of the action. Due to this event structure, the term 'media event' is to be preferred to Boorstin's concept of the 'pseudo-event'. The term 'pseudo-event' contains a depreciatory element and this concept creates the problem of having to distinguish 'real' events from 'non-real' ones.

Normally, media events consist of individual or social actions, or the products of these actions. The event may be represented as a mix of these elements, or relate to only one of them. As an aggregate event, media events themselves are communicative actions in so far as there is always a news item or message involved which is to be conveyed to a specific public. The presence of journalists or corresponding groups (e.g. a camera team) is a necessary prerequisite for such events: press conferences would become meaningless social actions if no media representatives attended them. Media events are structured either verbally or non-verbally (on the one hand, statements to the press, press conferences; on the other, environmental actions such as candle-light marches). In the political context, and particularly during election campaigns, it is important to schedule and shape social events (e.g. party congresses, visits abroad, meetings with other important/foreign/politicians) in such a way as to ensure an optimal presence of the media. Following Kepplinger, such events may then be dubbed 'mediatized events'. Election campaigns are strategically planned as a complex succession of media events. Thus 'events management' can be explained only with respect to the existence of the media.

The observation that not only the type of media event emerges alongside the development of the media, but that also part of the political system and its protagonists have been adapting themselves (including their behaviour) to the rules of the media system, has recently attracted scientific attention and caused media critics to sound some fundamental warnings.

From the reconstructive perspective, media events are treated as one type of events among others. The media are 'well aware' of the structure of media events, but must regard them as a subject matter to be reported in the same way as other types of events. For media events, the necessary relationship to the media belongs to the event structure itself, in contrast to natural or non-mediatized social events. As far as media events are a product staged for the media, the fact of staging itself must be regarded as part of the reality to be reported. In respect of the critical demand for objectivity, it can become apparent in the reporting process that they are media events with structures of their own transparency. Enlightenment about staged events would then be a genuine task of relevant reporting.

But it is a different question if public relations communicators are confronted with the moral demand to always disclose this character. At the moment it still seems to be true that in large sectors of professional public relations practice the transparency of media events, (the fact of their staging) is not held to be an essential feature of the communication. On the contrary, such staging of media events is often kept secret.

It may be assumed that most, but not all public relations activities are aimed at producing media events in a broad sense. This does not only refer to the 'events' – i.e. the special – experience-oriented – functions, but also to any form of work with the press (statements to the press, press conferences, talks with the press, press seminars), and to means of internal communication such as business reports, internal house journals, etc.

As far as the narrower concept of events – i.e. functions, is concerned, a study carried out by the BDW – Deutscher Kommunikationsverband in 1993, in which 209 firms were asked to describe their understanding of, and involvement in the matter of 'events', came to the conclusion that 96 per cent of the firms surveyed agreed with the definition of 'events' presented to them, and 80 per cent were found to carry out events defined in this way. The reasons cited for the organization of events were mainly communicative ones (product publicity, motivation, building of trust) and increasing competition. Up to now, service-to-the-customer and field-work functions as well as functions organized for the employees and product presentations have been the types of events on which attention has centred.

Kalt (1993), who analysed the content of the economic reporting of 'dpa', the 'Tagesschau' and the television news on RTL over a four-week period, concluded that 49 per cent of the news of dpa, 28 per cent of ARD news and 30 per cent of RTL news during the period investigated were 'staged' reports – i.e. news based on statements to the press, press conferences, manifestations and demonstrations. 'Nonstaged' events, i.e. non-public events as defined by Kalt, other public events and self-researched news made up 45 per cent (dpa), 59 per cent (ARD) and 58 per cent (RTL) of the reported news during the same period investigated.

Apart from the necessity of conducting further empirical studies of the different types of events, it can be argued that large parts of all the events to which reporting generally refers are media events in the sense described above.

CONCLUDING REMARKS

At present, it is not only hotels – as mentioned at the beginning – which organize functions as media events, it is both private and public companies and institutions which have to rely today on continuous and professional communication. A possible gradual separation in this communication lies in the distinction between media events and public communication. But even if all public information and communication were based on this type of event (which would neither be desirable nor seem really possible), public communication, including continuously produced media reality, could still be compared with the social reality portrayed there. This factually existing social reality of organizations, which can be perceived directly only by small segments of the public (the members of those organizations), provides the basis for any public relations activity. It cannot only be perceived and portrayed communicatively and will not disappear, in spite of all the artificially generated media realities and in spite of the development of 'virtual realities'. It will continue to exist and provide the criterion for the communicative realities constructed by man. For television spots, virtual reality and artificially generated media worlds do not satisfy people.

4 Community public relations in Germany – east and west state-of-the-art and development

Barbara Baerns and Anja Kutscher-Klink

INTRODUCTION

This chapter is concerned with traditions and developments in community public relations in East and West. It is also concerned with the opportunities and risks of two competing models, public relations (Offentlichkeitsarbeit) and public marketing in the public sector of Germany, and other European countries, today. In addition to the more theoretical approach, a survey of all 185 German cities and communities with 50,000 or more inhabitants reveals some of the developments in this field.

PUBLIC RELATIONS VERSUS PUBLIC MARKETING

Drawing on the idea of the central role that 'public' plays as a principle as well as a method in legitimizing the liberal constitutional state, the representative democracy of the Federal Republic of Germany guarantees comprehensive information as a prerequisite for their participation in, and control of, the democratic decision-making process. The basic right of freedom of information corresponds to this. The idea of individual freedom of information regarding the performance of state authority in the field of legislation and the idea of control through insight into processes in the area of jurisdiction have become fact, in that sessions of these bodies (namely parliaments and courts) are open to the public. There is a right to direct access. This right, however, is de facto restricted through lack of space, through geographic distances and inconvenient hours and is, therefore, dependent on information transmission facilities.

But even in the parliamentary context, on the local level, on the regional level (with the exception of the Land of Schleswig-Holstein) and on the national level, sessions of advisory committees generally take place behind closed doors. Moreover, the execution of state authority in the field of public administration altogether escapes public 'insight' and control. Whereas other democracies such as Sweden and the USA (also Norway, Denmark and Canada) grant their citizens access to information from the authorities without the condition that they are personally affected and as long as there is no higher valued public interest that demands secrecy, the individual citizen of the Federal Republic of Germany has no such right. Nevertheless, there are indications of openness towards a more direct citizens' participation on local levels. Thus, the amendment of the Federal Building Act (Bundesbaugesetz), which came into force as early as 1977, serves to let citizens have a say in planning before the final plans are decided upon and executed.

Existing information gaps are bridged by the basic right of freedom of the press which, broadly interpreted, includes the right to demand and exploit information from state authorities. This means that all national, regional and local authorities have to provide information when requested to do so by journalists. According to administrative law, the notion of authority includes 'all institutions that take over tasks of public administration', irrespective of their organizational form (Baerns 1993b). The rights of journalists to gain information, which are formulated, and the corresponding obligations of the authorities to provide information can 'legitimately' be characterized as constitutive for the democratic character of the Federal Republic of Germany, as long as individual access to information is restricted.

In contrast to the public political and state-run sector, we find that in the mostly private economic sector, the private societal sector and of course the intimate individual sector, there is little or no obligation to publish information.

The obligation to provide information has also contributed and led to the setting up of organizational forms of departments of public information and public relations in the public sector. Due to questions raised at the time regarding the mixing of public relations and election advertising in 1977, the Federal Constitutional Court took special notice of public relations carried out by the organs of state. In this context, public relations carried out by government departments has been viewed not only as admissible but even as necessary. Thereby, the Constitutional Court maintains that only the executive itself is able to redress the advantage it has over its citizens with regard to information and power. In 1988, the Higher Administrative Court transferred this judgement to the local level, recommending a kind of 'active obligation' to provide information, since it was recognized that only the informed citizen can participate creatively in the development of his or her community.

At the end of the 1970s and the beginning of the 1980s, new thinking emerged in this context which extended marketing beyond business management and into the public sector. This led to the emergence of terms such as 'non-profit marketing', 'non-commercial marketing', 'social marketing', 'socio-marketing' etc. In short, the **classical** approach to marketing which holds that firms can only be successful permanently with a market-oriented management, that is, only if the needs of the customers are taken as a point of reference for all activities of the firm.[1] Marketing is carried out not only by classical manufacturers who sell concrete products such as washing powder, drinks, cars or machines, but also by the service industry, banks or insurance companies. On this basis, it is then claimed that since the public sector also offers services, it is forced to apply various marketing instruments in order to effectively and economically reach the consumer with its services.

In our view, the scientific discussion of, and reflection on, the concepts and instruments of public marketing were already fully formed by the end of 1988 (e.g. Rober 1988: 1029–1035). Briefly summing up the arguments put forward in the literature regarding the advantages and dangers of marketing in the public sector, we obtain the following critical result.

The supporting arguments:

● By a purposeful application of modern marketing instruments of information gathering, public administration gains a considerably better data base for its decisions. If more information on the citizens' interests and needs are available and if these are interpreted as customers' wishes, then a creative administration (which is incidentally headed by politicians who have an interest in their own re-election) will adapt to these customers' wishes.

● Viewing the citizens as customers increases the awareness of communication barriers between citizens and the administration. Information about the public services of the social and welfare state is improved, as is their ability to work with it.

● With the application of marketing instruments, the public services are offered more efficiently and, therefore, employed less wastefully.

Marketing enforces reflections on an overall concept in accordance with a corporate identity. Authorities especially have to deal with many different acitivities and an overall concept does not become apparent for the citizens. Consequently, it makes good sense if the activities of the administration too are planned by way of rational criteria and made transparent and comprehensible with the help of corporate identity strategies.

Taken as a whole, marketing concepts enable the public sector to operate close to the citizens' needs (Burgernahe), since the citizens are viewed as customers whose wishes are recognized and fulfilled in the form of services.

The counter-arguments:

- Since the citizens' demands for services cannot be met without restrictions, the discussion of closeness to the citizens' needs (Burgernahe) is reduced to friendly contacts, to clearly-structured forms and to the provision of basic facilities. What we have here is a very narrow approach to closeness to the citizens' needs that only refers to the outward appearance of the contacts between citizens and administration and not to the dimension of content and politics.

- From its genesis, marketing is mainly a 'steering instrument 'with which the aims of a firm are supposed to be reached. In the public sector it may contribute to an intensification of the feeling of powerlessness, which many citizens already experience.

- Third, as a further restriction to which marketing in the public sector is subject, it is argued that the concentration on certain target groups contributes to a real or apparent neglect of other target groups. This bias in favour of some target groups may be unavoidable, but it is undesirable in principle in the public sector. Dealing with democracies, it may be inadequate, *per se*, to regard citizens and publics as target groups.

- Solutions by which a large part of these deficits could be overcome, if the methods of information gathering were improved and the marketing instruments thereby refined, should be regarded as dangerous. The intrusion in to citizens' private affairs by the state which could enable the state to compile a detailed information profile about a person would contradict the principle of informational self-determination as laid down by the Federal Constitutional Court in its judgement on the national census. It is not 'the transparent citizen' but the 'transparent townhall' which is desirable, as was suggested in the normative framework presented at the beginning of this chapter.

- Decisions in the public sector are usually based on compromises between competing interests (compromises that are often no more than formal compromises). If marketing is carried out in such a situation, it has the flavour of putting aside conflicts elegantly instead of overcoming them carefully. Even more problems occur if two-way-communication is used in such a situation. If managed professionally, such a 'phantom dialogue', some people think, may effectively hide the inadequacies of the public performance. For others, it seems reasonable to suppose that marketing is basically there to manipulate the citizens and to create propaganda.

• Marketing may become an unobtrusive, but effective instrument of those in power which could no longer be legitimized in the context of constitutional law. Accordingly, at the core of this discussion lies the problem of where to draw the line in controlling powers of the state in relation to its people, with which sovereign power must lie.

If we try to sum up the discussion so far and summarize the main argument, it becomes clear that a 'public marketing' cannot simply be developed within the micro-economic perspective of firms and then transferred to the public sector with only terminological adaptations. This is crucial, where problems of access and perception, as well as problems of information and communication are concerned. After all, the public forum of interests and opinions should not be confused with the market, where competitive haggling and selling takes place. It is only in the latter that marketing has its adequate place.

SURVEY DATA ON THE REAL SITUATION IN THE FIELD

To our knowledge, this theoretical discussion has had no deep impact on the practice of public relations for communities. In West Germany, a restructuring of public relations for communities towards 'community advertising' and towards 'image promotion' has been systematically carried out in some cities for years. After (re)unification, market-oriented strategies, as part of press and public relations for communities, have been seen on the one hand, as necessary as cities compete for tourists, workers, and the establishing of trade and industry not just by the German Congress of Municipal Authorities. On the other hand, the restriction of public relations for communities to community advertising and community marketing is still highly controversial, since the point of public relations for communities is seen in terms of making the decisions of the adminstration transparent and controllable in order to involve the citizens in decisions on the community level.

Against this background and in this context, it seemed useful to examine how far community public relations can contribute to more information for, and participation of, the citizens and to comply with the corresponding demands, even in a possibly modified framework and under modified working conditions. Our present investigation (Kutscher-Klink 1994) records that there are 185 communities in the Federal Republic of Germany with 50, 000 or more inhabitants (return rate: 77 per cent; former GDR = East Germany 25 questionnaires = 93 per cent, former FRG = West Germany 118 questionnaires = 75 per cent). The period of investigation was August 1993, and in essence it yields the following results.

Today, almost all German cities and communities with more than 50,000 inhabitants have a press office, that is 139 out of 143, or about 97 per cent. The number of community press offices is regularly published in the Statistical Yearbook of German communities (e.g. Kauffmann 1988: 409–19). Following these data, the figure was about 86 per cent in 1987. However, only 145 West German cities and communities were included in that survey, so that its results are only partially comparable with those of the present situation. Today, in only three cases (in West Germany), is there no press office. In one of these cases, such an office is being planned.

Since the objective is to study the organization and activities of community press offices, only cities with a press office have been included in the further analysis. These amount to 139 cities, to which the following results refer. The term 'press office' here stands for an overall number of 66 established different denominations for those departments in the administration that deal with public information and 'Offentlichkeitsarbeit' (The synonym 'public relations' is never used in the public sector in Germany). Among the denominations, classical terms such as 'press and information office', 'press >office', 'public relations office', or 'press and public relations office' are most frequently used. In summary, it was found that about one half (or 45.9 per cent) of the press offices are called by one of the classical terms.

However, around half of the press offices have other names. Among the titles used, four include the term 'marketing' or 'community marketing'. The terms 'information or advice for the citizens', 'promotion of trade and industry' and 'community advertising' occur three times each. If we assume that the denomination of a department indicates its scope of action, then combinations such as 'Department of Statistics, Elections, Procurement and Public Relations' or 'City Councillors' and Mayor's Affairs Office – Section for Public

Relations, Statistics and Elections' are almost bizarre, considering the declared aim of providing information for the citizens and also taking account of the background of constitutional jurisdiction.

Organizational facts

The organizational environment of a department crucially determines its scope of action and its status within an organization. The organizational environment includes its organizational assignment, its position within the hierarchy, co-operation with other departments, and, last but not least, finance and personnel.

The organizational assignment and the position within the hierarchy of the administration are of vital importance for the effectiveness of the press office. The press office has to rely on information from other departments. The exchange and transmission of information should not be dependent on the goodwill of the other departments but should be regulated through clear-cut responsibilities. In his study on public relations in the public sector in general, Frank Bockelmann found that a press office, in order to fulfil its duties adequately, ideally should be directly subordinate to the head of the administration and be organized as an independent office or as a department or departmental section of the main office (Bockelmann 1991). In practice, 72 of the 139 press offices examined were found to be organized as independent offices with their own budgets. A further 26 are situated at the main office in the form of a department, and another 18 as a departmental section. Thus, an overall number of 118 of the press offices included in the survey, 83 per cent, are subject to good organizational conditions. It is quite surprising that the number of independent offices was found to increase with a decreasing number of inhabitants. A particularly positive picture emerges from the investigation of the positions within the hierarchy. Of the 139 press offices 114 are directly subordinate to the heads of the administration. This figure also increases with a decreasing number of inhabitants. Compared with 1987, the figure has increased from 76 per cent then to 82 per cent now.

In most cities, press and public relations is formally carried out centrally through the press office. This is so in 124 cases. This figure includes a large number of administrations in which this only works 'with restrictions', that is in 60 of the 114 administrations, or about half of them. Accordingly, other departments often seem to ignore instructions and carry out their own press and public relations measures, bypassing the press office. Consequently, though most cities in

Germany do have a press office, press and public relations are still not completely run by this office in many cases. Since 1987, the average number of personnel working in such departments has increased by 0.5 to an average of 5.4 employees. The greater the number of inhabitants of a city, the larger the staff of its press office. However, these figures include personnel who are not exclusively dealing with press and public relations, like printers and messengers etc.

Additional probing revealed further insights into the operation of municipal public relations functions in cases where press and public relations were not managed centrally. This concerned 71 cases which form the basis for the following results. Of those other departments that carry out their own press and public relations measures the following were mentioned most frequently: promotion of tourism department; promotion of trade and industry department; departments for other subjects; limited companies (companies in which the community holds a share and which take on municipal tasks, such as a company for the promotion of trade and industry); community advertising department; community marketing department; others. In 23 of the 71 cases, the working of the various departments was found to be thoroughly co-ordinated. In twelve cases, such co-ordination did not take place, and in most cases, that is 34, operations were only partly co-ordinated. This, again, suggests that there are difficulties concerning the implementation of public relations programmes. The press office had responsibility for co-ordination in most instances (in 50 out of 71 cases). Only in very few cases did the administration transfer the task of co-ordination to a public relations or advertising agency or set up co-ordination committees in the form of teams.

Tasks and objectives versus actual activities

In our survey we dealt with information supplied by respondents only. This is regarded as a methodological handicap which might result in accuracies and misrepresentations.[2] In our questionnaire, however, we differentiated between tasks stipulated by regulations, objectives of the respective practitioner interviewed, and actual daily activities mentioned by them. By this approach, it was hoped that some of the methodological problems that might result from the survey approach might be overcome.

The **tasks** carried out by the press office according to job descriptions or instructions show the following scope: public relations (137) and press relations (132) were mentioned most frequently. Other activities mentioned included: providing information for citizens (114), community advertising (111), community marketing (91), advice for citizens (88), promotion of tourism (65), fairs and congresses (44) and finally, promotion of trade and industry (31). In terms of how far such tasks were carried out by the press office, answers ranged from 'completely', 'partially', to 'not at all'. However, it was noted that the press office only carries out partial functions on behalf of other functions, such as press relations for the promotion of tourism. In such cases, the figures presented here were reached by adding together the answers 'completely' and 'partially'.

As a result, it can be argued that the classical tasks of the press office score highest here. However, the offices are not able to concentrate on these tasks alone because, with varying degrees, they take on additional tasks which would normally come under the responsibility of other departments. These are, in particular, community marketing and advertising. This variety of tasks is already reflected in the countless different denominations given to the public relations function. In 1987, 46 per cent of the press offices had no additional tasks to fulfil. However, the situation has changed significantly and this is no longer the case today. Furthermore, the results show that typical tasks of the press office are only partially carried out. This is particularly so with regard to advice and information for citizens, two tasks which are obviously either taken on by other departments or discontinued.

The heads of the press offices were also asked to assess their most important objectives or aims ranking these on a scale of 1–7. The results revealed the following hierarchy:

1 to create transparency in the administration;
2 to improve the image of the city;
3 to inform the citizens about services;
4 to present the achievements of the administration positively;
5 to increase the degree of fame beyond the region;
6 to promote citizens' participation;
7 to increase the number of visitors.

It is remarkable that the original aim of community press and public relations, namely the promotion of citizens' participation, should again have such a low status in the assessment of the heads of the press offices. This table shows that the possibilities for the press office to promote citizens' participation are completely unrecognized. Twenty years ago, this aim took the third place. Today commercial aims, such as image optimization, are seen as more important.

This is all the more surprising, when taking account of the fact that the press office is the most important authority to be approached by the citizens! Of the 139 interviewees, 117 named the press office as the mechanism via which citizens could establish contact with local authorities. Other mechanisms identified included: citizens' assemblies, events for the purposes of informing the public, consultations and telephone advice services for the citizens. Departments other than the press office were seen to play only a marginal role as authorities to be contacted.

The status of the press office as a means for the citizens to establish contact with the authority is not readily identified and hardly finds expression in its daily activities. According to their frequency, the following activities were grouped into 'never', 'occasionally' and 'regularly'. If a hierarchy of the individual scores is set up, it turns out that the following activities take place 'regularly':

1 establishing contacts with the press;
2 collecting, selecting and processing information from the administration;
3 maintaining contacts with other departments;
4 planning and carrying out press conferences;
5 advising other departments;
6 making its own publications;
7 compiling a press review;
8 producing information material for internal use in the administration;
9 building up and updating an archive;
10 ghost-writing.

The following activities mostly occur 'occasionally':

1 carrying out lectures and discussions;
2 planning and carrying out events to inform the public;
3 producing television spots etc.;
4 advising the citizens;
5 dealing with citizens' enquiries;
6 attending to visitors and guests;
7 informing the administration about external affairs.

And the following activity rarely ever occurs: interviewing citizens.

However, in many communities, restructuring and reorientation processes concerning contacts with the public are in progress. They are often set up in the form of a variety of projects. These include projects for community marketing, mechanisms for more citizens' participation, more adaptation to the citizens' needs and projects for image optimization. The press office is involved in these projects to varying degrees. It may take over the management of such a project, it may restrict itself to carrying out public relations measures, or it may do both at the same time. In practice, however, the press office appreared to play only a limited role in carrying out public relations measures or in the implementation and management of public relations projects. In 64 per cent of the projects mentioned, the press office did not take part at all, but in 14 per cent of the cases it was appointed to manage the project. The press office had responsibility for management mainly in corporate design and image optimisation. Here, it was often in overall control. Projects intended to generate more citizens' participation or to improve adaptation to the citizens' needs were those in which the press office tended to play little or no part. In the field of community marketing, the press office was responsible in 37 per cent of the cases for the task of carrying out public relations measures. Here again, the press office was found to focus on commercially oriented projects, rather than concentrating on its original tasks.

COMPARING EAST AND WEST

A comparison between the situations in East and West German communities has shown that there are hardly any significant differences in the organization of community press offices. This is all the more regrettable, since there was an opportunity in the East to counteract negative developments in the organization of community press offices while building up a municipal administration. Furthermore, it can be argued that information and participation were particularly important following (re)unification.

However, a number of differences can be identified between the press office function in the East and West:

- As regards the reorientation processes far fewer East German press offices participate in the design of a unified image than their West German counterparts do.
- In East German communities, community advertising is more often not part of the tasks of the press offices than in West German communities.
- There are also some differences concerning the activities performed in East German press offices. It is considerably less

common for them to plan and carry out advertising measures than in West Germany.

• Moreover, the compilation of press reviews plays a more prominent role in the daily routine of press offices in East Germany than in the West.

• In contrast, dealing with citizens' enquiries is much more common in the Eastern part of Germany. While this task is carried out regularly in 38 per cent and occasionally in 50 per cent of the cases in the West, it occurs regularly in 61 per cent and occasionally in 40 per cent of the cases in the East.

Compared with West Germany, East German communities appear to be better at fulfilling the traditional goals of public relations. But the situation is somewhat ambivalent, since there is no evaluation, and theoretical backgrounds are not discussed. Thus, as far as future developments are concerned, the question remains open as to whether there is likely to be either a rethinking of the participatory claims of our political constitution, or whether marketing models will succeed in predominating. Maybe, the field of community public relations will finally be regarded as another illustrative example of the fact, that the socio-political change has not been taken as an occasion for societal innovation but for the further establishment of the Western status quo ante, as a routine (Baerns 1993a: 63).

NOTES

1 As a rule, marketing is divided into three dimensions:
  1 marketing philosophy, that is, the basic position of orientating all activities to the requirements of the market;
  2 marketing strategy, the subdivision into individual phases of decision-making processes in marketing such as analysis, planning, implementation, control, organization;
  3 marketing instruments, the tools applied in the sales policy of a firm such as product policy, pricing policy, distribution policy and communication policy. The latter, communication policy, with its subdivision into advertising, public relations, sales promotion, and direct sale.
2 There is too much focus on individual attitudes and individual characteristics; attention to attitudes instead of actual behaviour, reliance on interviews, questionnaires, or subject-supplied information – see D Nimmo: Political communication and research. An overview, in *Communication yearbook I. An annual review* (ed. B D. Ruben) New Brunswick and New Jersey: International Communication Association, 1977 pp. 441–52.

5 Towards a typology of MA and PhD theses projects in public relations

Benno Signitzer

INTRODUCTION

Whether public relations scholars (and practitioners) like it or not, the bulk of public relations research will, for some considerable time to come, be conducted by students in their MA and PhD theses. This certainly holds true in regard to quantity, but also to quality. And it holds particularly true in Europe where, notwithstanding some very promising developments since the beginning of the 1990s, the overall infrastructural basis for systematic public relations research (e.g. university chairs and departments for public relations, foundations emphasizing public relations research, publication outlets, etc.) continues to be rather weak. It would be quite reckless to build planning on the expectation of quick breakthroughs in this respect.

What are the consequences of this? We must take the above outlined basic fact seriously – for better, or for worse, and draw the obvious conclusion: if we want to increase the quantity and improve the quality of public relations research, we must increase and improve the quantity and quality of student theses and, possibly, re-allocate resources correspondingly. In other words, by ameliorating student theses, we will ameliorate public relations research overall.

Certainly, there is nothing spectacularly new about this idea, and it may apply to many fields of study, including the various sub-disciplines of communications. And there is no need to re-emphasize the specific contributions MA and PhD theses can make to an academic (and practical) field, not the least in view of the production of publications and the provision of consulting services. However, the very infancy of the public relations discipline (at least in some countries) makes our case quite specific leading us to the not-so-pleasant, but also challenging, alternative: either we develop sys-

tematic and sensible programmes for student public relations research
– or we have no appreciable body of public research at all.

The purpose of this chapter is to make a contribution towards more
systematic programmes for public relations research in MA and PhD
theses by attempting to develop a typology of such works at a rather
formal level. This is largely a discussion paper, not based on large-
scale empirical surveys of actual practice and perceived need. However, clearly discernable external inputs were provided and are gladly
acknowledged, inter alia, an investigation of German-language public
relations theses during 1980–1990 (Angerer 1990); by earlier
attempts at development of a systematization of the field (Pavlik
1987); and, of course, by this author's accumulated personal experience from advising many MA and PhD students over the past 8 or so
years at the University of Salzburg.

Overview of the typology of theses projects in public relations

1 basic research theses;
2 theoretical sector-based theses;
3 empirical sector-based theses;
4 theoretical theses on public relations programme areas;
5 empirical theses on public relations programme areas;
6 theoretical theses on public relations techniques;
7 empirical theses on public relations techniques;
8 theoretical theses on aspects of the public relations process;
9 empirical theses on aspects of the public relations process;
10 theoretical theses on the people doing public relations;
11 empirical theses on the people doing public relations;
12 largely empirical theses on the public relations industry as such;
13 largely practical theses, resulting in real-life public relations proposals.

Type 1 – basic research theses

Basic research theses would usually focus on the public relations
function in its totality, such as differing approaches to public relations (e.g. organizational, marketing, and societal approaches), theory of science issues, meta-research on public relations, historical
questions, criticism of public relations at different levels, conceptual
analyses of public relations (for example in regard to such functions
as marketing, corporate communications, integrated communications, propaganda, public diplomacy), models of public relations,

basic organizational and strategic issues of public relations management, basic ethical dimensions of public relations, etc. Most works would be of a general, theoretical nature, employing such methods as critical and historical. The outline here remains comparatively brief as these themes would not usually be considered a typical content for student theses.

Type 2 – theoretical sector-based theses

Theoretical sector-based theses deal with the public relations activities and functions of certain sectors of the economy or society. Examples would be such studies as public relations by airlines, public relations by universities; public relations in the textiles industry; public relations by local governments; public relations in the tourism industry, etc. The objective of such studies is to answer the following question: how does public relations help a certain sector achieve its goals in society or in the economy? Thus, a societal approach to public relations (with a good dose of a broadly conceived organizational approach) appears most appropriate. Methodologically, the most challenging aspect of such studies is to clearly and powerfully define and operationalize the dimensions of the communication component of the problems and opportunities of a given sector, as distinct from product, distribution and people problems. In addition, there may be (and very likely are) communication aspects in product, distribution and people problems which need to be just as carefully isolated and defined. Procedurally, such a study strives for a collection and systematization of the whole of the available theoretical and practical body of knowledge on the public relations function of a given sector. In practical terms, a vexing problem arises from the question: how much general knowledge about a sector is necessary in order to understand the public relations dimension of it and how competent are public relations students (and researchers) to selectively accumulate it? Or, more practically: how long and how deep should the typical general chapter describing the sector be? In this type of study, newness of the results usually stems from diligently collecting and creatively re-arranging existing knowledge along strong public relations theory lines, rather than from original data collection. This does not mean, however, that the use of some empirical social science methods were totally out of place; expert interviews, for example, may very well enrich and put into perspective the other sources. Even small case studies for the sole purpose of problem illustration may be in order.

Type 3 – empirical sector-based theses

Empirically orientated sector-based studies ideally can draw heavily on already completed works of type 2 theses in a given area. Examples would include the public relations programme of Lufthansa; the public relations programme of the University of Salzburg; the public relations programme of the city of Salzburg; the public relations programme of the Lubljana Tourist Board; or the public relations programmes of Austria's hotels etc. The objectives of such studies are two-fold: first, to measure the quality and sophistication of a given organization's public relations programme against a certain standard of excellence prevailing (or hoped for) in a specific sector as outlined in studies of type 2; second, to answer the question, to what extent an organization's public relations programme has managed to contribute to the achievement of this organization's overall goals. It becomes quite obvious that this kind of study needs to take into account overall sector dimensions. The organizational approach to public relations will dominate such studies, but, in some cases, a sprinkling of a societal approach may enrich the investigation with a view to the first question above. Typically, evaluation issues will be a central concern in the research. Methodologically, in addition to a careful discussion of the various social science methods employed, thorough and critical reflections on the strengths and weaknesses of the overall study design, namely of the case study method, appear imperative. Technical and source problems may arise when the sector in question is not sufficiently covered by knowledge usually produced by studies of type 1, thus leading to too-narrowly focused case studies bearing the danger of singularity.

Type 4 – theoretical theses on public relations programme areas

There are numerous programme areas of public relations, such as media relations, employee communication, community relations, financial relations, investor relations, consumer relations, customer relations, international public relations, crisis public relations, lobbying, governmental relations, fund raising, educational relations, issues management, marketing communication, etc. All those programme areas of public relations may constitute interesting themes for theses of a theoretical type such as 'an overview of community relations as a central public relations programme area', etc. The overall research question in such studies usually is: how does (or does not) a specific programme area contribute to the achievement of the public relations goals of an organization employing it? The goal of the study is to collect and put into a system all available theoretical and practical knowledge on a given programme area. As in other types of more theoretical and general studies (in our typology, numbers 1, 2, 4, 6, 8, and 10) a hierarchy of the sources used should be established and priorities set – ranking first, scholarly literature; second, practitioners' literature; and third, documents of practice, such as actual annual reports, PRSA Silver Anvil entries, etc. It appears also important in works of such type to critically discuss and make transparent the very method employed here, namely the literature review. A practical issue arises around the question of just how much knowledge of the contributing disciplines do we need in order to develop a reasonably sufficient understanding of a given public relations programme area, that is, how much are political science insights necessary to comprehend lobbying, how much community sociology do we need to gain an understanding of community relations, how competent must we be in finance so that our judgement in regard to investor relations will be sound, etc.

Type 5 – empirical theses on public relations programme areas

These are empirical theses on public relations programme areas with in-depth investigations into a given programme area as employed by a specific organization or else by a group of organizations belonging to a certain sector or a geographic area. Examples include: the investor relations programme of the BMW AG, Munich; the educational relations programmes of Austria's Municipal Theatres; crisis public relations programmes by selected chemical plants in the United States, etc. The purpose of such theses is, pretty much as in type 3, to examine, by way of case studies and the use of various empirical methods, to what extent an organization is conducting state-of-the-art public relations programmes in a specific area and to what extent this constitutes a contribution to its overall public relations goals (in terms of evaluation). Moreover, there is also room for theory testing in terms of the applicability of, say, a community relations theory to a specific situation. In some of the studies, students may also raise the issue of how to best organize a specific public relations programme area within the larger public relations function, including the management of overlaps with other organizational functions (e.g. financial relations located somewhere between the finance and the public relations departments). Theses of this type may also lend themselves to recommendations and proposals towards preferred courses of action.

Type 6 – theoretical theses on public relations techniques

No doubt quite a few of our students are preoccupied with the technical side of public relations – sometimes much to the chagrin of their more theoretically and strategically inclined teachers. However, there is room for theses exploring in great depth (by collecting and systematizing mainly practical information) such public relations techniques as press releases, press conferences, video news releases, speech writing, newsletters, public relations films, specials events, etc. Examples might include speechwriting as a public relations technique; video news releases – a new public relations tool; the evolution of annual reports as a public relations technique. The more ambitious students would go a long way towards integrating knowledge elements from such disciplines as rhetoric, film aesthetics, graphics, visual arts, journalism and effects research in order to develop a stronger argument for the usefulness of their public relations technique. The chief purpose of such studies is to establish sophisticated categories defining clearly how and when the employment of a specific public relations technique may provide a contribution to the achievement of public relations programme area goals.

Type 7 – empirical theses on public relations techniques

In such works, the use of a specific public relations technique is investigated in the context of certain public relations programme areas or overall public relations programmes by specific organizations, in certain sectors or else geographic areas. Themes may include changes in the function of the annual reports in the oil industry over the past 10 years; the use of seminars for journalists as a media relations technique by the top ten insurance companies in Switzerland; overview and analysis of the Austrian public relations film production in 1994. Typically, such studies must have carefully detailed research designs, e.g. quantitative and qualitative analyses of the contents, research on specific effects on specific publics, etc.

Type 8 – theoretical theses on aspects of the public relations process

Here, the focus is placed on the (strategic) public relations planning process as a whole or else on one or several stages of it. Largely theoretically orientated, the theses may have such themes as a comparison of different approaches to the public relations planning process; the concepts of publics and stakeholders in public relations; a state-of-the-art review of public relations evaluation; new theories of budgeting applied to public relations. The studies would usually involve fairly high-calibre literature reviews of specific communication and public relations theories, but also the application of novel approaches from management, organization, and the general social sciences to the public relations process – hopefully leading to a refinement of existing strategic public relations concepts and/or the development of new ones. This work should also lead to operationalization schemes making the concepts accessible to empirical test in subsequent research and practical application alike. While the organizational approach to public relations appears most fruitful, every effort should be made to integrate both marketing and societal approaches as well with a view to broadening the concepts.

Type 9 – empirical theses on aspects of the public relations process

Here, the emphasis is clearly on the hard-nosed testing of the concepts developed in studies of type 8. Students with strong empirical and methodological inclinations will find studies of this kind challenging and rewarding. The objective of such theses is the improvement of theoretical public relations concepts. Examples include development and testing of a stakeholder strategy for the BMW AG public relations programme; development of a research design for the evaluation of the public relations programme of the University of Cologne; development and testing of controlling and budgeting instruments for the public relations programme of Austria's Federal Chamber of Commerce. While the selection of a given organization and the knowledge generated about this organization are important, the very focus of the research interest rests on the refinement of the theoretical concepts. To put it in another way, as a result of such studies we know, of course, more about BMW's public relations programme, but we also – and this is crucial! – know more about the stakeholder concept.

Type 10 – theoretical theses on the people doing public relations

The various studies of this type may be placed under the umbrella term of professionalization in a broad sense; they deal both with the individual public relations practitioners (somehow similar to the classic communicator studies in mass communications) and the practitioners as an occupational group – addressing, *inter alia*, such issues as public relations roles, feminization of public relations, professional education, qualification profiles, professional ethics, labour market, role of professional associations, etc. In addition to a sound base in public relations theory, such theses need to integrate the most up-to-date advances in occupational sociology and professionalization theory. The classic attribute approach to professionalization seems to be no longer adequate as a single point of reference; the more recent market strategy and developmental approaches should also inform our thinking about public relations as a profession. Reviews and integration of both the scholarly and practical literature would be the most likely method employed. Considering the two-phases model of the professionalization process (moving from an economic phase to an ideological one), both organizational and societal approaches to public relations should be given equal attention.

Type 11 – empirical theses on the people doing public relations

Nearly all the themes of the studies of type 10 lend themselves to empirical investigations, mostly surveys of one kind or another. At the more individual level, oral history and other qualitative methods seem to be quite promising. Examples of such studies would include professional values held by Hungarian public relations practitioners; the evolving position of women pracitioners in UK public relations; thirty-five years in public relations practice: a professional biography of Horst Avenarius, former Head of Public Relations, BMW AG; practitioners' attitudes towards the German Public Relations Society (DPRG) etc. In most countries, there seems to be a priority need for data collection, as a basis for both further scholarly study and professional action. At the same time, the empirical testing of some of the theoretical propositions developed by studies of type 10 should not be neglected. For example, we badly need to know just what kind of profession, if any, public relations will or can or should ever be. Does the often uncritically adopted analogy with the classic professions of medicine and law really hold water? All in all, a tall order!

Type 12 – largely empirical studies on the public relations industry as such

As is the case with type 11 themes, knowledge collection rather than knowledge production still seems to be a priority when we look at the infrastructure of the public relations industry: numerical developments of public relations agencies in a given country; international agency networks, including models of co-operation; the evolving public relations function in organizations and institutional patterns; labour market developments at the macro level; broad descriptions of so-called public relations landscapes, as in The Public Relations Landscape of Norway; the evolving economic base for the public relations function in departments and agencies etc. One may phantasize about annual state of the nation-type reports of public relations, largely, but not exclusively, of a statistical nature, to be commissioned by the national public relations associations or else by CERP or IPRA.

Type 13 – largely practical theses, resulting in real-life public relations proposals

The primary focus of such theses is to produce a real-life public relations proposal, outlining implemenation procedures (including budgeting) and concrete actions over, say, a one or three-year period for a concrete organization, covering either the whole of a public relations programme or certain programme areas of it. The thesis may include the actual presentation (pitching) of the proposal to the organization, perhaps even in a competitive context. The actual real-life proposal running perhaps some 20 pages would be an integral part of the physical body of the thesis, often in the form of an appendix on differently coloured paper. The remaining 120–or so pages would consist of background information on the organization, its communicative status, the theoretical basis for the proposal, and a sort of workshop report on all the steps taken towards the development of the proposal (including its presentation). Obviously, a good working relationship with the organization in question is essential. Still, problems may arise as to scholarly independence and integrity, role of the thesis adviser, financial arrangements, etc. For some of our more hands-on-orientated students, this type of thesis can be an extremely rewarding experience.

It goes without saying that the above typology is one of ideal types, and overlaps will not be the exception, but the rule. Such a typology may be useful to the students in that it can help them more clearly focus on their central research question(s). From the adviser's vantage point, it might help him or her plan programmes of student research and identify uncovered research territory. On the other hand, however, my own advising experience suggests that one must be careful not to over-plan, thereby possibly stifling student creativity. Still, it does make lots of sense to strive for a system where empirical studies should be preceded by more theoretical ones, such as type 2 prior to type 3, type 4 prior to type 5, and so forth. Also, such a typology of student research projects may serve a useful educational function *vis-à-vis* the practical world of public relations, informing it about scope and priorities of the advising part of our work with the promise of more enlightened forms of co-operation. Finally, a typology of this kind may also further exchange processes within the public relations research community, both nationally and internationally.

It is the nature of such a typology that immensely different views on it will (and should) exist as to its overall structure, priorities, and hidden ideologies. After all, advising MA and PhD students in their thesis work is a complex pedagogical and social process involving a myrad of factors, of which consistency of product outcome is only one among many. Thus, the reader of this chapter is invited to criticize this proposed typology, to develop and refine it further, and, most importantly, to adapt it to his or her specific educational and intellectual setting. So, in the final analysis, it is not which typology one choses that is crucial, but that there should be some sort of typology at all.

Part III

UK perspectives of public relations

This section of the book contains three chapters by authors from the United Kingdom. These chapters offer insights into three quite different aspects of public relations practice and comprise examples of both fundamental and applied research.

Danny Moss, Gary Warnaby and Louise Thame examine the role of public relations within the UK retailing sector and compare how a number of leading retail organizations practise public relations. This study reveals marked differences between the retailers both in terms of the type of public relations activities practitioners perform and in the way in which each of the public relations functions are treated by the managements in each of the organizations examined. The study suggests that the role and scope of public relations function is strongly influenced by both the organizational context (in terms of traditions, size, culture and values) as well as by the retail industry's strong marketing orientation, both of which are found to constrain the scope of function to play a more strategic role.

Toby MacManus reports on the preliminary findings of a study designed to examine the interrelationship between public relations and culture, focusing primarily on public relations practices in three European countries. The chapter explores how the concept of culture and its impact on society have been treated in the literature and explores examples of more recent public relations research which has sought to explain the effect of culture on public relations. Mac-Manus concludes by outlining the findings of a comparative ethnographic study into perceptions of public relations in the United Kingdom, Austria and Sweden.

Jon White explores the consequences for business and organizational performance of recognition of the public relations practitioner's moral role. Drawing on the work of Hofstede (1980), White examines the contribution that practitioners can make to organizational effectiveness by acting to challenge prevailing values within an organization. Here White explores the question of what should be the fundamental nature of the relationship between organizations and its publics and considers the practitioners' role in helping to define the nature of this relationship. White argues that the debate is not simply a theoretical one, but can be found at the centre of recent studies, such as that being undertaken by the Royal society of Arts into the role of Tomorrow's Company, which are questioning the future relationship of business to society and other stakeholder groups.

6 Public relations or simply product publicity? An exploration of the role of public relations in the UK retail sector

Danny Moss, Gary Warnaby and Louise Thame

ABSTRACT

This chapter examines the role of public relations within the UK retail sector and seeks to determine whether retailers use public relations strategically: as a means of managing their relationships with key stakeholder publics; or simply as a tactical publicity function. An exploratory study was conducted in four major UK retail organizations indicative of the different types of retail institutions within the UK. In each case, the main characteristics of the public relations functions were identified and these were compared with those associated with each of the four models of public relations identified by Grunig and Hunt (1984). Here the aim was to identify whether the practices observed in each case could be matched to a single dominant model. The study also examined the relationship between the marketing and public relations functions, using Kotler and Mindak's (1978) framework as a starting point in analysing whether public relations operates as an independent function free of control from marketing or whether it operates simply as a sub-function of marketing. Finally, the study considers whether public relations can be said to play a largely strategic or tactical role within the UK retail sector. Here the study draws on the Grunig *et al.* (1992) work on 'excellence' in public relations and examines to what extent each public relations function could be said to be 'excellently managed'. Tactical publicity work (press-agentry) was found to be the dominant function performed by the public relations function in each of the retail organizations in the study. However, in at least two cases, evidence of more strategically-orientated activities was also found, involving both two-way asymmetrical or symmetrical communications practices. Although none of the public relations functions examined demonstrated the characteristics that would have allowed them to be judged to be 'excellently managed' (Grunig 1992), the work questions whether it would be realistic to expect them to have done so given the strong marketing orientation found within the retail sector. However, it highlights the considerable diversity in the way in which public relations is practised within the retail organizations studied, and suggests the need for more extensive research to identify the reasons for this diversity in the way the public relations function operates within the UK retail sector.

INTRODUCTION

Aims of the study

Increasingly retailers in the UK perceive themselves as, and are perceived by consumers as, brands in their own right. For example, Marks and Spencer is regarded as Britain's most recognized brand name (Davies 1992) and Laura Ashley, for example, is overt in its recognition of the company as constituting the brand rather than the merchandise sold.

This greater emphasis on corporate branding has led to increased pressures on the corporate and marketing communications activities of such companies. Communications objectives have become more wide-ranging and complex in scope as companies have sought to stretch the concept of the corporate image to accommodate both market and socially-orientated goals. This changing emphasis within corporate and marketing communications is a reflection of the changing balance of pressures facing modern corporations. Retailers, like companies in many other industries, have come under increasing pressures to demonstrate a greater sense of social responsibility and to temper their commercial policies with concern for their possible wider social and environmental impact. In short, retailers have recognized the need to develop a greater understanding of the possible wider social impact of their commercial activities in order to create or maintain a more receptive environment for their business and marketing activities. This greater social and environmental sensitivity within many company boardrooms has resulted in a greater recognition of the importance of establishing a more meaningful and effective dialogue with both customer and other stakeholder publics. The pursuit of this goal has resulted in a greater emphasis being placed on the role the public relations function.

It is against this background that this chapter explores the role which public relations plays within the UK retail sector and examines the extent to which UK retailers have used public relations as a means of strategically managing their relationships with their customer and other stakeholder publics, rather than treating public relations as simply a tactical publicity function. Because of the strong marketing focus within most UK retailers, we suspected there could be a considerable degree of overlap between the marketing and public relations functions. Here, we were conscious of the on-going academic and professional debate about the relationship between these two functions. Hence, in the course of our research we were also interested in exploring the way in which the marketing and public relations functions interact within the retail sector.

Developments in the retail environment

This study was conducted against the background of an increasingly competitive and dynamic retail environment in recent years. Significant developments in the retailing and business environments have resulted in a more pressing need for retailers to take a more strategic viewpoint. Walters and White (1987) compared the UK retail environment of the 1960s and the 1980s and noted the growth of the multiple retailer and the abolition of resale price maintenance; the latter enabling price to be used as a major competitive tool for the first time, reversing the balance of power between retailer and manufacturer. As a result, most consumer markets have become increasingly retailer dominated. Greenley and Shipley (1991) identified a number of specific changes in the retailing environment:

1 a decline in the number of retail outlets since the 1950s, leading to greater retail concentration;
2 changes in competitive rivalry, giving rise to oligopoly-type markets;
3 competitive conflict as a result of larger retail units with greater overheads leading to, along with other influences, different forms of store;
4 general improvements in productivity across all retailing sectors;
5 a shift within the distribution channel to give, in general, retailers more power than other channel members, especially *vis-à-vis* manufacturers, thus changing trading conditions in favour of retailers;
6 most mainstream retail sectors have moved into the maturity stage of the industry life-cycle.

These developments have necessitated the development and application of increasingly sophisticated management techniques by retailers, encompassing a more scientific approach to product and assortment development, trading style, customer communications and marketing. In short, most retailers have needed to adopt a more long-term strategic perspective (particularly those with nation-wide or strong geographical presence). Many of the leading retailers have come to be regarded as brands in their own right. As Davies and Brooks (1989) pointed out, the typical retailer seems to have acquired many attributes of a manufacturer's brand. However, achieving this strategic perspective has not been accomplished easily. One of the main themes in the retail marketing literature is the specific characteristics of retailing that militate against the adoption of such a perspective. These include the very rapid rate of environmental change in retailing; the predominant influence of a few individualists; the size and consequent diversity of the retail industry; the low cost of change for many of the dimensions of retail competition, leading to imitation and inter-firm homogeneity (Gilligan and Sutton 1987; Porac *et al.* 1987).

The problems of imitation and inter-firm homogeneity, in particular, have resulted in an emphasis in the academic treatment of retail strategy on the need for differentiation (Walters and White 1987; Wortzel 1987; Davies 1992; Davies and Brooks 1989; McGee 1987). Davidson and Doody (1966) defined differentiation, in the retail context, as an attempt on the part of the retailer to adapt his offer to the differences that exist in the needs and wants of customers. Indeed, evidence of such efforts is apparent throughout the UK retailing sector. Davies and Brooks (1989) argued that the differentiation of the offer in the eyes of the customer is 'the one key task for retail management', and as a result, retailers have shifted the emphasis of their competitive strategies towards variables such as store design and ambience, product offerings, service and branding.

However, factors such as the low barriers to entry in retailing and the fact that many aspects of retail strategy can be easily replicated by competitors (Lees and Worthington 1989; Porac *et al.* 1987) raise questions as to the sustainability of any particular form of differentiation over the long term. As a result, it can be argued that in order to achieve a form of differentiation that is as sustainable as possible, retailers must strive to achieve differentiation in terms of more intangible, less easily imitated, image-related variables rather than through the provision of physical products and services, which by their very nature are more easily replicated by competitors.

As a consequence of this growing emphasis on image-related variables, the role of such factors as branding, corporate image, and the use of public relations is likely to become increasingly prominent within the retail sector.

The development of public relations

There is little doubting the fact that the importance of good public relations has been increasingly recognized by the business community throughout the 1980s and early 1990s. This can be seen in the increasing size of public relations budgets and in the number of personnel working in public relations functions. This growing recognition of the importance of public relations has resulted, at least in part, from the increased social, political and consumer pressures experienced by firms of all complexions to act and to be seen to act in a more socially responsible and accountable manner. The emergence of more professionally-managed pressure groups; the increased scrutiny of government regulatory bodies; and the growing attention of investigative journalism have all combined to force firms to pay far greater attention to the way their activities may impact on society and influence public opinion. Firms have recognized the need to court public opinion and have realized that *ad-hoc* or poorly managed communications can have extremely damaging consequences for them. As a result, many firms have either established their own in-house public relations functions or appointed outside consultants to help them develop more effective and strategically managed communications programmes that can assist them to achieve their business goals.

A number of writers have articulated the growing importance of public relations to the business community (e.g. Moore and Kalupa 1985). However, it would be misleading to suggest that the importance of public relations has been universally accepted by all sectors of industry. Moreover, it is probably true to say that public relations is still regarded with a healthy degree of suspicion by many firms in the UK. In many firms in the UK, public relations has tended to be treated primarily as a sub-set of the marketing function. This perception has also been reflected in the way public relations has been treated in much of the academic and professional management literature. This marketing orientation has resulted in public relations being viewed primarily as a tactical publicity function. As such, it has struggled to gain recognition as a senior management function. Until the mid 1980s, it was comparatively rare to find public relations represented at company board level in most UK companies. Although there are signs that this situation has begun to change, particularly during the late 1980s and early 1990s, there is still little evidence to suggest that public relations personnel have been successful in gaining acceptance as equal members of the dominant management coalition in most UK companies.

The evolution of the professional practice

The role and scope of public relations has changed dramatically since its appearance as a form of 'press agentry' at the start of the twentieth century (Cutlip *et al.* 1985). In reviewing the historical development of public relations as a professional practice, Grunig and Hunt (1984) identified four models to explain the broad differences in the way in which public relations has been practised since the mid 19th century – 'press agentry', 'public information', 'two-way asymmetrical' and 'two-way symmetrical' public relations. Although these models were originally conceived as a means of explaining the evolutionary development of public relations, the authors maintained that these 'models' also provide a means of broadly describing and explaining the differences in the way in which public relations is practised in organizations today. However, the authors acknowledged the limitations of the models as a means of capturing the wide variations in modern public relations practice, and hence, acknowledged that they should be treated as simplified representations of the spectrum of contemporary approaches to public relations practice. Although subsequent studies by public relations researchers have found that the four models do provide a means of classifying the principal forms of public relations practice found in organizations today, their limitations have been exposed by a number of scholars (e.g. Miller 1989 and Van der Meiden 1993). While acknowledging the criticisms of Grunig and Hunt's (1984) original models, Grunig and Grunig (1992: 291) nevertheless maintained that subsequent studies have shown that they do represent a sound positive (descriptive) theory of public relations as it is practised today.

Grunig and Grunig (1992) argued that the two-way symmetrical model provides a normative theory of how ethical and effective public relations should be practised. However, they accepted that, in practice, 'excellent' public relations normally involves a hybrid between the two-way symmetrical and two-way asymmetrical models – what Murphy (1991) suggested might be described as a 'mixed-motive' model, combining both symmetrical and asymmetrical tactics.

Reflecting on the criticisms of the original four models as a means of explaining the reality of modern public relations practice, led

Grunig and Grunig (1992) to re-conceptualize the models along two continua of 'craft' and 'professional' public relations which they suggested provide a better reflection of the way practitioners practise public relations today.

In this new paradigm, practitioners of 'craft' public relations are seen to have a predominantly techniques-orientation, viewing the effective application of communications techniques as an end in itself. Practitioners of 'professional' public relations, in contrast, see public relations as having a broader strategic role in which communication is used to help resolve conflict and manage organizational relationships with strategic publics that may limit the autonomy of an organization to pursue its goals. Here, professional public relations practice is identified as ranging between asymmetrical compliance-gaining tactics, and symmetrical problem-solving tactics. While restating their belief in the superiority of the two-way symmetrical model as representing the most excellent way in which public relations should be practised, Grunig and Grunig acknowledged that organizations often fail to practise public relations in this way.

In examining the role of public relations within the UK retailer sector, we sought to determine to what degree the practices observed might correspond to any one, or combination of, the models identified by Grunig and Hunt (1984), or for that matter, whether the practices observed might be explained better in terms of the models advanced by Grunig and Grunig (1992). Here, we also sought to identify the factors that might account for the type of practices adopted. To this end, we were conscious of the fact that the most common form of the practice found by US researchers was the 'press agentry model' and we were interested to discover whether this finding would be mirrored within the UK retail sector.

Public relations and marketing

The relationship between public relations and marketing has always been a somewhat ambiguous and controversial one. Much of the controversy has centred around the issue of delineating between the respective roles of the two functions. From the marketing perspective, public relations has tended to be treated primarily as a publicity function whose main role is normally seen as that of providing tactical support for marketing campaigns. This view largely ignores what public relations practitioners and academics see as the more strategic role of public relations, namely that of managing the relationships between an organization and those strategically important constituencies (both customer and non-customer) within its environment (e.g. Grunig and Hunt 1984; Cutlip *et al.* 1985). The former extremely restricted view of the role of public relations (public relations as company propaganda or persuasive communications) recurs throughout the marketing literature. For example, Shimp and Delozier (1986) view public relations and publicity as activities that 'serve to supplement media advertising, sales, and sales promotion'; Schwartz (1982) sees public relations as 'another form of consumer-oriented sales promotion'; and Kotler (1982, 1986, 1988), one of the most prolific and influential marketing authors, while acknowledging that public relations and marketing are two distinct disciplines, has continued to subsume public relations under the control of marketing throughout most of his writings. For Kotler, public relations is seen as primarily a communications function, and as such plays a far narrower role than marketing in defining and achieving business goals.

In one of the first studies of its kind, Kotler and Mindak (1978) considered the relationship between the marketing and public relations functions and postulated five possible models to describe the organizational relationship between marketing and public relations: separate but equal functions; separate but overlapping functions; marketing as the dominant function; public relations as the dominant function; and public relations and marketing as the same function (the view that the two functions comprise rapidly converging concepts and methodologies). While accepting that no one model would be likely to prove applicable to all organizations or to all situations, the authors argued that the divisions separating the marketing and public relations functions are breaking down and that there is likely to be a growing trend towards a closer convergence between the two functions. Although there is little concrete evidence to substantiate how far Kotler and Mindak's predictions about a growing convergence between the marketing and public relations functions can be said to be true, there is considerable anecdotal evidence to suggest that the traditional barriers between the two functions have, and are continuing to, become more blurred.

The continuing controversy surrounding the relationship between marketing and public relations and the strong marketing orientation within the retail sector, suggested the need to extend our exploration of the role of public relations in the UK retail sector to include an examination of the relationship between the public relations and marketing functions. Here, we took as our starting point Kotler and

Mindak's five conceptual models of the marketing-public relations relationship.

Excellence in public relations

The 1980s and early 1990s have witnessed an upsurge of interest in the pursuit of 'excellence' and the associated concept of 'quality' throughout the corporate sector. The publication of Peters and Waterman's (1982) study of the characteristics of 'excellently managed' US companies, undoubtedly served to fuel this interest in the measurement of excellence. Despite subsequent criticisms of the approach adopted by Peters and Waterman and other researchers who have focused on identifying examples of excellent management practices (e.g. Kanter 1989), there is little doubt that these studies have served to focus attention on the question of how organizations can best optimize their performance. Here, the concept of excellence has been closely linked with that of organizational effectiveness in the sense that 'effectiveness' is taken as the yardstick by which the excellence of an organization is judged.

While considerable academic and professional energy has been directed to answering the question of how to improve the effectiveness of organizations, relatively little consideration has been given to how the management of the public relations function might be made more effective, or how the performance of the public relations function might contribute to improving an organization's overall effectiveness (and by implication the achievement of excellence). Grunig *et al.* (1992) attempted to address this gap in the literature by constructing a general theory of excellence in public relations and communications management. Here, Grunig *et al.* set out to answer two related questions. First, how does public relations contribute to the achievement of organizational objectives, and thus to organizational effectiveness; and second, how should public relations be practised and organized so as to contribute most to organizational effectiveness. In seeking to answer these questions, Grunig *et al.* recognized it was necessary to determine how public relations should be practised at the programme, departmental and organizational levels. While the authors acknowledged that theirs was an essentially normative theory of how public relations should be practised so as to make organizations more effective, nevertheless they maintained that their normative model describes the conditions under which public relations is able to contribute most to the achievement of organizational objectives, and hence, it describes how 'excellent' public relations programmes and departments should be managed.

Building on a set of twelve key characteristics of excellent organizations distilled from a review of the literature on excellence, the authors identified a series of characteristics of excellent public relations practice at the programme, departmental, and organizational levels. A number of the more important of these characteristics which we identified as likely to be of particular relevance to our research into the role and practice of public relations in the retail sector are summarized below:

- public relations programmes should be managed strategically;
- there should be a single integrated public relations department;
- public relations should report directly to senior management;
- public relations should be a separate function from marketing;
- communications should adhere to the two-way symmetrical model;
- the senior public relations person should be a member of or have access to the organization's dominant coalition;
- the organization's view of public relations should reflect the two-way symmetrical model.

Here, Grunig (1992: 248) maintains that 'excellent public relations, in short, seems to be the glue that holds excellent organizations together, because of the importance of symmetrical communications and collaboration in organizations that are organic, value human resources, are innovative, have leaders that inspire rather than dictate, and have strong participative cultures'. Symmetrical communications, Grunig argues, is a key factor in excellent organizations and he maintains that the public relations department is the logical location where responsibility for managing such communication should reside.

While we did not set out specifically to assess the degree to which public relations as practised by UK retailers might be judged 'excellent' according to the criteria defined by Grunig *et al.*, we were nevertheless, conscious of the fact that the 'excellence' criteria could provide a useful frame of reference in assessing how effectively UK retailers organized and managed their public relations functions. Here, our starting point was to examine the extent to which each public relations function appeared to meet the objectives set for it. However, we recognized that in the course of this research we might also gain some indication of the degree to which each of the public relations functions examined might meet the criteria (as defined by Grunig 1992) that would allow them to be judged to be excellently managed.

METHODOLOGY

This study was intended to form the first exploratory stage of a more extensive research project to investigate the role of public relations in the UK retail sector. The results of this exploratory study were intended to inform the approach adopted in the subsequent stages of the research project. This initial stage of the study comprised a series of semi-structured in-depth interviews with senior managers drawn from a small sample of UK retailers, indicative of a range of retail institution types – department stores, variety chain multiples, specialist multiples and co-operative societies. The data gained from these interviews was augmented by observations of the way the public relations functions operated in practice, and by a review of secondary data in the form of company publications gathered from each of the retail companies in the sample. The data collected was examined to ascertain the role, scope, organization, and performance of the public relations function in each of the retailers in the sample. In each case, the public relations function was analysed in terms of a number of relevant variables drawn from the work of Grunig and Hunt (1984) and Grunig (1992), and also using variables identified as relevant to the organization of the communication and marketing function in UK retailing (Piercy 1987a and b; Piercy and Alexander 1988; Greenley and Shipley 1991). These variables included:

1 the location of responsibility for PR;
2 the title of the department responsible for PR;
3 the title and reporting responsibility of the senior PR executive;
4 the size and composition of the PR department;
5 the main functions performed by the PR department;
6 the PR department's perception of its main publics;
7 the dominant mode of communication practised by each company;
8 the nature of the interaction between the PR and marketing functions within the organization.

Based on data collected from each retailer, we also sought to identify whether the public relations practices in each case could be said to correspond to any dominant model of public relations practice, drawing on the work of Grunig and Hunt (1984) and Grunig and Grunig (1992). Respondents were also questioned about the position of the public relations function within the management hierarchy and the significance of its contribution to the strategic management function. While the principal aim of our study was to gain a better understanding of how public relations is managed and practised within the

UK retail sector, we were also concerned to try to ascertain as to whether public relations is perceived as a strategically important function by retailers, or whether it is viewed as fulfilling a largely tactical marketing support role.

As it was anticipated that most retailers would display a strong marketing orientation, we were also interested in exploring the nature of the relationship between the marketing and public relations functions, in particular. Here, we began our investigation by asking respondents to identify whether the relationship between the public relations and marketing functions might approximate to any of the schematic models devised by Kotler and Mindak (1978). The key findings of the study have been summarized in tabular form to allow comparison between each of the retailers examined. The conclusions and implications for further research are considered in the following sections of the chapter.

FINDINGS

The four retail groups chosen for this exploratory study represented an example of each of the main institution types prevalent in the UK retail industry – department stores, variety chain multiples, specialist multiples and co-operative societies. Independent retailers were omitted from the sample as they were felt not to have the critical mass necessary to justify a separate public relations function. Brief details of the companies included in the sample are given below.

Harrods

Harrods is a large privately owned department store based in Knightsbridge, London, and is part of the House of Fraser department store chain. With over 20 acres of selling space and over 300 separate merchandise departments its daily turnover is approximately £1.5 million. The store has an international reputation for the provision of a wide range of high quality products and services. The merchandise emphasis is on top quality manufacturers brands, some exclusive to Harrods, as well as some premium quality own-branded merchandise, which is of particular interest to the tourist market. This tourist market is exploited by a number of 'signature' shops selling Harrods merchandise in international airports.

Russell and Bromley

Russell and Bromley is a family owned chain of shoe shops, dating from the early nineteenth century, currently operating 43 stores retailing quality high fashion men's, women's, and children's shoes and accessories. Much of the merchandise is own branded, although some manufacturers ranges are stocked, particularly sportswear ranges.

Marks and Spencer

Marks and Spencer is a multiple variety chain store, employing over 52,000 people in more than 300 stores in the UK, and also has 69 franchise shops in 17 countries. Overseas operations include Brooks Brothers Menswear and Kings Supermarkets in the USA. The company also has financial subsidiaries. Merchandise ranges sold include ladieswear, menswear, childrenswear, home furnishings and food. The company has, over the last century, built a very strong brand awareness by promoting an image of quality, value and service. Indeed, the company is regarded as 'the UK's best-selling brand' (Davies 1992). The company structure splits into three main areas – head office departments, stores and overseas operations.

Co-op Wholesale Society (CWS)

The CWS was set up in the 1860s to provide goods and services to the growing number of retail co-operative societies, which originated in the nineteenth century through shoppers forming their own societies to buy groceries and household items at preferential prices, with any profits generated passed back to members in the form of annual dividends. It is only in the last twenty years that the CWS has become a retailer in its own right. The CWS still continues however, to provide manufacturing and distribution services to the society retailers, and also acts as a major funeral director and travel company. The CWS, based in Manchester, now directly operates stores across most of England, Scotland and Northern Ireland. The CWS organizational structure comprises a board of 35 directors, elected by the member societies, which meets once a month. There is also a seven strong executive board of the top managers who are equivalent to the board of a plc. They run the business on a day to day basis.

The main characteristics of the public relations function in each of the retailers studied are summarized in tables 6.1, 6.2, 6.3. The respondents' views about the dominant 'model' describing the relationship between the marketing and public relations functions in their respective organizations are also illustrated in table 6.3. The data gathered has been presented in the form of a series of brief descriptors relating to the variables that were identified earlier as relevant to the organization of the public relation and retailing functions. Comparisons between the various retailers in terms of the organization and management of their respective public relations functions together with the implications of the findings are considered below.

DISCUSSION

Although each of the retail organizations examined in this study can be seen to have experienced more or less the same market and socio-economic changes that have affected the UK retailing sector as a whole in recent years, the impact of these changes and the way in which each of these retailers have chosen to respond to them has been markedly different. These differences can be seen to reflect the diversity among these retailers in terms of their traditions and culture, ownership, mode of operation, leadership and type of merchandise offered. Such factors, we believe, are also likely to play an important part in explaining the differences in the way in which each of these retailers has approached the management of their respective public relations functions.

The dominant model of public relations practice

Given the diversity in the nature of the retail operations in each of the organizations examined, it is perhaps not surprising that their public relations functions differed significantly in terms of their size, organization and operating practices. Our research suggests, however, that the retailers could be divided into two distinct categories. First, those retailers where the public relations function appears to operate primarily as a product publicity function (Harrods and Russell & Bromley), and those where public relations has a broader role involving responsibility for a wider range of communication activities directed towards both corporate and customer stakeholders (Marks & Spencer and CWS).

When we compared the observed characteristics of each retail organization's public relations function with those associated with each of the four models of public relations devised by Grunig and Hunt (1984), we found that, with the exception of Russell & Bromley,

Table 6.1 Research findings: summary of characteristics of the public relations function found in the four retail organizations examined

Characteristics	Harrods	Russel & Bromley	Marks & Spencer	CWS
Title/location of the PR function	Press Office – operating on a tactical store basis. Corporate communications handled by the Chairman & Corporate Press officer whose brief extends to all House of Fraser stores	Press Office – working closely with store merchandising managers	Corporate Affairs Division (split into Corporate Affairs and Commercial Publicity	Public Affairs Department
Objectives of the PR function	● To optimize product publicity ● To maintain good media relations with regard to corporate and product issues	● To optimize product publicity ● To promote customer relations ● To maintain liaison with the fashion media in particular	● To maintain effective media relations ● To promote and enhance the corporate reputation ● To promote customer relations ● To promote employee relations	● To promote good media relations ● To optimize product publicity ● To support marketing activities ● To promote the reputation of the CWS
Title and reporting responsibility of the senior PR executive	Press and PR Director reporting to the Chairman	Press Office Manager reporting to the Chairman, but does not sit on the Executive Committee	Public Affairs Director reporting to the Board of Directors	Public Affairs Director who is a member of the Executive Board
Composition and size of the PR function	2 PR Managers 8 Press officers – each with specific product line responsibility	1 PR Manager and Assistant Press Officer	Corporate Affairs Department comprises 50 staff	2 Public Affairs Managers 2 Press Officers and one assistant 4 Regional Press Officers

Table 6.2 Research findings: summary of characteristics of the public relations function found in the four retail organizations examined

Characteristics	Harrods	Russel & Bromley	Marks & Spencer	CWS
Main activities performed by the PR function	• Production of: – press releases; – publications; – photography; • Employee communications • Event management • Corporate communication • Issues/crisis management – on a tactical level – no input to policy decisions	• Liaison with the fashion media – largely reactive to press enquiries • Production of: – product publicity; – photography; • Event management • Support for new product launches	• Production of: – press releases; publications – both corporate publications and the company's customer magazine; – photography • Media relations • Employee communications • Event management • Product publicity • Corporate communication • Community relations • Issues/crisis management • Market research	• Media relations – on a proactive basis • production of: – press releases; – publications – both employee magazine, product, and corporate publications • Product publicity • Support for new product launches • Event management • Corporate communications • Crisis/Issues management • Community relations • Sponsorship
Perception of the key target publics (prioritized)	• Print & Broadcast media – to influence opinion leadership • General public – as potential store customers • Store employees	• Print and Broadcast media particularly fashion press • Employees (but personnel department responsible for employee communication) • Customers	• Customers • Employees • Shareholders • General public and local community • Media	• Customers • Employees • Competition – other co-operative societies who buy from the CWS in its role as a manufacturer
Dominant model of communications (using Grunig & Hunt's classification	Primarily one-way press agentry/publicity	Primarily one-way press agentry/publicity but some two-way asymmetrical practices	Both two-way symmetrical and asymmetrical practices but also press agentry tactics employed	Both two-way symmetrical and asymmetrical practices but also press agentry tactics employed

Table 6.3 Research findings: summary of characteristics of the public relations function found in the four retail organizations examined

Characteristics	Harrdos	Russell & Bromley	Marks & Spencer	CWS
Orientation of the form of professional practice (in terms of Grunig and Grunig's two continua of 'Craft' and 'Professional' Public Relations)	Primarily a 'craft public relations' orientation	Primarily a 'craft public relations' orientation but with some Professional asymmetrical (mainly asymmetrical) public relations practices	Primarily a 'professional public relations' orientation involving both symmetrical and asymmetrical practices. But also Craft public relations tactics frequently employed	Primarily a 'professional public relations' orientation involving both symmetrical and asymmetrical practices. But also Craft public relations tactics frequently employed
Marketing and Public Relations relationship Dominant model based on Kotler and Mindak's five schematic models	Mkt PR Seperate but overlapping functions	Mkt PR Seperate but overlapping functions	Mkt (PR) PR part of marketing function	Mkt PR Seperate but overlapping functions
Other departments with which the PR department works closely	Advertising Promotions Buying Display	Buying Display	Buying In-Store Mercandising	Most other departments/ areas of business

it was impossible to identify a single model that would describe satisfactorily the way public relations was generally practised in each case. Rather, the typical pattern that emerged in most cases was for public relations to alternate between press-agentry and two-way symmetrical, or more often, asymmetrical-type practices. Only at Russell & Bromley did the public relations function seem to adhere to a single dominant model of public relations practice – namely, the press-agentry model. While press-agentry also appeared to be the dominant form of public relations practised at Harrods, we also found some evidence of two-way asymmetrical practices being employed (e.g. in the case of employee communications). At both Marks & Spencer and the CWS a combination of press-agentry, two-way symmetrical and asymmetrical practices were found to be used. Press-agentry was the predominant mode where public relations was being used as a tactical promotional support function to assist in the marketing of merchandise. However, in situations involving communication with non-customer audiences such as employees or shareholders, the emphasis switched to the two-way symmetrical or asymmetrical modes of practice. We believe that this use of a combination of practice modes at Marks & Spencer and the CWS probably reflects the broader scope and responsibilities assigned to the public relations function within these two organizations. These findings would seem to suggest, therefore, that at least in the case of three of these four major retail organizations, public relations practitioners alternate frequently between different forms of practice models. Hence, the way in which the public relations function operates in these three organizations may be best explained in terms of Grunig and Grunig's (1992) two continua of 'craft' and 'professional' public relations – with practitioners operating in different modes along both continua at different times. However, our research suggest that neither models of public relations developed by Grunig and Hunt (1984) nor those suggested by Grunig and Grunig (1992) are capable of capturing fully the degree of diversity in the type of public relations practices adopted by these retailers.

    In addition to the problems of identifying a single dominant model that would describe the form of public relations practised by different retailers, we also found it difficult to identify the reasons for the observed differences in the way public relations is practised. Here, we suspect that the differences between the public relations functions might be explained more by traditional operating practices corporate culture and the underlying attitudes of the senior management toward public relations, than by such factors as the size of the organization, types of markets served, or the background and experience of the practitioners employed within each of the public relations functions.

Public relations objectives

Significant differences were found between the type and emphasis of the public relations objectives set by each of the retailers in the study. As might be expected, at Russell & Bromley, the public relations objectives were almost entirely focused on achieving product publicity to support the marketing of merchandise. At Harrods there was also a strong emphasis on product publicity objectives, but other objectives relating to employee communications and external corporate communications activities were also cited by respondents. At both Marks & Spencer and CWS a far broader range of public relations objectives (in terms of longer-term image building) were found to exist than at either Russell & Bromley or Harrods. Although the generation of product publicity remained an important objective for the public relations function at both of these retailers, there was an equally strong emphasis on achieving a more strategically-orientated range of objectives relating to each company's relationships with both external and internal corporate stakeholders.

The importance attached to product publicity objectives by all of the retailers probably reflects the fact that they all identified customers (or potential customers) as their most important target public. Judged purely in terms of their success in achieving product publicity objectives, the public relations function at each of the four retailers was perceived to be highly effective by their respective managements. However, it proved more difficult to assess the degree to which any broader corporate communications objectives that may have been set had been achieved. Such assessment was inevitably more problematical because of the longer-term image/reputation-related issues with which corporate communications objectives tended to be concerned. It also proved impossible to gauge accurately to what degree public relations had been able (or was expected) to contribute to the achievement of each retailer's wider organizational goals – a fact that may reflect the lack of a clear link between the public relations and corporate planning functions in all cases.

Given the generally strong marketing orientation within the retail sector, it is understandable that marketing support in the form of product publicity figured prominently amongst the priorities for most retailer public relations activity. However, this does explain why both the CWS and Marks & Spencer have placed greater emphasis on achieving longer-term (strategic) corporate public relations objectives, whereas at Russell & Bromley and perhaps to a lesser extent Harrods, there appears to be a greater emphasis on achieving shorter-term tactical communications objectives. We suspect that the main reason for these differences may again lie in the nature of management attitudes towards public relations within each of these companies.

Marketing and public relations

Given the controversy surrounding the relationship between the marketing and public relations functions identified earlier, we were naturally interested to explore how the relationship between the two functions operated within the retail sector. Here we were conscious of the fact that one of the conditions for excellent public relations departments identified by Grunig (1992) was that public relations should operate as a separate function from marketing.

In examining the relationship between the public relations and marketing functions, we began by asking each of the retailers to identify which, if any, of schematic models devised by Kotler and Mindak (1978) best described the nature of the working relationship between the two functions. Three of the four retailers – Russell & Bromley, Harrods and CWS – each identified the most appropriate 'model' to describe this relationship as that in which marketing and public relations operate as separate but overlapping functions. At Marks and Spencer, however, public relations was identified as operating as part of the marketing function. This response was unexpected and somewhat surprising as Marks & Spencer was known to possess one of the largest and perhaps most sophisticated public relations functions in the retail sector. Public relations was, in fact, described as part of the company's overall 'marketing communications function'. However, we believe it may be misleading to accept this response at face value, since it may reflect the monolithic nature of the Marks & Spencer 'brand' which identifies the merchandise and the company as one. Thus, all communications and mainstream marketing activities are directed towards promoting and enhancing the company's brand image.

Further probing of respondents, however, revealed considerable variation between all of these retailers in terms of the way in which their marketing and public relations functions worked together in practice (the degree to which the two functions 'overlapped'). Given the strong publicity orientation of both their public relations functions, it was perhaps surprising that respondents at both Russell & Bromley and Harrods maintained that the marketing and public relations functions worked together only occasionally, whereas at Marks & Spencer and the CWS the marketing and public relations functions were said to often work closely together. In all four cases, however, public relations was also found to work closely with a range of other operational departments, most notably with the buying, merchandising and display departments. Here, public relations was used to provide tactical publicity support in the form of brochures, point-of-sale material and media relations. At the CWS, it was claimed that public relations worked with all other departments within the organization, not simply those concerned with marketing and sales-related activities.

The limitations of using Kotler and Mindak's models as a basis for examining the relationship between marketing and public relations functions clearly emerged during the course of the research. In particular, it was apparent that these models were unable to capture either the variations in the degree to which these two functions interact in practice, or the differences in the degree to which particular activities were perceived to fall within the ambit of marketing or public relations. Such differences could only be discerned by further careful probing of respondents and observation of practices 'on the ground'. In short, Kotler and Mindak's models were unable to reveal the degree of functional 'overlap' between the two functions. For example, at Russell & Bromley the two functions appeared to work together only very occasionally (limited degree of overlap), whereas at the CWS, where a strong and independent public relations department clearly exists, the public relations function appears to work closely with marketing as well as other departments on a regular basis (high degree of overlap). Equally, the regularity of contact between the marketing and public relations departments does not necessarily reflect the nature and division of functional responsibilities between the two departments, i.e while the marketing and public relations departments at Russell & Bromley may work together only occasionally, most of the work of the public relations department consists of promotional support activities.

The excellence criteria

When we examined the characteristics of each of the public relations functions and compared these with the set of 'excellence' criteria identified by Grunig *et al.* (1992), we found that none of the retailers' public relations functions exhibited all of the characteristics of excellence (at the programme, departmental, or organizational levels). In fact, in most cases, the public relations functions appeared to display relatively few of these characteristics of 'excellence', particularly at the programme and departmental levels. Therefore, judged in terms of Grunig *et al.*'s excellence criteria, none of these retailers could be said to possess excellently managed public relations departments. However, this general finding obscures the fact that significant variations were found to exist between each of the retailers in terms of the prevailing 'world-view' of the role of public relations, the type of communications programmes typically used, and in terms of how the public relations function was organized in relation to other organizational functions. For example, because of the role assigned to public relations and its position within the organization at both Marks & Spencer and the CWS, it was perhaps only to be expected that both public relations functions tended to exhibit a far greater number of the characteristics of excellence than was the case at either Russell & Bromley or Harrods. This was particularly evident in terms of two of the most important of the characteristics of excellence postulated by Grunig (1992), namely that public relations programmes should be managed 'strategically', and should characteristically adhere to the two-way symmetrical model of public relations. However, not all public relations programmes used by these two retailers could be said to be strategically managed, nor was public relations always practised as a two-way symmetrical function by either Marks and Spencer or the CWS. Nevertheless, both of these retailers' public relations functions appeared to display these two key characteristics of excellence to a far greater degree than was the case at either Russell & Bromley or Harrods.

The prevailing understanding of ('world-view'), and attitudes towards, public relations held by the senior management team in each of the retail organizations examined appeared to be the most important factor determining the role and scope of the public relations function and type of programmes used by each respective public relations function. However, because of the nature of the retail trade, it was perhaps inevitable that the type of public relations programmes most commonly used by retailers were found to consist largely of tactical publicity-gaining activities designed to help promote the sale of merchandise. Clearly, such public relations programmes were unlikely to be seen to have a strategically important role, nor would they be likely to involve two-way symmetrical communications.

Although this study was conducted amongst only a small sample of retail organizations, we believe it raises some fundamental questions about whether it is possible to prescribe a general set of criteria for excellence that can be applied to public relations functions across all retailers, or for that matter, across all industry sectors without regard to the particular priorities and operating practices found in each respective sector.

Here, we believe that Hickman and Silva's (1984) suggestion that each organization tends to create its own unique criteria for excellence might offer a more realistic approach to determining a set of benchmarks by which the 'excellence' of any particular organization's public relations function might be judged.

CONCLUSIONS

Despite the limited scale of this study, it has revealed considerable differences in the role assigned to public relations and in the way in which public relations is practised among retail organizations. While the data collected does not allow us to generalize about the nature of public relations practice in the UK retail sector as a whole, it has highlighted a strong emphasis on the use of public relations as a tactical marketing support activity (to generate product publicity) by retail organizations. Only limited evidence was found to suggest that retail organizations view public relations as contributing significantly to the achievement of their strategic goals, and little evidence was found to suggest that public relations personnel are frequently involved in, or consulted about, the formation of either corporate or business strategies. However, it was notable that at two of the retailers examined in this study – Marks & Spencer and the CWS – the role of public relations was found to extend beyond simply supporting the promotion of merchandise, and was seen to play a significant part in supporting each of these retailer's broader corporate and business strategies.

Although this study did not set out specifically to examine the degree to which public relations departments within the UK retail sector could be judged to be 'excellently managed'; nevertheless, our research has highlighted the difficulties of applying Grunig *et al.*'s (1992) set of characteristics of excellence in a sector in which marketing considerations clearly predominate. Clearly, the dominant marketing emphasis within the retail sector appears to influence the prevailing 'world view' of the role of public relations which, it can be argued, makes it extremely difficult for the function to operate in a way that would allow it to demonstrate many of the characteristics of excellence defined by Grunig *et al.*

Although it is impossible to generalize at this stage, our initial findings suggest that, at least as far as the UK retail sector is concerned, public relations appears to be treated predominantly as tactical publicity function whose main role is to support retail marketing strategies. However, there appear to be quite marked variations in the way in which public relations is practised by different retail organizations which, we suggest, may reflect their different traditions, cultures, modes of operation, and type of merchandise offering, rather than any ideological view about the nature and role of public relations per se. The role assigned to public relations and the type of communications practices that are generally adopted also appear to vary significantly according to the type of situation which the particular retailer organization faces. Thus, we suggest that the way in which public relations practitioners within the retail sector generally operate might be explained in terms of Grunig and Grunig's (1992) two continua of professional practice styles, with practitioners operating in either the 'craft' or 'professional' mode according to the perceived needs of the situation in hand. Here, however, their scope for action appears likely to be constrained by the dominant world view of public relations held within the organization.

Thus, while this study found limited evidence of public relations operating on a broad strategic level (in terms of managing longer-term strategically important issues and relationships) within the retail organizations examined, public relations was, nevertheless, perceived to play an important marketing support role by all of the retail organizations examined in the study. In this latter role, public relations inevitably tends to involve predominantly press-agentry or two-way asymmetrical communication, rather than operating in the two-way symmetrical mode which Grunig has argued characterises 'excellently managed' public relations programmes and departments. Further empirical research is now needed to examine whether the findings of this initial study do, in fact, reflect the way in which public relations is generally practised within the UK retail sector.

7 Business and organizational consequences of the moral role of the public relations practitioner

Dr Jon White

ABSTRACT

This chapter explores the consequences for business and organizational performance of recognition of the moral role of the public relations practitioner. This role has been alluded to, in discussions of the public relations practitioner acting as a conscience for the organization, and in specific recommendations made by Geert Hofstede. Hofstede suggested in a 1980 paper that there is a need within organizations for individuals who can challenge organizations' prevailing values. He saw this role as belonging to an individual that he described as a director of external relations. The business benefit of such challenges is that organizations that allow for their values to be questioned are less likely to be surprised and damaged by value shifts in the wider society of which the organizations are part.

Public relations is a practical management and business discipline, partly because it is also a moral practice. It is a moral practice in that it raises questions of right and wrong in considering relations between organizations and their publics. Realistically, it asks what is the current state of relationships between organizations and significant groups, and how should they be influenced so that organizational objectives may be achieved. The practice goes beyond these questions to ask what should the relationships between organizations and its publics be? This raises further questions about the interests of publics, and the wider public interest.

The argument in this chapter is that the practitioner becomes more effective and valuable to the organizations he or she serves by recognizing and embracing the moral role. The argument is not an abstract one, but is bound up in current discussion in the United Kingdom of the role of business in society. This discussion, carried on through a lengthy study now being undertaken by the Royal

Society of Arts of the role of 'Tomorrow's Company', is focused on the obligations of business to society: What should the relations of business be to society and to a number of stakeholder groups? The chapter concludes that public relations practitioners have an important part to play in answering these questions, because of the moral role of public relations. Implications for the development, effectiveness and success of business and other organizations of this role will be drawn out.

INTRODUCTION

Hofstede (1980) described the experience of a Dutch company importing coffee from the Portuguese colony of Angola, which ran into difficulties when it refused to recognize the strength of public feeling against its action. After a consumer boycott of its business activities, the company was forced to change its policy on the imported coffee it was using. Hofstede concluded his discussion of the company's experiences by arguing the need for corporations to have 'a modern equivalent to the medieval king's court jester, a person with direct access to the highest decision-makers, whose institutionalized role it is to challenge values' (1980: 39). The court jester could, he suggested, be the external relations manager, which some enlightened corporations have institutionalized, if the position is taken seriously.

This chapter revisits Hofestede's suggestion, to re-examine the moral role of the public relations practitioner, a role which should allow the practitioner to challenge accepted values within an organization, and which should, if fulfilled, bring in its train organizational and business advantages. The chapter is mainly concerned with some of the practical consequences of the practitioner's moral role.

The idea that practitioners have a moral role is not a new one, and is discussed in more or less detail in recent books on public relations practice. Finn (1959) argued that public relations performs the function of keeping management in line, by providing an 'anvil' against which management morals can be hammered. Grunig and Hunt (1984: 72) stated a belief that 'ethical practitioners [confronted by an organization which refuses to exercise public responsibility] should stay on the job and **argue for ethical organizational behaviour**, even if they are not always successful' (emphasis added). Harrison (1990) studied books commonly used to teach public relations and found that although most mention ethics and moral rules governing practice, treatment of these subjects, especially in advanced texts, is scanty.

Codes of conduct, such as those upheld by the Public Relations Society of America, the United Kingdom's Institute of Public Relations and the International Public Relations Association, all contain provision for public relations to be practised with the public interest in mind ('with proper regard to the public interest', Institute of Public Relations; 'with respect to the public interest', IPRA; 'in accord with the public interest', PRSA). However, the nature of this obligation is left vague.

It is timely to return to questions about the moral role of the practitioner in view of debates now taking place – in the United Kingdom and elsewhere – about the future of the company, and approaches to corporate governance. These topics are being discussed in a study being carried out by the Royal Society of Arts (RSA), the Tomorrow's Company study (Interim Report), in reports such as Business International's *New Directions in Corporate Governance* (1991) and books such as Hampden-Turner and Trompenaars' *The Seven Cultures of Capitalism* (1993). The thrust of these discussions is that the company of the future will be based on values different from values which now prevail.

The RSA study argues for what is called the 'inclusive' company. This will include groups other than shareholders and investors in the future of the company. The RSA study's interim report believes that 'to achieve sustainable success tomorrow's company must take an inclusive approach'. Tomorrow's company, the report continues, 'will understand and measure the value which it derives from all its key relationships, and thereby be able to make informed decisions when it has to balance and trade off the conflicting claims of customers, suppliers, employees, investors and the communities in which it operates' (RSA 1994: 1). Throughout the report there is an emphasis on the need for clarity about values and obligations to 'reciprocal relationships'. The approach recommended in the report is contrasted with current British management and organizational practices, which are focused on developing and providing value to shareholders and negotiating adversarial relationships with other stakeholders.

Hampden-Turner contrasts the performance of British capitalism with that of emerging economies in the Far East, and draws the conclusion that UK management could learn from the approaches to relationships evident in Asia. These, he suggests, are based on mutuality and norms of reciprocity: the relationship defines areas of agreement, with room for flexible change, while relationships in UK management are based on rational-legal rules. In the UK, he suggests, individuality and self-interest are transformed, as though by an invisible hand into the public interest. In China in particular, he suggests, an emphasis on the community and social concern is changed by the norm of reciprocity into personal interest (Hampden-Turner 1994: 47). He believes that the economies of the Far East are examples of 'catch-up' capitalism, based on a dominant ethic of co-operation. Since the best solutions for the problems of industrialization have already been found, populations in the Asian countries need to work together to emulate examples drawn from elsewhere.

His arguments do not have to be accepted, of course, but they are evidence of a new willingness to question dominant values in western economies which are proving unable to deliver consistent economic success and related social benefits, such as adequate levels of employment.

Questions of corporate governance have been on the public agenda since the early 1990s in the United Kingdom, when the Cadbury Committee on Corporate Governance began its work. This committee produced its recommendations for improvement of corporate governance in 1992, advocating a strong role for non-executive directors on the boards of companies to provide a check on management and to ensure that the interests of stakeholders in companies are taken into account. The committee's recommendations were aimed at identifying best practice, which it encouraged companies to adopt. A Business International Report (1991) on new directions in corporate governance described the findings of research in the Anglo-Saxon countries, and in particular in the US, which shows that executive managers, especially the CEO, will dominate boardroom deliberations. The report also advocated the appointment to boards of strong and informed non-executive members, but said that their presence will not ensure good corporate governance. The report suggests that 'it takes an act of extraordinary will to stand up to a strong CEO when the company's performance is high and there is no immediate storm on the horizon' (ibid.: 101). The report argues that good corporate governance is likely to develop as opportunities for better communication between companies and major shareholders, particularly institutional shareholders are increased.

Better organizational performance in many areas of organizational life as a result of dialogue between organizations and important groups is a theme running through the literature review contained in Grunig (1992). In Grunig and White (1992), it is argued that public relations should be based on a view of the world that incorporates ethics into the process of public relations.

The next section of this chapter argues that ethical and moral questioning are part of the process of public relations. It also argues that by embracing this part of the process of public relations practice and making it explicit, practitioners can contribute to the changes recommended in the studies of company performance and corporate governance cited and discussed briefly above.

THE ROLE OF THE PRACTITIONER

Figure 7.1 is a graphic representation of the task of the public relations practitioner, developed by Walton (1987), as an aid to explaining his role as director of government and public affairs with the British Petroleum company to the company's senior management. He argued that the company exists in a network of social relationships, and has to manage these relationships as it makes its case and pursues its objectives. The figure is useful because it demonstrates the potential complexity of the social environment and the fact that important groups are also in relationship to each other. It demonstrates that the task of public relations involves the management of important relationships and that relationships are developed, maintained and influenced through communication.

The figure can also be used in training and as an aid to public relations management. Programme planning elements of research, analysis and the development of programmes of action can be followed through using the illustration to identify important questions relating to an organization's stakeholder relationships. This line of questioning leads on to ethical and moral questions. Such questions involve the following specific issues:

1 What are the objectives of the organization?
2 In order for the organization to achieve its objectives, what will it need from important relationships – support from employees, minimal opposition from identified pressure groups, favourable decisions from government regarding intentions for legislation, for example?
3 What will need to be done to influence important relationships so that groups behave towards the organization in ways which will support the achievement of objectives?
   To this point, questions are pragmatic, concerned with the achievement of objectives, and what will be needed in order for objectives

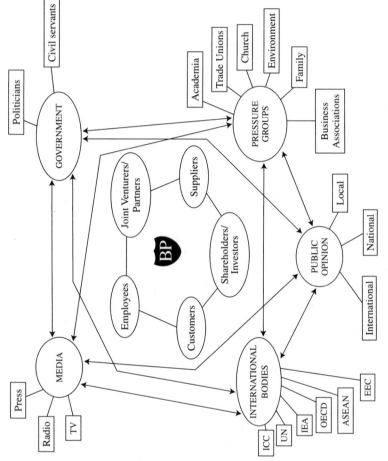

Figure 7.1 The task of the public relations practitioner (Source: Walton 1987)

to be achieved. Beyond this point, questions become ethical questions, questions of what sort of behaviour would be appropriate.

4 To what extent can the organization pursue its objectives without regard for the interests of others?

Once questions are raised about the interests of other groups, a further question follows:

5 What should the relationship between the organization and other groups be?

The line of questioning which starts with questions of approaches to the achievement of organizational objectives which require public relations support leads inexorably to questions of morality: how should the organization behave towards, take account of the interests of important groups, what should the relationship be between the organization and important groups?

These are defined as ethical and moral questions according to some of the simple definitions offered for ethical and moral behaviour: 'Ethics is a set of rules that define right and wrong conduct. Ethics deals with fundamental human relationships. Ethical rules are guides to moral behaviour.' Frederick *et al.*(1988: 52).

In practice, it is recognized that the line of questioning will come to an end when pragmatic conclusions have been reached. Budd (1991: 3) argued in a chapter on ethical dilemmas in public relations that 'a business executive's genuine sensitivity to his social responsibilities is realistically constrained by economics . . . economic pressures tend to limit contemplativeness when faced with those uncharted gray murky areas of ethical dilemmas'.

It is precisely at this point that the public relations practitioner's role becomes important, in the light of the discussion in the earlier part of the chapter. The pragmatic approach to business activity, which would suggest single-minded attention to the bottom line, to return on investment, to cost minimization, profit maximization and shareholder benefit is the approach which is now being questioned in the reports and other material discussed earlier.

Practitioners themselves recognize the role implicated in the questions they pursue, as Finn's comment quoted earlier indicates. They are faced with several options when considering this part of their role. They can, like some of the pragmatic managers and clients they serve, deal only with what will work, and with what will produce the results needed in order to achieve objectives.

They may, as Olasky (1984) has suggested, act so as to obscure the ethical and moral questions that their work raises. This may be from ignorance, where they have been unwilling to think through the ethical and moral issues that their work involves, or it may be by design. In these cases, the practice of public relations is itself called into question, as in the recent so-called 'dirty tricks' campaign waged by British Airways against its much smaller competitor, Virgin. A third option would be to acknowledge the line of questioning and pursue it to its conclusion, examining the consequences of answers as they suggest themselves. This option raises new possibilities for the contribution which can be made by the public relations practitioner to business and organization effectiveness, and also raises questions about the practicality of the practitioner playing this role and the training needed for it.

IMPLICATIONS FOR BUSINESS AND ORGANIZATION PRACTICE AND FURTHER RESEARCH

Hofstede's 1980 case study suggested that if, within organizations, there were individuals who could challenge established values, a number of benefits would accrue to the organization. In the case he described, the organization would have been presented with a realistic assessment of the pressures developing against the organization's activities. The organization would also have been presented with advice as to what it should do, advice on appropriate conduct. It would still have been a management prerogative to ignore such advice, but the advice would have been presented. If acted upon, the advice would have saved the organization time, minimized damage to the organization's reputation or have enhanced it, and would have saved the organization money.

The Conference Board, describing benefits to be derived from issues management programmes, has suggested that issues management programmes help companies to avoid mistakes. Allowing practitioners to pursue their role as questioners of their organization's or client's moral behaviour would also have the same effect, with similar benefits to those mentioned above.

A good current example of where practitioner questioning might have been of benefit is provided by the British company, British Gas. Privatized some years ago, British Gas is a large monopoly, providing gas to commercial and domestic customers. Since late 1994, the company has made a number of announcements and found its activities questioned in ways which suggest that the process being described in this chapter has not been in place. The company's troubles began with an announcement that its chief executive was to receive an increase in compensation in the order of 75 per cent over his previous compensation level. This announcement was followed days later by an announcement that staff in the company's retail outlets were to have their already relatively low salaries reduced and were also to be asked to work longer hours. These announcements were followed by the release or discovery of information suggesting that the company's safety standards were slipping, because less money was being spent on safety inspections, that the company's service standards were lessening, and that the company was thinking of reducing, or charging for, services to the handicapped.

Media commentary on British Gas raised questions about how the company was being managed. If the company was so inept at managing its public relations, how could it possibly be managing other aspects of the company's operations effectively?

It will not be clear until the British Gas case is thoroughly researched what the role of the company's public relations practitioners was during this period. But the argument in this chapter is that difficulties such as the difficulties now being encountered by British Gas would be avoided if practitioners are allowed to question the rightness of management decisions on moral grounds.

Other important benefits of the practitioner playing a moral role might follow in a number of other areas. The additional questions raised might serve to improve the quality of management decision-making, the climate for communication within the organization, and the organization's capacity to be innovative, competitive and successful – the concerns of the RSA study discussed earlier.

Innovation, which is described as the process of taking new ideas effectively through to satisfied customers, depends on a willingness to accept change and regard it as an opportunity. It also depends on a culture which is conducive to managed risk taking and an open communicative style of management (Hedron 1993). Communication is one of the main factors contributing to innovation, which is seen in a United Kingdom Department of Trade and Industry and Confederation of British Industry report (1993) as synonymous with good management. The best companies have a clear sense of mission and purpose, which is communicated throughout the organization. A Department of Trade and Industry memorandum on competitiveness suggests that quality of management is probably the key issue in innovation.

Recognition of the moral role of public relations practitioners and of the contribution they can make to management decision-making by adding moral dimensions which might otherwise be missing would contribute to the quality of management. There are, however, several practical barriers to practitioners playing out their moral role:

1 Practitioners will simply not be allowed to play this role. Consultants may only present a limited number of obstacles to their clients before they may find their services dispensed with, and in-house practitioners are subject to the same limitations faced with strong management as are non-executive directors.

2 Managers will not perceive practitioners as having this contribution to make. A Gallup study of senior managers' perceptions carried out in 1990 found, for example, one manager who said 'It could be questioned whether public relations advisers should provide advice on social affairs . . . what is their job?'

3 Practitioners may not have the inclination, training or skills to play the role. This is not a criticism of practitioners. They may find themselves in close sympathy with the organization or client objectives they are asked to support and see no reason to challenge them, even in the role of a devil's advocate. They may not have been trained to work through the analysis involved in public relations programme planning. Their skills may not permit them to argue comfortably with senior management about the approach that is being taken to the organization's objectives.

4 The role may not be seen as important. Grunig and White (1992) argue that the idealistic approach to public relations practice is, in fact, a practical one, but this is not a widely held view.

The RSA study cited earlier implies a need for practitioners to play this role if business and other organizations which contribute to the achievement of social goals are to be successful in future. It may well be that the future of public relations practice is bound up with development of the practitioner's moral role (Bovet 1993).

Arguably, public relations may develop in future in two ways. In the first, it will be a largely technical practice, using communications techniques to support marketing activities and becoming involved in work on product and corporate branding, corporate reputation, market penetration and development. Discussion of the practice in the United Kingdom in the pages of the country's trade publication, PR Week, which mirrors similar discussions in the United States, suggests that this view of the scope of the practice is coming to dominance.

In the second form of development, public relations will increasingly become a social practice, helping organizations fit into their social environments, and working on relationships between groups to help to bring about social and economic development and to help in the resolution of social problems. This approach is embodied in public consultations, in which practitioners take the lead in bringing organizations and their publics together to discuss and resolve their possibly conflicting interests.

These twin paths have interesting implications for public relations education, and the relationship between practitioners and public relations academics. A Delphi study of research priorities in public relations practice in the United Kingdom (White and Blamphin 1994) found that academics contributing to the study asked, 'if public relations is practised in the public interest, how can it be used to support the marketing of fast-moving consumer goods?' Those involved in public relations education tend to see the practice in idealistic terms, while practitioners are impatient with this view and ask what will work in practice. Educators recognize that although they may argue for the idealistic view, they have still to prepare students for work in the 'real' world, and that the credibility of the programmes they offer will depend on real world acceptance of the students they graduate.

A difficulty in the relationship between practitioners and educators is that there are no suitable meeting places in which these views can be aired and reconciled. At this stage in the development of public relations education and practice, the dilemmas raised by consideration of the moral role of the practitioner are dimly perceived and not seen as priorities against other pressing questions in the practice, such as how can its effects be measured and evaluated, and how can its place in management be secured?

8 A comparative analysis of public relations in Austria and the United Kingdom

Toby MacManus

INTRODUCTION

The concern of this chapter is a comparative analysis of the perception and practise of public relations in Austria and the United Kingdom. It considers briefly existing research into how public relations manifests itself internationally and the concept of culture is subject to a short analysis to clarify its application in public relations research. Arising from this discussion are research objectives which form the starting point for the second part of the chapter. This considers the methodologies for a comparative analysis of public relations and identifies the approach adopted. A presentation and discussion of the preliminary results of an empirical study being undertaken forms the final section.

INTERNATIONAL PUBLIC RELATIONS RESEARCH

Interest in the way public relations is understood and practised in different countries has grown noticeably over the past four to five years from a small base (Botan 1992: 154). Although possibly unacknowledged by mass communications theorists, it forms a part of what Ang (1990) has described as an intense interest in culture in contemporary communication studies.

The majority of this research comprises single country studies rather than a comparative analysis. Since 1990 there have been, among others, studies published about public relations in China (1990), India (Sriramesh 1992), Germany (Baerns 1994) and Russia (Ivanov 1994). However, Coombs *et al.*'s (1994) study is notable because of its comparative approach, examining practice in Austria, Norway and the USA. The focus of this chapter takes a similar approach by initially considering public relations perception and practise in two countries, later to be extended to include Sweden. The methodology adopted however is slightly different. Other international public relations research has been more wide ranging in approach. Botan (1990; 1992) noted that developing nations may use public relations as a tool for nation building with less emphasis on the business context. He therefore warns against basing research on enthnocentric assumptions of public relations, a reference to American research largely portraying public relations from the perspective of practice in the United States. An understandable development since modern public relations is predominantly of United States origin and research presented in the English language is overwhelmingly from the USA.

More recently, Verčič, Grunig and Grunig (1993) have drawn on evidence from Slovenia to support their proposal that global principles of public relations apply across cultures where suitable conditions exist. Mackey (1994), in a quite different, but also wide ranging enquiry, has sought to explore the relationship between culture and public relations from a philosophical standpoint. He suggests that conventional public relations practice tends to operate from a utilitarian view of the world stemming from Hobbes, yet this is a view which has been challenged by academics in the social and cultural theory area for some years.

A feature of single country or comparative studies has been a pronounced cultural emphasis in the methodology. Coombs *et al.*'s (1994) study used Hostede's cultural dimensions as a basis for a cross cultural analysis that explored the relative degree of professionalization of public relations. MacManus (1990) suggested that cultural factors were influential in shaping the different nature of health care public relations in Sweden and the UK, and Gunn (1994) points to the strong influence of Bhuddism in Thai society, affecting the scope and form of public relations practice in Thailand. The area of culture and public relations has also been skilfully considered by Sriramesh, Grunig and Buffington (1992) focusing on corporate culture, and Sriramesh and White (1992) on culture. Their literature reviews provide a valuable context, although European cultural studies do not feature strongly. International public relations research also led Grunig and Grunig (1992) to postulate the likelihood of two further public relations models, in addition to the initial four American derived models (Grunig and Hunt 1984), the two being a 'personal influencer' and 'cultural interpreter' models.

Culture is also a well-defined area in management studies, (see the *Journal of International Studies of Management and Organisation*;

Granovetter 1985; and Whittington 1993), and in international marketing the issue of standardization or customization is a fundamental strategic decision which draws on cultural factors as part of the analysis. Usunier (1993) has adopted a more explicitly cultural approach to international marketing, taking a cross-cultural view in comparing national marketing systems, and an intercultural perspective to address interaction between people of different cultures. Arguably such a text should be complemented by a similar appraisal of international public relations.

THE CONCEPT OF CULTURE

In suggesting that cultural factors are a growing and significant area of public relations research the question of what is meant by culture has been left open. This section examines some of the many interpretations and aspects of culture[1] and proposes some ways of understanding its relationship with public relations.

A popular notion is that culture is essentially about quality, it represents what is judged to be a positive reflection of society, its production of fine buildings, poetry and painting. The emergence of interest in Cultural Studies in Europe of the 1950s however, was based on a perspective that democratized culture as a concept. It was not simply about the best that has been thought or said but something pervading the whole of society, a general social process of the giving and taking of meanings, with commonly accepted understandings slowly evolving. Raymond Williams (Hall 1986: 35–36) expressed it in this way: 'Culture is those patterns of organization, those characteristic forms of human energy which can be discovered as revealing themselves . . . within or underlying all social practices'.

Culture is therefore analysed by trying to discover how these complex relationships are organized and begins with a discovery of characteristic patterns. Seeking out characteristic patterns provides a basic objective for this research, although whether cultural factors are in fact being examined by the methodology is another matter, since economic, political, legal and geographic factors will play a role in shaping the public relations of a country.

Writing about the dynamics of culture Namenwirth and Weber (1987) criticize the use of surveys of individual opinions or values. They propose that to conceive of 'personal values' is a contradiction in terms, values are collective properties of culture, and individual attitudes and belief systems are only reflective of psychological properties, not cultural ones.

Furthermore, individuals are unequally informed about their culture and society, but survey research to produce national value profiles treats individual view points equally. To sum responses of individuals through survey research therefore produces biased social indicators.

For Namenwirth and Weber the more appropriate methodology for analysing culture is content analysis (procedures designed to draw inferences from texts). It is presented as an unbiased approach relying as it does on the analysis of material produced by collective actions. In this context culture is 'a design for living' and has only a 'programmatic and conceptual existence'. Here there is no place for culture as behaviour or material artefacts, and investigation of the relationship between public relations and culture would concentrate on texts produced by organizations through public relations departments.

Although the proposition is detailed and clearly presented, it is ultimately unconvincing as a perspective on culture, being a narrow conception apparently lacking in empirical support. The criticism of individual views as unequally formed should not be a major problem of methodology provided the bias is random, in which case differences will be likely to cancel each other out.

By contrast the possible influence of culture on personality led Hofstede (1984: 23) to reason that 'culture is the collective programming of the mind which distinguishes the members of one human group from another'.

His presentation of culture as mental software corresponds with Williams' definition; it is the broad conception commonly taken by social anthropologists.

Hofstede suggests cultural traits can be identified in personality tests and the relationship between culture and the human group is the same as that between personality and the individual. The strength of this perspective lies in the remarkable empirical investigation of employees of the multinational company IBM in its national offices in over fifty countries. The relevance of Hofstede's work for this study will be picked up in the discussion of methodology, but his influence is already apparent in research on public relations and culture. Although Hofstede's thorough and illuminating study has had a substantial influence on subsequent cultural research (see Sondergaard's 1994 analysis of its impact), it is argued that it has three major limitations. The cultural dimensions developed from the data are artefacts of the periods of analysis – an inescapable methodological bias; there are obviously constraints imposed by population of IBM employees; and the problem of inferring values from the use of a single measuring instrument of attitude questionnaires (Sondergaard 1994: 449).

Another fundamental aspect of culture relevant to its relationship with public relations is language. The Wharf-Sapir hypothesis (Usunier 1993: 99) on the influence of language on culture contends that an individual's perception of the world is largely created from the language habits of the group. Differences in the way reality is perceived and organized are therefore a function of language. The validity of this hypothesis has however been contested by linguists and anthropologists.

Examples of different culturally-derived meanings for the same words or the absence of a direct translation of one word into another language are prevalent in literature on language and communication, such as the absence in the American Hopi indian language of grammatic constructions that refer directly to time (Carroll 1956). More germane examples are the Swedish and German equivalents for democracy and public relations respectively (MacManus 1992).

An exploration of the meaning of words linked to public relations could be a useful starting point for culture-based public relations research. This would address both distortions and the development of commonly accepted words or phrases such as 'PR' and 'press release' and perhaps in the future 'VNR' and other information technology based words. On a broader scale Hofstede (1991: 42) contrasted countries where a 'Romance language' is spoken with those where a 'Germanic language' is spoken. There seemed to be a relationship between language area and 'mental software' in respect of his cultural dimension of power distance relationships.

The new language of science and technology which is often pervasive across cultures, has been criticized by Habermas (Jenks 1993: 4) for penetrating the 'life-world' in a way that undermines the maintenance of democratic society. The adoption of such linguistic terms in public relations might conceivably be interpreted as a part of this process, but a more general and obvious link between public relations, dominant social groups and culture is its relationship with the media, and the process of lobbying.

The interface between public relations, the media and culture is the last element in these comments on culture. The aim is to highlight the research context, draw on some of the ideas put forward to explain the shaping of culture in societies and point to their significance for the study of public relations.

This conceptualization of culture starts with an assumption that the production and reproduction of sense and meaning in society is a question of both signification and power. A focal interest in cultural studies should therefore be on how signifying practises and the exercise of power are interconnected (Ang 1990: 245).

If organizations play a large part in the process of signification at a societal level, and public relations is the means by which they mostly effect their involvement, then the role of public relations should be one of the primary areas of analysis, and not just by public relations researchers. However, cultural studies researchers have tended not to be interested so much in the process by which this organizational signification occurs, as in the nature of effects (Scannell 1992).

The historical development of mass communications research has been categorized as falling into two traditions, the pluralist and the radical (Gurevitch *et al.* 1982). The pluralist tradition is usually associated with American cultural studies, of which Carey (1989) is a representative. The more cynical, radical approach, which draws on Marxist philosophy, is associated with European (particularly British) cultural studies. However, while the dichotomy was clearly apparent in the early 1980s there has since been a growing together of the two research traditions (Curran 1990). This can be seen in the weakening of the case for a radical class conflict model, as a result of work by Michel Foucalt (1980) and John Fiske (1989) among others, and in the pluralist thinking evidenced by Tunstall's work on the autonomy of journalists (1981) and Sigal (1987) exploring the interconnections between centres of power in society and media organizations.

Given the centrality of the media in much of public relations practise, and the preoccupation of cultural studies with the media, (Ang 1990: 241), the traditions just mentioned provide a further conceptual basis for research. The perspective here for public relations is one that recognizes the legitimacy of the concept of hegemony, but does not automatically assign it a privileged role in analysing culture. Public relations research should therefore draw on the strengths of both the pluralist and radical traditions.

A similar view has been advanced by Toth and Heath (1992) advocating a greater plurality of research methodology in public relations. For the most part public relations research has followed the positivist method that Ang (1990) notes has been the route taken by mainstream communication research into culture and the media. The alternative set of principles, which Ang identifies with cultural studies, embodies an interest in '. . . historical and particular meanings rather than in general types of behaviour, process oriented rather than results oriented, interpretive rather than explanatory.'

In discussing culture and communication Ang emphasizes ethnography as a method, as does Moores (1993) who edited a book devoted to the ethnography of media consumption. In doing so they follow a long history of ethnographic studies in sociology and anthropology which have sought to understand culture from the point of view of its people. Whyte's (1943) classic study of an Italian slum is an example of this tradition.

In this section a number of conceptions of culture have been outlined. The value some hold for analysing public relations, has been pointed out, as well as the desirability of adopting both qualitative and quantitative techniques in methodology.

RESEARCH OBJECTIVES AND METHODOLOGY

The research objective of the project reported in this chapter is to explore two questions in the context of Austria, the United Kingdom and, in later research, Sweden.

1 To what extent is there evidence that the perception and practise of public relations differs significantly between these countries?
2 How can any differences or similarities be explained, and what do they signify for the theoretical basis of public relations?

A third objective to be addressed in more detail in further research, is to ask to what extent can a methodology be developed and applied to give meaningful measurements or insights into these differences?

Comparative international public relations research is unavoidably problematic, as Oyen (1990) eloquently puts it: 'All the external and unsolved problems inherent in sociological research are unfolded when engaged in cross national studies'. Here I am going to refer briefly to some of these methodological issues and set out the approach taken, and to be taken, in later stages of the investigation of public relations in Austria and the UK.

First there is the justification of the choice of countries, why Austria, the UK and Sweden? They cannot be said to be representative of public relations in Europe, there is no balance between rich and poor countries or between the north or south of Europe. The study however is neither concerned with sampling in a representative manner, if that were possible, public relations activity in Europe, nor is there an interest in defining a European character to public relations, as opposed to a North American or Japanese public relations. But there is an interest in exploring public relations in Europe and the influences which shape it. Austria, Sweden and the UK are all on the periphery of Western Europe yet a part of the European Union. They are bound by a common set of union laws and regulations, that affect the opportunities for business, the way it is transacted, and the social framework of the countries.

However, the countries also have quite distinct characters. Austria and Sweden since the end of the Second World War have maintained positions of political neutrality. Austria is culturally part of the German speaking area of Europe. Sweden has close cultural and economic links with its Scandinavian neighbour states.

Although all three countries have ties with the USA through immigration, the UK has a close relationship because of a common language and deeper historical ties.

For research purposes both Austria and Sweden are attractive because many people speak English and the populations are quite small.

The data to be discussed derives from an exploratory questionnaire survey. Problems of external validity apply such as, how far and successfully does the measuring instrument seek to probe and record the perception and practise of public relations? How representative is the sample and, crucially, how does one take account of the problem of respondents, either consciously or unconsciously, portraying one set of beliefs and behaviours in their answers while others may be applied in different and more challenging circumstances?

To bring this last issue closer to home, practitioners may have a self-image of professionalism which is drawn on when answering a questionnaire from public relations researchers/educators. But in reacting to a hostile pressure group or demands from senior management, a different set of beliefs and behaviours may come into play. In other words their behaviour is situational.

If the researcher feels reasonably confident about the validity and reliability about the data and clear differences emerge between the two countries, what then? How is it possible to decide whether such differences are due to national, regional, local, organizational or professional influences? In this research differences, or similarities, may be more a function of the stage of professional development achieved by the respondent, than other influences that might be cultural or personality based.

This position is supported by Scheuch's suggestion that in highly industrialized and pluralistic countries differences may not be so marked and survey research may more appropriately be regarded as observation under differing conditions, rather than as 'a test of meanings, and effects of a culture, of a society or of a polity' (Scheuch 1992: 30). The differing conditions can be argued to relate to the level of professionalization of public relations.

However such an argument would have to contend that the substantial cultural differences which Hofstede identified in his cohorts for Austria, the UK and Sweden (Table 8.1), have no bearing on public relations. Since Hofstede's main tenet concerned the cultural relativity of management theories, and public relations is widely regarded as a management process (Grunig and Hunt 1984; Crable and Vibbert 1986; White 1991; Baskin and Aronoff 1992) the potential for culture to influence public relations is clear and already explored in the studies mentioned earlier.

On the other hand should a difference be suggested to relate to Austrian customs, how can we be sure this is Austrian culture, rather than diffusion across cultures, that is causing the effect? (Galton's problem: Scheuch 1992: 28.)

Cross cultural researchers also point to the often mistaken assumption that countries are 'variance reducers', that there will be less variance between internal regions than between the country as a whole and other countries. Finnish research found the country to have one of the highest rates of coronary heart disease in Western Europe, which became a much publicized finding. In reality, the high incidence was restricted to farmers and foresters in the north of the country. Heart disease rates in the more populous south of the country were the same as for other Scandinavian countries.

Table 8.1 Hofstede's cultural dimensions for Austria, the UK and Sweden.

Country	Dimensions			
	Power distance	*Uncertainty avoidance*	*Individualism*	*Masculinity*
Austria	11	70	55	79
UK	35	35	89	66
Sweden	31	29	71	5
Overall mean of 53 countries	57	65	43	49

Source: Usunier 1993

In the sampling frames used respondents were selected on a random basis, and it seems likely that organizational and personality influences will cancel each other out. It is expected therefore that the two main influences forming the background to respondents' answers will be professional and or cultural, whether national or regional.

But the method adopted here relies on postal questionnaire data, and this has limitations as a tool for probing professional and cultural factors because it does not allow the researcher to get close to the respondent and consider the intersubjectivity of his or her experience as a public relations practitioner. In order to examine the 'everyday life' of the subjects, perhaps, for example, the ten staff in a London based public relations consultancy specializing in health care, we need to turn to the qualititative investigation of social processes using the interpretive, ethno-graphic approach referred to earlier. Here, a research strategy might adopt the framework of symbolic interactionism, examining the 'social meanings' that are shared by groups of public relations practitioners, and seeking to interpret those meanings in terms of relationships with other groups. Or the strategy might be based on ethnomethodology and examine the activities rather than the actors. So it becomes an enquiry into the specific nature of public relations activity, in an Austrian or UK context which 'makes' meanings possible (Cuff *et al.* 1990: 191–2). Such methodologies are concerned with issues of agency and meaning that shape micro-social situations, as opposed to a macro level perspective (theories of structure) considering factors such as institutional processes that shape public relations.

The limitation of adopting ethnography as a research method for public relations is that it portrays only partial truths and the cultures described are partly influenced by the author's imagination and prejudices. Moores (1993) highlights the tendency of researchers to spend only short periods of time with a limited number of subjects. He contrasts Morley's (1986) sessions talking about television in the sitting rooms of eighteen South London homes with Malinowski's (1926) two years' living with the Trobriand Islanders.

The problems inherent in positivist and ethnographic procedures for examining the perception of practice for public relations are real but not overwhelming; one can draw encouragement from outstanding examples of both techniques, for example, Bourdieu's (1984) investigation into the sociology of taste was based on a large scale questionnaire survey of 1,200 respondents in France. His work has been described as 'probably the most important statement to date on the patterned practices of consumer cultures' (Moores 1993: 118).

Having considered methodological issues relevant to this study the following section describes the approach taken. First, it was considered important in order to obtain a balanced view of the public relations practitioner population that the questionnaire should be directed to both practitioners who belonged to the main professional associations in Austria and the UK and to those who did not.

After its design the questionnaire was seen and commented on by six professional colleagues from the UK (4) Austria (1) and Sweden (1) and changes were made to the wording and format. It was subsequently piloted with twenty-six practitioners in the UK and following minor changes, translated into the German and Swedish languages. Discussions over meaning and content were held with the German translator and as a result further changes made to the original text. The Swedish translator had her first draft scrutinized by a Swedish business man working in the UK and fluent in English. Suggestions for improving the translations were also made by colleagues in Austria and Sweden before a final version was produced. These discussions and cross checking brought to light the inevitable imperfections involved in translation from one language to another.

The outline results presented here represent a sample of responses received from a continuing process of data collection that will give the project a longitudinal dimension. Since the results discussed here are a sample of the total responses they must be treated with extreme caution. That does not prevent a discussion of the results; there is value in identifying the possibilities raised by the data, which if affirmed by subsequent research can lead to more focused questions on the nature of public relations in Austria and the UK. For Austria, subjects were selected from the members' list of the 1993 handbook of the Public Relations Verband Austria (PRVA), and for non-PRVA members selection was made from the 1993 Austrian press handbook's public relations counsel section. These latter selections were crosschecked against the PRVA list to ensure their members were not being included. Both samples were randomly selected but the large majority of the initial phase of questionnaires on which these results are based, were sent to PRVA members.

All questionnaires had a covering letter from the researcher but in addition, the Austrian cohort received a further letter of recommendation from Professor Benno Signitzer of Salzburg University. The Austrian response rate was 35 per cent from 206 questionnaires sent out.

In the UK, random selections were made from the Institute of Public Relations (IPR) membership list and a public relations industry handbook published by Hollis. In a two stage process 465 questionnaires were sent out with an overall 29 per cent response rate. The lower rate may be a result of a shorter deadline given in the covering letter to the first stage which achieved a 26 per cent response rate against 33 per cent in the second stage.

These response rates can be compared with surveys of professional public relations practitioners conducted by Lindenmann in 1990, who achieved a 27 per cent rate in a survey of 945 members of the Public Relations Association of America (Watson 1994) and Watson's 26 per cent response rate recent survey of 1000 members of the UK Institute of Public Relations (Watson 1994), and Coombs *et al.* (1994) three surveys of professional membership in Austria (72 per cent) Norway (50 per cent) and the USA (54 per cent). It is difficult to judge why some response rates are better than others; the fact that this research did not use a postage paid return envelope, as was the case in the Watson and Coombs' studies, could have influenced some potential respondents not to reply.

The questionnaire was initially split into three sections. (See Appendix 8.A). The first section contained questions about respondents' beliefs and values in connection with public relations, and about structure and the practitioner's role.

Section two addressed styles of approach to public relations tasks. It was based on a learning styles questionnaire developed by Honey and Mumford (1986). The questions relate to four categories: activists, reflectors, theorists and pragmatists. Although the questions were originally designed to enable people to identify their particular learning styles, it is considered they can equally relate to modes of behaviour in relation to management tasks – in this case, public relations. The purpose of including this section was to see if there was any indication that styles might differ across cultures, or between professional and non-professional members; and additionally to see whether any particular style appeared more suited to public relations practitioners. The expectation was that there would be a uniform distribution of styles across these samples. However, this section was removed after the initial survey as feedback from respondents suggested it was confusing and lacked empirical value.

The final section sought background information that, as well as standard questions on age and sex, enquired into the business of the organization, and the education of the respondent.

On completion of the full postal survey the results will be used to help generate questions for the second stage of in-depth interviews with public relations practitioners, and subjects who are able to take an outsider's view of industry. A further option will be to secure interviews with a sample of respondents to explore the reasons behind some of their answers.

PRELIMINARY RESEARCH FINDINGS

One hundred and fifty questionnaires were selected for the preliminary analysis. Initially 50 each from Austria and the UK, but an additional 50 questionnaires were later included following the second stage of the UK survey. Of Austrian responses 60 per cent were by PRUA members and 90 per cent of UK responses were by IPR members. The difference could affect the results if it is assumed that professional membership will be likely to result in different answers, being more supportive of research, education and ethical conduct. However, unlike the UK, there are several other professional associations in Austria that public relations practitioners may join as individuals. Moreover, it is unsafe to suppose that membership of professional association leads automatically to professional behaviour, or that people cannot be 'professional' if they don't 'join up'. The difference between the two samples may not, in this respect, be so important. The responses to seven questions have been analysed with the findings listed below. To enable comparability between Austrian and UK results and future scores, percentages have been used, although the correct use of a percentage could not strictly be applied to the Austrian population of 50 responses.

The first question asks respondents to say how much they agree or disagree with three definitions of public relations. The definitions come from the United Kingdom, the USA and Germany. The first definition (1a) is virtually that of the United Kingdom's Institute of Public Relations up to 1994 when it was amended:

> Public relations practice is the planned effort to establish and maintain goodwill and mutual understanding between an organization and its publics.

The second definition (1b) is, except for the inclusion of the word 'strategic', the one given by Grunig and Hunt (1984):

> Public relations is the management of communication between an organization and its strategic publics.

The third definition in question (1c) is by Heinz Flieger (1988):

> Public relations is a specific mode of social action to be regarded as a basis for the existence of developed industrial societies with a

high level of organization . . . Basically public relations is the cultivation of social relations.

The definitions emphasize different aspects of public relations. The first two indicate the relationship between an organization and its publics, however the first has a stronger ethical, two-way connotation in emphasizing goodwill and mutual understanding. The second has the benefit of being more concise and more clearly emphasizes the strategic management nature of public relations. The third definition takes a sociological approach seeking to explain public relations' place in society. In essence then, the first is more ethical, the second more pragmatic and the third more philosophical in their explanations of public relations. The expectation was that UK respondents would be more likely to agree or strongly agree with the first definition. There was no expectation on the form of responses for the second definition, but for the third definition it was expected that the Austrian cohort would show more agreement and less disagreement than the UK cohort.

These expectations have been confirmed by the preliminary data. Of UK respondents 94 per cent agreed or strongly agreed with the first definition. By contrast 80 per cent of Austrians agreed or strongly

Table 8.2 Response to Question 1

Q.1 Here are three definitions of public relations. How much do you agree or disagree with each of them?

	UK	*%*	*Austria*
Definition A			
Agree or strongly agree	94		80
Disagree/strongly disagree	6		20
Undecided	–		–
Definition B			
Agree/strongly agree	88	%	66
Disagree/strongly disagree	8		34
Undecided	4		–
Definition C			
Agree/strongly agree	12	%	50
Disagree/strongly disagree	64		42
Undecided	24		8

agreed, but 20 per cent indicated that they disagreed with this definition. It will be interesting to see whether this proportion of disagreement is maintained when all the results are analysed, and to follow up
in personal interviews why it is found wanting.

For the second definition the divergence between UK and Austrian
opinion becomes more distinct. Eighty-eight per cent of UK respondents either agreed or strongly agreed with the definition; for Austrian
respondents the figure was 66 per cent. Only 8 per cent of UK
respondents disagreed/strongly disagreed whereas the figure for Austria was 34 per cent. A possible explanation for Austrian disagreement might be that this is too short a statement to describe public
relations.

The third definition was disagreed or strongly disagreed with by 64
per cent of UK respondents and 42 per cent of Austrian respondents.
The expected divergence emerged with only 12 per cent of UK
respondents agreeing or strongly agreeing, whereas 50 per cent of
Austrian respondents agreed or strongly agreed with this statement.
For this definition we therefore have a roughly even split between
agreement and disagreement with Austrian respondents, but while
most UK respondents agreed with it, 24 per cent were surprisingly
undecided.

Question 5 takes an indirect approach to practitioner perceptions,
asking their views on public agreement or disagreement with four
statements about public relations (see question 5, section 1 in Appendix 8.A). The first statement that public relations accurately explains
an organization's viewpoint portrays a one way ethical process. The
second statement is that public relations tries to sell an organization's
products or services, and presents public relations as a tool of marketing. The third statement suggest public relations seeks to manipulate
public opinion and represents the unethical and asymmetrical dimension, and finally the fifth statement provides a contrasting view that
public relations seeks a dialogue to create mutual understanding and
represents the ethical and symmetrical dimensions. Taking question
1, there was clarity in disagreement or strong disagreement between
the two countries, but rather more UK practitioners were undecided
(26 per cent) than Austrians (18 per cent).

The second questions presenting a marketing view was agreed or
strongly agreed with by 66 per cent of Austrian and 81 per cent of UK
respondents.

A similar divergence emerges for the question on manipulation
with agreement or strong agreement by 58 per cent of the Austrian
and 84 per cent of the UK respondents.

The final question on mutual understanding showed more convergence over agreement and strong agreement with 38 per cent of Austrian and 28 per cent of UK respondents falling in this category. However, 50 per cent of the Austrian cohort disagreed or strongly disagreed against 37 per cent in the UK as with the first question many more UK respondents were undecided: 30 per cent compared to 12 per cent.

It appears from these answers that UK professionals believe the public has a lower opinion of public relations than Austrian counterparts. It would be interesting to explore this question further with respondents by asking them on what they based their judgement about public opinion, or more specifically, how did they think public relations becomes identified in the minds of the public? To what extent, for example, do they think the media plays a part in providing the setting in which public relations is perceived? In the United Kingdom public relations seems to be rarely, if at all, portrayed in a positive light by national newspapers (either broadsheet or tabloid), or on television as exemplified by the Channel 4 screening in 1994 of a programme titled 'I hate PR'. It may well be that the representation of public relations is not so negative.

Question 6 asks how valuable higher education degree courses in public relations or communication science are to the practise of public relations. It could be argued that positive answers indicate a more professional perspective of public relations since a fundamental element of a profession is a foundation of research, theory and a higher education training programme. On the other hand, negative answers might not be so much to do with the value of higher education in principle, but more linked to scepticism about the quality and depth of current research, theory and education programmes. The results from the 150 questionnaires provide a striking difference in views on the value of education in public relations. Fourteen per cent of Austrian and 41 per cent of UK respondents thought it was very valuable. Forty-six per cent of Austrian and 85 per cent of UK respondents thought it was either of some value or very valuable. Thirty-two per cent of Austrian and 9 per cent of UK respondents believed public relations education to be of little or no value.

Such divergence was not expected and it may well be a statistical anomaly due to the small sample. A factor that might have influenced a positive UK response is the rapid growth of higher education courses in public relations in the UK over the last six years. These have received favourable publicity in the Institute of Public Relations' journal, and over a five year period the public relations industry has experienced an increasing number of students working on industrial placement, with high levels of motivation because of the vocational nature of the degree. Typically these placements are for 20 to 40 weeks duration. It may also be the case that Austrian degree courses, which are at masters level, have a much stronger theoretical emphasis than the courses in the UK, and so are not perceived as being so relevant by Austrian practitioners. However, this is not borne out by answers to question 12 which asked whether a knowledge of theoretical models of public relations is relevant to practice. Seventy-six per cent of Austrian and 54 per cent of UK respondents believed that is was relevant. The Austrian replies appeared to contradict the views on higher education since that represents the process by which new entrants into the profession gain a knowledge of theory. For the UK respondents it may suggest that the value of higher education in public relations resides in developing practical skills and a knowledge of the broader management context.

Question 9 asked whether in the future public relations would become more allied with marketing or more distinct from marketing. Here there is a convergence of views: 66 per cent of Austrian and 75 per cent of UK respondents believed that public relations would become more allied with marketing, whereas 26 per cent and 25 per cent respectively thought that it would become more distinct from marketing. The belief in the closing relationship between public relations and marketing raises an issue of whether respondents are confident that public relations will continue to develop as a distinctive profession, and what for them defines professional public relations practice. Although as academics we may seek to make clear important distinctions between public relations and marketing, do such distinctions have the same significance for practitioners who may see greater integration between public relations and other forms of public communication used by organizations.

Practitioners' sensitivity to what may or may not be justifiable in public relations was probed by inviting them to say whether or not they thought disseminating inaccurate information was justifiable in four contexts (question 11). It was expected that a measure of professionalism would be indicated by the extent to which practitioners recognized that none of the contexts were acceptable behaviour. Codes of professional conduct in public relations, such as the European Code, 'Code of Lisbon' (Clause 3) and the Code for the UK Institute of Public Relations (Clause 2.2) both recognize that professional practice is essentially founded on the truthful use of information.

Since 100 per cent scores on each category were unlikely it was considered that a high degree of professionalism would be indicated by 90 per cent of answers falling in the 'No' category for each context. This was achieved in all four of the categories by UK respondents, as illustrated in Table 8.3.

In the first and fourth contexts neither group fell below the 90 per cent base line. But in the second, concerning conflict with another company, only 76 per cent of Austrian respondents did not think it was justifiable to disseminate inaccurate information, and 22 per cent did. The Austrian response also dipped below the base line (86 per cent) in respect of the third context concerning threat of unwelcome government intervention.

Will these preliminary results stand the test of an analysis of the full sample of replies? On the basis of current data, Austrian practitioners are more willing to use inaccurate information in conflict with another company. What can be made of these initial results? First it has to be asked whether Austrian respondents might simply be more honest in their answers. Could a questionnaire from a foreign researcher whose results will be published in another language make it easier for respondents to be more open? On the other hand, might UK respondents simply be opting for the safe reply of ticking all the 'No' boxes, whatever their real actions may sometimes be?

A further line of enquiry is to ask why one context makes the use of inaccurate information justifiable when another doesn't? In Austria does conflict with another company create more motivation to avoid uncertainty and lead to greater aggression in response (Hofstede 1994: 125).

Table 8.3 Percentage of 'No' responses to Question 11 by UK and Austria

	%	
	UK	Austria
Category 1 – to improve some aspects of the market share for product:	96	90
Category 2 – a tactic in a conflict in another company:	93	76
Category 3 – in response to the threat of unwelcome government intervention:	94	86
Category 4 – in response to a hostile pressure group:	90	92

The final issue dealt with here concerns the extent to which public relations in Austria and the UK is similar to that practised in the USA. Respondents were asked to what extent did public relations differ in their country from the USA. Once again a clear difference emerged, more UK respondents (29 per cent) thought that UK public relations was similar or very similar to the USA, than did Austrians (14 per cent). Austrians were much more clear about the difference; 56 per cent said that their public relations was different or very different from USA. There was a far larger number of UK respondents (46 per cent) who answered 'Don't Know' than Austrians (28 per cent). These answers are not surprising given the closer cultural ties between the UK and the USA referred to earlier. This is supported by the much closer alignment of scores for power distance, uncertainty avoidance and individualism between the UK and USA than between Austria and the USA (Hofstede 1991).

The survey also sought to discover reasons for differences with the United States. In line with the greater sense of difference, Austrian answers tended to be more specific. There was however agreement between the two countries on a number of distinctive features of public relations in the United States:

- more extensive and sophisticated use of lobbying;
- a different marketing environment, such as consumer buying trends;
- more emphasis on events, 'show public relations'.
- Austrian respondents also mentioned that there is little in the way of non-profit making public relations in Austria;
- better collaboration in the United States with other forms of marketing communication;
- stronger moral components in public relations strategy in the United States.

Some of these comments are not surprising. A high level of lobbying activity is a well-recognized feature of public relations in the USA. It has been estimated that there were in 1988 between 15,000 to 20,000 commercial lobbyists in Washington, substantially more than estimates for lobbyists in Brussels, the location of the European Commission (Moloney 1994: 20–21). The emphasis on events shows public relations is also consistent with a stereotypical view of the high value placed on entertainment in the United States' society. But such an assumption has to be balanced by sensitivity to cultural variety in North America which led Garreau to propose the existence of nine distinct regions (1981).

One result not expected from the question on differences between the USA compared with Austria and the UK were the comments that little in the way of non-profit making public relations existed in Austria. The same cannot be said for the UK; if the distinction is sustained by subsequent research it provides a further avenue of enquiry.

CONCLUSIONS

This discussion began by noting the growing body of international public relations research and considering concepts of culture and the frameworks they offer for understanding public relations. It then critically assessed issues of methodology connected with a comparative analysis of public relations in different countries, concluding that such research is strengthened by qualitative and quantitative methods to the questions being addressed.

In presenting the results of the study, selected data from 150 questionnaires was examined to give a preliminary view of public relations in Austria and the United Kingdom. The central questions were, to what extent does the data indicate differences or similarities between the countries, and how might these be explained?

The initial analysis of the questionnaire suggests there may well be significant differences in what practitioners do and how they think of public relations in Austria and the United Kingdom. In the opening questions on definitions it is of note that a significant number of Austrians disagreed with each of the definitions, whereas in the United Kingdom practitioners were only strongly in disagreement with the final sociological definition, which originated from Germany. The definition was accepted by only 12 per cent of respondents. A significant proportion of Austrians (46 per cent) were content with this definition but almost an equal number (42 per cent) were unhappy with it and 20 per cent also disagreed with the UK definition.

It may be that this group found the concepts of mutual understanding and goodwill unrealistic and not sufficiently commercially oriented. But there appears to be a body of practitioners in the UK which is also unhappy with the concept of mutual understanding, saying that its inclusion in definitions was at a time when public relations was concerned to distance itself from the charges of being associated with propaganda. This line of thinking argues that mutual understanding is too idealistic for the modern context of public relations where its management function needs to be more firmly emphasized (Newman 1993). A broader question referred to in the discussion of methodology is whether practitioners practise the principles to which they say they aspire? So although there are differences in agreement about definitions, does this mean that the representatives of both countries in reality practise public relations any differently?

In question five respondents indicated how they thought the general public viewed public relations. While practitioners' opinions on how they are perceived by the general public is a legitimate area of enquiry, it is also possible that answers to this question give some indication of practitioners' own opinions on public relations, because of the possibility of the projection of their views onto the public they are thinking about. It is interesting to note here that practitioners in Austria also thought their public would disagree with the notion of public relations seeking to create mutual understanding.

Differences were evident in all the other questions except for question nine, which asked whether public relations would become more allied with marketing or more distinct from marketing. The broad agreement that public relations would be more closely allied with marketing may well reflect the realities 'on the ground' in the two countries, and possibly elsewhere in Europe.

Earlier on in the discussion of the results it was asked whether the differences might relate more to separate stages of professional development rather than the influence of culture. The results of this preliminary examination give an indication of cultural influence when looked at from Hofstede's dimension of uncertainty avoidance (Table 8.1).

In Hofstede's values for this dimension, Austria scores high for uncertainty avoidance (70 per cent) and the United Kingdom low (35 per cent) the overall mean for 53 countries is 65 per cent. Uncertainty avoidance measures the degree to which people tend to feel threatened by uncertain, ambiguous or undefined situations. Where uncertainty avoidance is high in an organization or society there will be a much greater tendency to produce rules and procedures that define the context of behaviour. Hofstede (1991) notes that 'Societies in which uncertainty avoidance is strong, are also characterized by a higher level of anxiety and aggressiveness'. This may explain why a significant number of Austrian practitioners were unhappy with the UK definition, seeing its defining aspect 'mutual understanding', as a vague and imprecise concept.

In the answers to question 11, on disseminating inaccurate information, uncertainty avoidance may also explain why a significant number of Austrian practitioners considered the use of inaccurate information justifiable in dealing with conflict with another company and the threat of unwelcome government intervention. Both these situations could be perceived as creating a high level of uncertainty, and therefore legitimatizing an aggressive response. Such a suggestion is highly speculative, but it is reasonable to hypothesize that the distinctly different levels of uncertainty avoidance scores that Hofstede found in an organizational environment do affect the way public relations is perceived and practised.

A further cultural dimension, power distance, may also be relevant in explaining differences between the two countries. Power distance measures the extent to which society and its members tolerate an unequal distribution of power in organizations and in society. In low power distance situations, members of the organization tend to feel equal and close to each other in their daily work relationship. In high power distance societies superiors and subordinates are likely to feel separated from each other; the real power tends to be very much concentrated at the top of the hierarchy. Austria's score of 11 for power distance was the lowest amongst all 53 countries surveyed. The UK score of 35, although below the overall mean of 57, is still substantially greater than Austria's. This may well have an effect on the way public relations is organized and the decision making process. An ethnographic methodology would seem to be a particularly appropriate way of exploring this possible relationship further.

It is important to underline that the findings in this study are tentative, but a number of questions have emerged as a result of the analysis. If sustained in the full examination of the data they will serve to propel further research into the nature of public relations in Austria and the United Kingdom, and the development of a methodological approach for exploring differences in public relations between countries.

NOTE

1 The abstract notion of culture may have originated in Germany in the 18th Century where the word Kultur was used to denote civilization. In 1952, Kroeber and Kluckhohn reviewed the definitions of culture and identify 164, many of which derived from the work of anthropologists. This was, coincidentially, close to the time when the British civil servant Pimlott came up with a list of more than 400 definitions of public relations (Grunig and Hunt 1984, Chapter 1). For a more detailed discussion of the cultural process and dynamics see Usunier (1993: 38–97)

APPENDIX 8.A

PERCEPTION & PRACTICE OF PUBLIC RELATIONS IN THE UK

This survey is part of doctoral research into Public Relations in Europe. Your assistance by completing this questionnaire would be much appreciated. You can answer most of the questions by placing a tick in the appropriate space. The survey takes approximately 10 minutes to complete.

SECTION 1. This section addresses some conceptual and practical aspects of public relations

1. Here are three definitions of public relations. How much do you agree or disagree with each of them?

A. 'Public relations practice is the planned effort to establish and maintain goodwill and mutual understanding between an organization and its publics.'

Strongly Disagree	☐
Disagree	☐
Undecided	☐
Agree	☐
Strongly Agree	☐

B. 'Public Relations is the management of communication between an organization and its strategic publics.'

Strongly Disagree	☐
Disagree	☐
Undecided	☐
Agree	☐
Strongly Agree	☐

C. 'Public relations is a specific mode of social action to be regarded as a basis for the existence of developed industrial societies with a high level of organization . . . Basically public relations is the cultivation of social relations.'

Strongly Disagree	☐
Disagree	☐
Undecided	☐
Agree	☐
Strongly Agree	☐

2. Listed below are a number of forms of public relations. Please indicate the level of involvement of your organization in each of these:

1= Low   5=high

Media Publicity
(Press, Radio, Television)   1☐ 2☐ 3☐ 4☐ 5☐

Governmental
(Local, National, International) 1☐ 2☐ 3☐ 4 ☐5☐

Business to Business   1☐ 2☐ 3☐ 4☐ 5☐

Consumers   1☐ 2☐ 3☐ 4☐ 5☐

Local Communities   1☐ 2☐ 3☐ 4☐ 5☐

Investor/ Financial   1☐ 2☐ 3☐ 4☐ 5☐

Employees   1☐ 2☐ 3☐ 4☐ 5☐

Issues/Crisis management   1☐ 2☐ 3☐ 4☐ 5☐

Other (please specify)   1☐ 2☐ 3☐ 4☐ 5☐

3. What is your primary role as a public relations practitioner?

....

....

4. If you have more than one role, please rank them in order of importance.

Media Relations   ☐

Employee Relations   ☐

Counsellor/ Adviser to management   ☐

Investor/ Financial Relations   ☐

Managing public relations staff   ☐

5. Below are a number of points of view about public relations. Thinking of the general public in the UK, how strongly do you believe they agree or disagree with these views of public relations? Please indicate in the range 1 to 5.

**1=Strongly Disagree 2=Disagree 3=Undecided 4=Agree
5= Strongly Agree**

It accurately explains an organization's viewpoint?
1☐ 2☐ 3☐ 4☐ 5☐

It tries to 'sell' the organization's products / services?
1☐ 2☐ 3☐ 4☐ 5☐

It seeks to manipulate public opinion?
1☐ 2☐ 3☐ 4☐ 5☐

It seeks a dialogue to create mutual understanding?
1☐ 2☐ 3☐ 4☐ 5☐

Other please specify...
....
1☐ 2☐ 3☐ 4☐ 5☐

6. Thinking of higher education degree courses in public relations or communication science, please indicate how valuable you think they are to the practise of public relations?

No value   ☐

Little value   ☐

Some value (50%)   ☐

Very valuable   ☐

Undecided   ☐

7. What proportion of your public relations activity is practised in a marketing context? Please circle the appropriate percentage range.

20–30% / 31–40% / 41–50% / 51–60% / 61–70%/ 71–80%/ 81–90%

8. What do you believe to be the national proportion for public relations practised in the marketing context?   . . . .%

9. In the future will public relations:

• become more allied with marketing;   YES☐ NO☐

• become more distinct from marketing?   YES☐ NO☐

10. In what other way will public relations change over the next 5 years?

....

....

....

....

11. Please indicate by ticking against 'Yes' or 'No' whether you think that disseminating inaccurate information is justifiable in any of the following contexts.

    i. To improve some aspects of the market share of a product or a service.

                  YES☐ NO☐

    ii. As a tactic in a conflict with another company (e.g., a take over bid).

                  YES☐ NO☐

    iii. In response to the threat of unwelcome Government intervention.

                  YES☐ NO☐

    iv. In response to a hostile pressure group.

                  YES☐ NO☐

12. Do you believe that a knowledge of theoretical models of public relations is relevant to the daily practise of public relations?

                YES☐ NO☐ Don't Know☐

13. To what extent, if any, does public relations in the UK differ from the United States of America?

Very Similar   ☐

Similar   ☐

Different   ☐

Very Different   ☐

Don't Know   ☐

14. If in answering question 13, you believe there are differences, please indicate what they are, placing your answer in the following categories:

ECONOMIC..

....

....

....

SOCIAL ....

....

....

....

OTHER ....

....

....

....

Part IV

Central and northern European perspectives of public relations

This final section of the book contains chapters by authors from the Netherlands, Denmark and Slovenia. The chapters again reflect the diversity of research traditions in public relations and offer insights into both fundamental and applied research being undertaken by academics in these two European regions.

Henrik Rebel's contribution offers an extensive literature review and re-examination of various theoretical constructs concerned with the concepts of 'image' and 'identity' which he suggests are central themes in a **normative** theory of public relations. Rebel criticizes both practitioners and academics for their misuse of many of the original core concepts of image and identity as well as for their practice of 'manipulating' the scientific contexts. In particular, he highlights the apparent lack of regard amongst practitioners and academics for the relationships between identity and image and he argues for a more eclectic approach to identifying these dimensions. Pursuing these and other issues, Rebel proceeds to formulate and synthesize his propositions to construct a theoretical model of the relationship between image and identity.

Some contentious areas do exist, however, such as problems of incommensurability brought about by the author's apparent stance, which is signified by his constant use of the term **scientific**. Indeed, during his quest he enters many different epistemological domains. Rebel's efforts to deconstruct and metaphorically interpret the corporate situation continually adopts many diametric perspectives, such as symbolic interactionism, cognitivism and hermeneutics. Nevertheless, this piece of work deserves serious thought not least for its foresight to question the **meanings** of PR terms, and their ability to **translate** well across both European and international boundaries.

Inger Jensen examines the central importance of concept of legitimacy in public relations and develops a theoretical framework for clarifying the assumptions, social values and norms which underpin the legitimacy of various organizations. Here the author argues that the traditional distinctions between profit and non-profit organization offer little assistance and may not be appropriate. The chapter suggests that a far more subtle and complex analysis of an organization's economic and social objectives is needed in order to understand the basis of its legitimacy.

Betteke van Ruler explores how public relations practitioners in the Nertherlands view their professional roles and argues that most have a rather unclear view of the type of communications roles that they fulfil. Here the author argues that the failure on the part of practitioners to fully appreciate the communications concept has resulted in a lack of clarity in their understanding of their professional roles. The chapter reports the results of a large scale study conducted in the Netherlands which confirms the confusion that exists among practitioners about the nature of the communication process in which they are engaged. The author argues that this confusion explains, at least in part, why many practitioners fail to make use of research and undervalue the importance of formal training in public relations.

Dejan Verčič offers an interesting insight into public relations decision-making systems in Slovenia, examining how environmental issues relating to the Sostanj power station were handled. The chapter demonstrates how the application of the situational analysis of publics and media analysis resulted in recommendations to the plant's management about how they should attempt to tackle the environmental problems they faced. The chapter also reviews recent business literature and highlights what the author sees as the new ethical and moral dilemmas facing businesses as we approach the new millennium. Here the author postulates the emergence of a new set of challenges for public relations practitioners, what the author terms the development of the 'fourth wave public relations'

9 Towards a metaphorical theory of public relations

Dr Henrik Rebel

ABSTRACT

This chapter purports to outline a normative theory of public relations (PR) which might help to clear up some conceptual misunderstanding and to build a coherent conceptual framework. The meaning and use of the concepts which are generally considered as core concepts of public relations, viz., image, identity and ideality are debated and from the analysis that follows, an assessment is made of the scientific use for those concepts. The chapter builds on this discussion of the scientific usage of these terms and goes on to consider the means by which these concepts can be researched. Connected to the scientific usage are the means by which the core concepts can be researched. The chapter concludes by presenting an empirically testable and normative theory of public relations.

INTRODUCTION – SOME COMMON CONCEPTUAL FALLACIES

One can hardly imagine concepts of science that are so poorly and inconsistently delineated as those core concepts of public relations, image and identity. There seems to be no common understanding of these concepts either in the domain of PR professionals or among its researchers or the scientific community. Three main causes seem to underly this unsatisfactory situation.

First, it should be realized that public relations is an applied science in a double sense of the word. For the essential theories of public relations are mainly derived from the more general 'communication science'. The latter, in turn, is an application of the 'pure' social sciences of sociology and psychology. If public relations researchers are to develop their own theories arguably they should draw on both

these 'pure' sciences for inspiration and insight. The remoteness from
its theoretical origins causes gaps in public relations theorizing which
need to be filled. In fact, the lack of clear scientific concepts is
addressed by the use of well-known colloquial concepts drawn
from everyday PR practice.

Williams (1981: 130) designated the 'image-concept' as a **jargon-
term** in commercial advertising and public relations. Jargon, as we
should realize, has more the function of social signpost in a community, than of a clear scientific concept (Rebel 1993: 40). Recently,
Van der Meiden (1994: 6) complained in this respect: 'We often use
in our profession terms and concepts [in the Dutch version he used the
term **jargon** here] that are treated like tomatoes for Cold Buffets; we
hollow them out and fill them again with non-tomato-related stuff-
ing.' [cited from the English edition]. Among PR practitioners and
PR researchers there seems to be neither sense of the etymology of
the original concepts nor of their usage in the original scientific
contexts. Originally derived concepts become instruments of wilful
manipulation in the hands of 'crafty vendors' who try to sell their
customers an image and an identity. A tendency signalled for over
thirty years by Daniel Boorstin (1962).

Specific local traditions in diverse PR-minded countries only
aggravated the obtuseness of the present PR conceptualization. In
the Anglo-Saxon tradition, admirably represented by David Bernstein's *Company Image and Reality*, the author chose a definition
of identity as 'strictly physical – it comprises visual cues – but it
serves also as a guide to corporate behaviour' (1984: 156). And,
earlier, he spoke about identity as 'the outward manifestation of an
inner set of beliefs, a company persona' (ibid.: 58). He used these
descriptions despite a far more insightful and complete discussion he
presented in another chapter (ibid.: 60–8), to which we will return
later in this chapter. It seems as if Bernstein's origin as founder of
The Creative Business can be held responsible for this leap towards
the visual cues. In the same vein, Paul Hefting described corporate
identity in a designer's study as 'the image a company strives to
achieve' (1990: 2). Earlier Garbett (1988) wrote a comparable study
How to Build a Corporation's Identity and Project its Image.

In the Dutch tradition, represented by Blauw (1986) and Van Riel
(1992), one meets a different instance of complying with the popular
usage in a scientific conceptualization. Since the mid-sixties it has
become a habit in the Netherlands to translate the image-concept into
the seeming Dutch equivalent 'imago' (Vos 1992: 23–24). As Blauw
recently commented [personal conversation] he had been fully aware

of the problems of translation, for 'image' (English) is 'beeld' (Dutch) and 'imago' (Dutch) is 'imago' (English). But he did not succeed in convincing his contemporary partners in the discussion to abandon this mistaken usage. Finally, he refrained from making an issue of the matter and conformed to the popular sayings. As the originator behind the major Dutch school on Corporate Communication at the Erasmus University, he thereby advanced a conceptualization, which generated a false expectation. Many followers came to believe that merely changing a logo (a part of the imago, as we will see later) would inevitably result in, or necessarily meant, a change of corporate image.

Not knowing in which context the conceptualization has been developed, one can imagine how the encounter of Dutch and Anglo-Saxon PR-researchers and theoreticians may thus cause all kinds of mutual misunderstandings. Third parties (German, French, or other language speakers) will probably never realize how complex the mixing-up of those ideas and concepts may be. This in its turn is detrimental to international education programmes.

Scientific concepts should not be merely derived from ordinary usage, but they should be chosen in such a way as to reflect logical, semantic and epistemological principles (Silverman 1994: 196–211). The first, being the application of **logical** principles such as mutual exclusiveness. For if one assesses or measures contaminated concepts one will never be able to estimate if their relationship is causal or only semantic. Second, **semantic** principles such as knowledge of the semantic category and the semantic model behind the concept must be considered, because only in this perspective can operationalization be tested accurately. Third, **epistemological** principles such as a clear reference either to concrete phenomena or to early dubbing or to an agreement among a scientific community (Putnam 1977; Donnellan 1977; Evans 1977) must be considered.

SOME QUESTIONS OF MEANING DEVELOPMENT

What we may deduce so far is that we should look to the original sciences than to linguistic communities such as designers or industries for the grounding of PR concepts. In fact, the core-concepts of present day public relations theory are mainly borrowed from the sphere of personality and cognitive psychology. Through **metaphorical reasoning** the PR theoretician compares the organization to an individual person. This brings public relations theory in to the orbit of an 'open-systems theory'. We should be aware, however, of the tacit assumptions behind such reasoning. Metaphors are not just the adoption of verbal expressions, but they are the transfer of a whole series of ideas connected to an original source in order to shed light on a more opaque phenomenon (Boyd 1981). The metaphor is a 'vehicle' to turn an original meaning (a 'tenor') into a new sense (Hawkes 1972: 61–76). If we would realize the wealth of ideas connected to the psychological realm, we would be able to infer several fruitful approaches to public relations theory from it.

The concept of 'image', for example, is derived from the Latin concept 'imago', which united two semantic fields, viz. 'imitari' [to imitate] and 'aemulor' (to strive for) (Muller *et al.* 1963: 422–3). Both fields discriminate the conceptual meaning in specific contexts, but we may also discern an interaction of the two meanings. For instance, a statue (a specific form of imago) is both an imitation of reality and a certain idealization of the object it represents. From its incipience, this duality of meaning has always been connected to the concept-in-use. It need not concern us as long as the concept is used in a realistic sense. But when more virtual (psychological) meanings develop we are obliged to make sharper distinctions.

Although the virtual meanings were known in Latin, the more specific development of this form belongs to the French culture from about 1100 up to about 1800. In the Middle Ages the fourth form of imago, viz. **imagenem**, by which a result is expressed became the indication of the 'product of imitation': l'image. Around 1600 this 'image', which originally had simply referred to concrete statues, pictures and the like, received the more psychic meaning of 'perception'. A hundred years later the connotation of 'conception' was added (Dauzat *et al.* 1971: 382). 'Perception with conceptory elements' forms the basis of the image-concept as it is realized in psychology under a wealth of other names (Denis 1991; pp. 16–17), such as: operant seeing (Skinner), stereotype (Lippmann 1922), and schema (Kant, Bartlett). We will return to this psychological meaning when we examine image-theory below.

The **imago-concept** did not vanish completely, but returned around 1800 in the realm of biology to indicate the adult stage of the butterfly (larva → pupa → imago). It is the full realization of what is hidden inside the origin, the ova (egg) (Mish 1985: 600). A century later it obtained the connotation of 'the manifestation of an – as such – unknowable godhead' in the science of religion. The godhead can only manifest itself in the world of earthlings in disguise – as it were – that is in the form of his imago (or in Greek: his icon). The imago (icon) cannot be seen apart from its origin, but it does not exhaust the latter's essential being (his identity) either (Van der Meiden 1993: 52–6). The purely psychological construction of imago comes with the development of Jungian psycho-analysis. Here it indicates a 'target-image', a return of the striving aspect of the original meaning. Recently, McAdams described the imago in the same sense as 'the idealized and personified image of the self' (Emmons 1989: 88–91). We will adhere to the differential meanings of imago and image when we transfer the psychological constructs to the realm of organizations, companies, associations, administrations, and to their behaviour and impact.

The **identity concept** is straightforwardly derived from the Latin 'identitas' (from: idem = the same and entitas = being; Mish 1985: 597). The etymology which is indicated by Bernstein, who stipulated that an association with 'identidem' (i.e. over and over again) is certainly not correct. Although the idea of identification (the assessment of an identity) is clearly connected to the original concept, it is incorrect to assume that someones identity is **only** in the eye of the beholder. This view seems to be common among designers. Although Bernstein's analysis is in itself an indication of the complexity of the identity concept, he did not follow his own surmise. According to Bernstein's definition, the lemma of identity comprises three entries (1984: 63):

1 the quality or condition of being the same; absolute or essential sameness;
2 individuality;
3 (a sign) that serves to identify the holder.

As indicated before, Bernstein decided to use only the last meaning, whereas the other elements were in his eyes merely indications of qualitative constraints of the identification. The first meaning reminded him of 'the need for consistency', whereas the second indicated its relationship to 'personality'. So he concluded: 'My identity is what I was born with, partly what I have become, but chiefly *what I choose to present*. My identity is largely my concept and image of myself.' (Bernstein 1984: 63 italics in the original). He did not seem to realize how close he was to the modern conception of identity in psychology. Nor did he realize how fruitful it could be to stay close to the original scientific meaning.

As for so many psychological insights, we may fruitfully return to the conceptualization by William James. He attempted to associate the concept of 'Personality' with the concept of 'Identity': 'Personality [or 'self' as he also called these phenomena] implies the incessant presence of two elements, an objective person, known by a passing subjective thought and recognized as continuing in time. Hereafter let us use the words 'me' and I for the empirical person and the judging thought.' (cited in Burns 1981: 6). James himself added a third element to his conception of personality/identity: 'Pretention'. This is a state of self which I strive for, which I want to become. It is my 'ideal self'. This concept corresponds closely to the 'imago concept' if we maintain a short-term perspective. If we take a longer-term view it resembles conceptions as 'ideal' and 'ideality'. The latter sense also plays a role in image-theory.

Instead of the rather philosophical term 'I', the technical concept of 'Ego' is preferred as one of the three constituing parts of Self, besides the 'Me' as indication of self-image (in the tradition of Mead (Mead 1934) and the 'Imago' as indication of the 'Presentation of Self', to use Goffman's terms (Goffman 1959). Thus resulting in a tri-partite composition of personality: ego, me and imago. In an earlier study these three concepts were described as: the 'self as agent', the 'self as object' and the 'self as project', respectively (Rebel 1991: 684–740). The concept of Identity has been superimposed in a systematic fashion to these constructs of Emmons (1989) and of Schlenker and Weigold (1989). There it possesses a meaning that can be described as the 'public elements of self', comprising major elements of 'me' and 'imago', plus the conscious parts of 'ego'. 'Ego' is mere possibility and tendency, while 'identity' is daily actuality. Ind described Identity as the 'sense of self' (Ind 1992: 19).

In the phenomenology of religion it was recognized much earlier that identity and imago are connected inextricably, such that one could not speak of 'identity' without also speaking of 'imago'. However, one should not identify the phenomena either (Van der Meiden 1993: 53). Identity changes when ego, me (self-image) or imago change. This implies that there is a **functional** relation between 'Identity' and its constituent parts. Identity is not only something superimposed on disparate personality elements, but it is the result of their interaction. A summary of the present general scientific understanding of 'self' (personality) is depicted [leaving out most psychological details] in Figure 9.1.

TOWARDS A MODEL OF CORPORATE IDENTITY

A metaphorical theory of corporate identity must start with a discussion on the common concepts in public relations – these were largely derivations from psychological constructs. Many PR concepts were

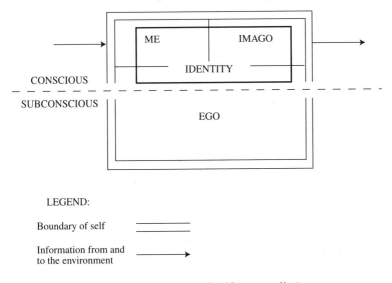

Figure 9.1 The psychological system of self (personality)

metaphorical expressions taken from the domains of several psychological disciplines: cognitive psychology, psycho-analysis and social psychology. It would seem fruitful to systemize those derivations and make them into a coherent whole, however, there are dangers involved when taking over an original concept from a different domain without being conscious of the differences between both contexts. Those differences can be very conspicuous, but may also remain somewhat hidden. Conceptualization with metaphorical meanings must take place in a very prudent manner. Individual personalities and corporate personalities, for example differ quite substantially.

Corporate personalities, for example, may change drastically or even overnight by a merger, a buy-out, a take-over or a bankruptcy in contrast to the average individual personality, that seems to be quite stable (Ind 1992 rev. ed: 28–44). The larger the firm, arguably, the less chance of showing a coherent **imago**. One cannot control every aspect of the organization. Someone's **self-image** may be shattered because of the reception of different interpretations of his actions by his significant-others (friends, colleagues and relatives). A corporate self-image can only be conceived of as a combination reflecting the **set** of individual experiences of the employees with the organization and of their perceptions of the 'generalized outside reactions towards the organization. It is a **shared** internal public image. Finally, the concepts of **corporate structure and corporate culture** must be dealt with, although there were no corresponding psychological constructs in the sphere of 'ego'. However, an analogy of reasoning may be used by taking the original psychological constructs and likening them to sociological concepts. These may then be translated into a corporate situation.

Psychologically, an individual is a member of a **culture** whose elements he has to internalize. Sociologically, an individual contributes to a culture by his and others' patterned actions. In that perspective, the analytical definition of the Dutch sociologists Van Doorn and Lammers seems to bridge the different domains when they described 'culture' as 'The set of norms, values, goals and expectations shared by many and transferable to others' (Van Doorn and Lammers 1979: 108–9). The norms, values, goals and expectations are psychological constructs whereas the ideas of sharing and transfering indicate the sociological part. We may use the idea of 'set' later, when we arrive at the operationalization of our constructs. The idea of **corporate structure** bears no apparent relationship to psychological structures which generally refer to brain functions and regularities of mind (Fodor 1983). Only some vague similarities can be identified, such as: between the biological-genetical substratum of the brain and the foundation and the past of an organization; between differential functions of the brain and the divisionalized or matricized structure of a corporation; and between the nervous transfer of signals and managerial communications.

Finally, it is necessary to redefine the psychological concepts of 'conscious' and 'subconscious' in terms of the more sociological concepts of 'overt' and 'hidden', with their Mertonian overtones of 'manifest' and 'latent' functions (Merton 1949: 63–139). This is a projection of the terminology as developed into the original model of Personality (depicted above) and represents a first approximation of a consistent theory of Corporate Identity.

The identity-concept can now be defined operationally, with the corporate identity being defined as an 'inferred concept' – consists of the logical product of three components:

1 the image which inner publics have of the organization and of its performance in the environment;
2 the public presentation of the organization in **words, deeds** and **physical presence** (the visual cues belonging to the last); and
3 a set of structural and cultural characteristics of the organization, as far as the organizational population is conscious thereof.

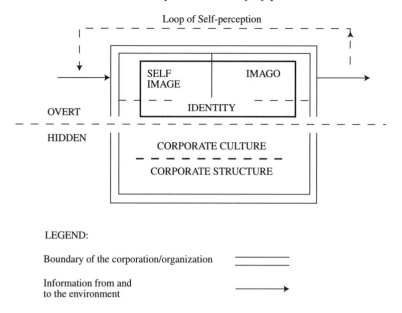

Figure 9.2 A model of corporate identity

Conceptualizing identity as a logical product instead of a logical sum gives rise to the connotation that identity is a kind of **core-personality**. At the same time it points to operations with which a researcher may infer the quality of the identity. From this perspective we can identify and distinguish three typical situations (Vos 1992: 102–4; Ind 1992: 121–4):

1 If there is a large commonality between self-image, imago, structure and culture of the organization, then we identify a **strong identity**. At corporate level the 'unitary or monolithic identity' of corporations like Philips is intended to be a strong identity. But if the corporate culture does not fit such an imago the identity is weakened considerably, such that merely an 'umbrella-identity' remains.

2 If there is only a small overlap between self-image, imago, structure and culture of the organization, then this results in a **weak identity**. At the corporate level most so-called 'branded identities' like Unilever and Pepsico, actually portfolio-holdings, are weak identities. However, in the case of Unilever, the corporate culture is much stronger than would have been expected, probably due to its company history. In such a case an 'endorsed identity' may develop, like the Dutch-Swedish AKZO-Nobel company achieved.

3 If there is no commonality whatsoever between self-image, imago, structure and culture of the organization; then a **split identity** results. A good instance of the last phenomenon would be the umbrella-organizations which can be found in almost all Western countries during the Cold War period: viz. trade agencies as cover-up for the Soviet Russian espionage organization KGB. Other instances are 'diversified identities' grown out of mergers or buy-outs, for example in the UK, Kingfisher plc, present owner of Woolworth (retailer stores), Comet (electrical retailers), Superdrug (chemists), and B & Q (Do It Yourself stores).

This model and classificatory schema has three advantages:

● it is systematic, which makes it suitable for further theorizing, as we will show below;
● it is apt for empirical research by providing operational definitions;
● it may figure in corporate identity programmes as starting point and as target of the internal corporate policy (Ind 1992:113–20).

Although we may infer the corporate identity, we need to 'measure' or 'assess' its constituent parts more directly.

Imago

The concept of imago consists of three broad sets of perceptable phenomena: words, deeds and physical presence. Each of them can be researched with traditional means:

1 **Words** can be **content-analysed** or in its qualitative counterpart **text-analysed**. The universe of words to be analysed may consist of anything from press release to conference texts and public interviews with the CEO.

2 **Deeds** are much more ephemeral than words. Unless patterns of action are recognizable, most deeds are strictly one-off events. If the researcher happens to be present he may observe them, but otherwise we can only get at them indirectly. Unobtrusive methods such as **content/text-analysis** of complaints might be very useful here. Other methods involve **interviewing** specialized publics (customers, financial world, government officials) about their experience with the organization under scrutiny. **Participant observation** of daily routines can be useful, too.

3 **Physical presence** is mainly concerned with the visual presentation of the organization. **Semiotic analysis** can be used for analysing the creative radiation of the firm. The logo and the consistent

use of symbols and colours are meaningful in themselves, but also the condition of the hardware (trucks, engines, buildings) may signify the firm's way of life. Those three aspects can be seen as 'facets' of the imago. By understanding them we can estimate the implicit and explicit messages which the organization sends out to its environment.

Personality

Personality is more difficult to assess than imago, especially the cultural side of it. Culture is the kind of life-style which exists in an organization and it is not very easy to get a good grasp of this rather hazy concept. The structural part, on the other hand, is more easy to detect, albeit that sometimes private owners of a company are reluctant to be candid about the exact juridical construction of ownership.

1 **Structure** as the backbone of an organization can be assessed mainly through **desk research**. The company chart, the official use of documents, the number of official and unofficial meetings, core figures of the industry, the use of diverse channels of communication, etc. can all be assessed through the use of in-company documents, library research, data from the Chamber of Commerce and official branch-statistics. Sometimes an unstructured interview with the board of directors or the CEO will yield additional information and a check on the validity of the data. In this type of **investigative research** triangulation (Denzin 1978) is imperative.
2 **Culture** as the flesh of the organization consists of many subjective experiences in all ranks of the organization. Experiences that can be reduced to the analytical categories of values, norms, goals and expectations. Each of those categories can be operationalized with traditional means, choosing indicators like attitudes (for values), expectancies (for norms), policy measures (for goals), and hidden suppositions (for expectations). In some instances a 'mission-statement' will be a good guide for this endeavour, at least it will be a starting point. **In-depth interviewing** with a purposive sample from the organization will often be the most convenient method of data-collection in this case. However, it will often be impossible to obtain a standardized response to the questions on the interview-guide, as each organization has its own peculiarities. Nevertheless, Geert Hofstede (1980) succeeded in making a cross-cultural comparative study to assess the 'corporate culture' of 40 subsidiaries of the IBM corporation.

Self-image

When we come to the self-image part of identity we must direct our attention to image-measurement in general, for self-images in this context are just images of the organization held by internal publics. They tend not to differ substantially from images of external publics, only in the respect that they will be based more on inside information and direct experience. This implies that they will probably be also more elaborated, more specific, and richer in attributions than the more Gestaltist external public image. For this reason we may resort to a less standardized form of information collection, the semi-structured **open-interview** (used in motivation research). The external images, on the other hand, are mainly researched in a standardized form, unless we deal with a very specialized public, like investors. Sometimes it is possible to make use of press clippings. Exogeneous messages about the organization contribute to the overall impression employees have of their own firm to a substantial degree. It is important to realize what could have been the input into the self-images before one starts to ask specific questions.

Identity

Referring to our discussion of images in general we can assume that the research methods discussed above will provide enough information to infer the identity of the organization. As we already said before, logical reasoning on the basis of our assessment of imago, self-image and personality will suffice to arrive at the corporate identity. When research on image, self-image and personality show considerable overlap, we may assume that the overlap as such will be a good indicator of identity. The elements in this overlap show that the organization has a concrete basis, as such experienced by its members, which is radiated out to the environment. All other elements, not shared, may indicate instances of misperception and/or of window-dressing. A final caveat is necessary here, if one wants to infer an identity; one has to be sure that the measurement/assessment procedures chosen for the three different facets are not contaminated. Pretesting interview-schemes used for this measurement is highly recommended. As a final point, this type of investigation will generally result in a **narrative** rather than in some standardized profile.

TOWARDS A MODEL OF CORPORATE IMAGE AND IDEALITY

The concept of corporate image is much more taken for granted in public relations theory than the identity concept. Almost all authors who tackle the image question seem to be united about the idea that corporate images are receptions of messages about an organization or the result thereof. But this unanimity is absent when more closely inspected, for when social scientists try to interpret the image-concept in social-psychological terms, some of them move into completely opposite directions. For instance, Pruyn (1992) describes (mature) images as a kind of attitude, whereas Grunig (1993) subsumes attitudes under images. Others (Kotler and Fox 1985) describe images as impressions, the sum of beliefs and ideas, whereas still others (Vos 1992: 27) add an evaluative and appreciative element. Some consider them as 'reality based' others as mere 'fancy', some say it is 'public' and others stress it is 'private'. The picture is really quite complex. In this section we will try to work out a systematic view of images from a 'cognitive' perspective. Subsequently, we will elucidate what possible impact a specific kind of message sent by an organization, viz., **ideality**, may have on the 'public' image.

Images

The image concept in psychology has its roots in functional and social psychology. For example, from around the turn of the century the advent of Walter Lippman's 'stereotypes' ('standardized pictures in our heads'), Bartlett's reintroduction of Kantian 'schema' and Tolman's 'cognitive maps' to the domain of perception-research (Denis 1991: 16–17; Lippman 1922; Anderson 1981). However, the first author who looked exhaustively at images was the system-theoretician and economist(!) Kenneth Boulding (1956). In a nutshell he suggested a complete research programme, when he remarked: '... behavior depends on the image. The image is built up as a result of all past experiences of the possessor of the image. Part of the image is the history of the image itself. The meaning of the message is the change it produces in the image' (Boulding 1956: 6–7). Implicitly, he thereby put three major questions on the research agenda:

1 How do images come into being?
2 How can they be influenced?
3 How do they affect behaviour?

The first question falls mainly into the domain of cognitive psychologists, who consider images as Gestalt-like impressions in a framework made up by earlier experiences (Anderson 1990: 243–78; Denis 1991: 16–67; Shanteau 1988; Snodgrass, 1984: 3–22). Images are formed and changed through a combination of **impression** and **imagination.** Impressions are prone to all messages a person may encounter; it is quite unlikely that an observer would only meet imago-like information directly from his employer's voice. Messages in the press, rumour, concurring voices from competitors in the market – besides the words, deeds and physical presentation of an organization – all add up to the impression the observer undergoes (Schultz *et al.* 1993: 114–22).

Imagination comes from within, so to speak. The framework of memory, consisting of earlier experiences within the organization, earlier experiences with other organizations in the same domain (stereotypical reasoning), and analogies and inferences from mundane knowledge together constitute a receptive network for perceptory elements offered daily. The interaction of impression and imagery – often described as 'selective perception' – yields the Gestalts, which we call 'images' (Dretske 1981). Images, therefore, are personal, time-bound and rather inarticulate. Only on thinking through an image, may a person be able to articulate attributory elements. Which elements will surface mainly depends on the interest a person has in an organization. The financial specialist will focus on performance in the market, the future employee on the reputation of the employer, the client on the eventual chance that the firm would cease to exist, etc.

There is one specific aspect that needs to be elaborated a little further. Baskin and Aronoff (1988: 63) consider image as a 'container-concept': 'An organization's image is a composite of people's attitudes and beliefs of the organization.' Grunig (1993) suggests a similar view in a more complex way. He reached the conclusion that we may better refrain from using the image concept, because it is so inarticulate. This approach, however, fails to do justice to the modern cognitive theories which treat images as 'cognitive phenomena' and the present main view of attitudes as 'evaluations', i.e. as affective phenomena (Rokeach 1969; Fishbein and Ajzen 1975; Rajecki 1982). For the same reason we cannot accept Pruyn's approach who subsumes, the other way around, images under attitudes (1992). The main reasoning behind this last view is that images can be measured with the same method as attitudes. The misunderstanding here, is that

both terms are (epistemologically) **disposition terms** (Armstrong 1988: 127–44).
Disposition terms can only be measured or assessed in indirect ways, e.g. statements which ask for a reaction. The difference between a reaction on image-statements and attitude-statements is the answering format. An image-statement is reacted upon with a 'true – false' judgement. In ordinary language we speak of an image **of** an object, which corresponds to external reality. An attitude-statement is reacted upon with an 'agree – disagree' statement. In ordinary language we speak of an attitude **towards** an object, which refers to internal (limbic) reality. Those differences in speech habits, which exist in all European languages, and the distinct domains of reference leave no room for treating the two as identical.

The measurement of images

Images are disposition terms, as we said before. It means that images are never observable directly, but we should be able to 'calculate' the existence of an image from indirect evidence. We also indicated that images are Gestalts, undifferentiated wholes. This means that analytic procedures like scaling will always remain palliative. Images are best assessed through free interview procedures, like asking for **associations** on hearing the name of the organization or seeing its logo. Those associations can be analysed through cluster-analysis procedures, and respondents can be differentiated along their respective images (the *Associative Group Analysis* by Szalay and Mir-Djalali 1991: 213–50).

Other procedures focus on the actual imago which might have been received by the public. These procedures can be of additional value, because they allow for a better comparison because of their standardization and, finally, their reality value might be calculated quite straightforwardly. The two most important techniques in this respect are the '**facet-design**', originally developed by Louis Guttman and later elaborated by his successor Shlomit Levy (1990: 155–79) and the more traditional methods of (multi-dimensional) scaling (Schiffman *et al.* 1981). The difference between these techniques is mainly connected to their first stages of battery construction. The measurement procedures do not differ in a principal way. **Facet designs** are really paper and pencil designs. The researcher tries to elaborate the main characteristics of the image-object and assesses contextual aspects of the characteristics in advance. The logical combination of those aspects (a so-called 'mapping sentence') yields the eventual instrument of measurement.

In the traditional **scaling methods** we proceed by first performing some exploratory interviews or focus groups with key figures from the external publics about their organization's corporate-image. This information is supplemented with the result of an identity study, which examines the corresponding elements of imago, self-image and personality. From both sources a set of statements is drawn, of mixed character: both statements that are objectively true and statements that are objectively false in a known ratio. Four possible combinations might thus emerge: objectively true attributions, subjectively true attributions, objectively untrue attributions and subjectively untrue attributions. By assessing these statements it is possible to estimate the difference between image and identity, and to trace which elements are problematic from the company's point of view. This approach is comparable to the method of the Image Measurement System of the American Opinion Research Corporation, which asks to pick both favourable and unfavourable statements from a set that applies to the firm in question. It is also known as the **cafeteria technique** (Bernstein 1986: 212–15).

Many researchers, however, are not always interested in the relation between identity and image, but seek a means to compare several companies along particular dimensions. Therefore they need to standardize their research instrument. Here a **semantic differential** scale may be used for this purpose. For example, the Corporate Image Barometer used by the Dutch Decision-Makers Survey uses the following image dimensions with a grading format: quality of management, profit/yield, sense of social responsibility, employee friendliness, innovativeness, market orientation, contribution to the country's economy, future expectations regarding the organization, quality of products/services, and active dissemination of information about the company (Vos 1992: 111). One should be careful, however, not to indulge in the temptation to ask evaluative questions, for as we have seen, attitudes are the evaluative phenomena, while images have cognitive characteristics. It is important to separate perceptual from preference data in such research.

Ideality

The concept of 'ideality' is not very common in Public Relations. As far as we can trace its origin, we found Vélu (1988) one of the few to use the idea until recently. From this perspective ideality can be described as the change of identity strived for or, alternatively, the projection of the company's policy goals into the future. As has already been indicated the imago concept bears a halo of idealism. The presentation of a company or an organization, especially when carefully planned, is often slightly better than an insider might perceive it to be. The ideality concept represents the often unrealized aspect of a company which is taken for granted and even propagated. Communicating an ideality has a dual function:

● internally, to present a future perspective which the members of the organization may use as a motive to do something extra;
● externally, to arouse the expectations of stakeholders, opinion-leaders and special publics and, sometimes, to gain some extra time for internal change.

Idealities also have a relationship with images. By being just a projection of ideals, there is no difference between images and imagos in the future. Ideality belongs to the conception of the new identity that exists at the horizon of our consciousness (external) image and (internal) identity. When we approach the desired situation *in vivo* we run the risk that image and identity will fall apart. If insufficient measures are taken to assess the course of our external image, we may soon discover that significant publics have gone off in a different direction. Disappointment about a course of action that held great promise but actually worked out too slowly, or plain rejection (after initial silence: we wait and see) of the direction in which the organization is heading, may lead to severe damage to the (ideal) image strived for. Thus, great care is needed with the overt presentation of a worked out ideality.

Communicating idealities inside an organization can be a motivating force, provided that the organization's members judge it to be realistic. Idealities may seem out of reach to the rank and file member of the organization. Theories of motivation point to the necessity of breaking down the seemingly unattainable goals into a range of clearly recognizable objectives that can be accomplished step by step (Pervin 1989: 7–10; Wright and Brehm 1989: 169–210; Lee, Locke and Latham 1989: 291–326). The possible process in the development of an Ideality is illustrated in Figure 9.3.

In short, by communicating an ideality which substantially differs from the identity of the organization, a CEO may cause an external motivating force. Internally, however, an image may create a motivating force for change. Such motivating forces may lead to attitudinal or behavioural change.

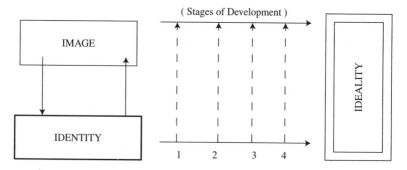

Figure 9.3 Image, identity and ideality in perspective

The measurement of ideality

Ideality is mainly expressed by an organization's decision-making unit, either in public statements or in writing. It is from the analysis of this verbal data that we are able to assess the corporate ideality. **Hermeneutic text-analysis**, especially means-end theory based on Kuypers' *Final Method*, can be a useful research instrument in this respect (Rebel, Postma and Snellen 1993).

TOWARDS AN EXPLANATION OF THE COGNITIVE ROLE OF IMAGES

From the aforementioned analysis, images appear to be important concepts of a theory of change. Two forms of change are important to the public relations theorist and researcher, viz. attitudinal change and incitement to behaviour.

Images and attitudes

The analysis above must not be taken too literally, i.e. images and attitudes should not be seen as completely separate phenomena. On the contrary, in the broad perspective of cognitive science it is quite clear that (rudimentary) images or frameworks always constitute the basis of an attitude. An attitude is 'about' something, and without that 'something' no attitude will ever come into existence. On the other hand, there is not a single element of thought that is not influenced by affective elements, albeit that those elements are not necessarily of the secondary and durable character of attitudes. In many respects images are the counterpoint of attitudes, two sides of the same coin

(Holbrook 1978: 545–56). Recent theories stress the idea that attitudes are 'activated automatically' as soon as a first impression is offered for mental processing (Fazio *et al.* 1986; Dovidio and Fazio 1994). This makes perfect sense if one realizes that on the first preconscious perception – the proto-image – identical messages are processed in a parallel way, both in the cognitive regions (the neocortex) and in the affective regions (the limbic system) of the brain. Recognition and evaluation occur as soon as the outcome of both processes are projected in the same (prefrontal) lobes of the neocortex (Schadé 1984: 168–72; Frijda 1986: 393–4).

The process conjectured in Figure 9.4 seems also to be substantiated by the results of Krosnick and Abelson's recent review of experimental research on attitudes (1994). They inferred from their results that 'attitude strength' is dependent upon three general factors: cognitive elaboration (knowledge, i.e. proto-images); emotional commitment (intensity cum certainty of existing attitudes); and ego-preoccupation (values/needs) (1994: 183). This view of attitudes, in its turn, corresponds closely to the explanation of behaviour that Minsky suggested (see below).

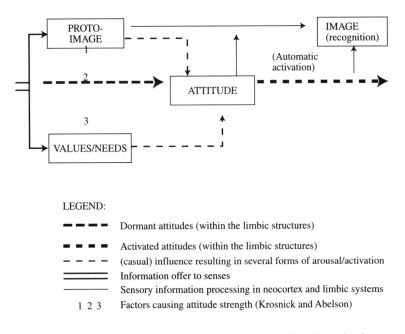

LEGEND:

▬ ▬ ▬ ▬	Dormant attitudes (within the limbic structures)
■ ■ ■ ■	Activated attitudes (within the limbic structures)
– – – –	(casual) influence resulting in several forms of arousal/activation
════════	Information offer to senses
────────	Sensory information processing in neocortex and limbic systems
1 2 3	Factors causing attitude strength (Krosnick and Abelson)

Figure 9.4 The cognitive relations between images, attitudes and values

Images and behaviour

The third question which concerns us relates to Boulding's work on the relationship between images and behaviour. Among most PR theoreticians it seems to be taken for granted that images are a causal factor in the explanation of behaviour. But it is seldom problematized in exactly what way images are a factor in decision-making. Reviewing explanatory research one may see both instances of a quite substantial correlation and of a very poor relationship between images and action.

It seems to be the case that when images are not problematic in view of the values and norms that people hold, there is no reason to behave in a specific way. But when there is a tension between images of reality and one's own conviction about the 'rights' of the situation, there will be a tendency to bring both elements more in line. Motivational tensions (arousal) are supposed to be engendered along those lines. 'Man is a Difference Engine, having "actual inputs" [images] and "ideal inputs" [values and attitudes], the interaction of which leads to reactions to diminish the differences' (Minsky, 1986: 78–9, 165, 175). (Figure 9.4 above illustrates the mechanisms supposed to be active here.)

Three general tactics are used in this perspective:

1 cosmetics (a change of image only showing itself in verbal behaviour);
2 a change in conviction (Festinger's (1957) cognitive dissonance principle – which, parenthetically, is better described as 'affective dissonance' – preceded by actual behaviour); or
3 a combination of the two.

It is for this reason that someone's verbal behaviour often seems contrary to his non-verbal behaviour; they are often opposite movements of the mind. So images may exist which are more or less neutral to behaviour and, at other times, the same images can be quite powerful causative factors. In addition to images, therefore, one should always assess the attitudes, values and norms held by the diverse publics. For instance, a banker possesses norms derived from his financial tradition and if the image of a company is poor in this respect he will probably refuse a loan. But the same attribute, e.g. a high level of wages and salaries, may be an asset in the eyes of the unions. If they are interviewed they probably will utter different opinions (contingent evaluations of their images) about the company. Summarizing the previous analysis requires a general theory of behaviour from a Cognitive (with capital C, i.e. cognitive **and** affective) point of view. Personological theory is devised especially for that purpose (Rebel 1991). A dynamic view on personality marks the essence of personological theory. It starts from three basic assumptions, based on cognitive, brain physiological and emotion-psychological findings:

1 The human mind is hierarchically structured. The lower levels – containing attitudes, memory frames, needs and values – serve as regulators (e.g. selectors), moderators (e.g. executors), and motivators (enhancing or blocking the information process); the top level – containing perceptions, images and judgements (interpretations) and intentions – harbours the mechanisms of information processing, among which the process of opinion formation.

2 The lower levels are generally formed in earlier periods of life. Youth experiences constitute the basis of our value system, whereas attitudes are more the fruit of adolescence and formal tertiary learning.

3 The flow of information at the upper level is characterized by a process of mental calculation, triggered by arousal. An immediate reaction to information input in the form of **expressive behaviour** will only occur with high arousal. In case of intermediate to low arousal a fully blown decision-making (information) process will normally set in.

The outcome of this information process – any form of behaviour – is always characterized by three modes of duration: **choice or decision**; (n.b. opinions are considered to be a kind of verbal decisional behaviour, an act of reasoning) **habits** (or roles); **life style.**

Images play the role of realistic yardstick in this theory, which makes them much less mythical than in most PR theories. They are the core of what W. I. Thomas called 'The Definition of the Situation' – an expression which became common wisdom in Symbolic Interactionism.

It should be clear by now that mere image measurement is of very limited use to a principal. It should at least be accompanied by the assessment and measurement of the core values which specialized publics hold in the situation in which they meet the company in question. This latter topic is the main interest of stakeholder and opinion-leader research in the 'issue-management' tradition in public relations (Ferguson 1994: 69–73, 88–9). On the other hand, researchers who devise image scales that go beyond the mere cognitive domain run the risk of missing the main motivating factors by

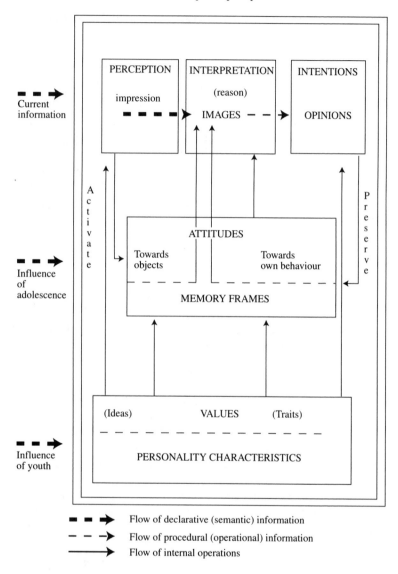

Figure 9.5 The role of images in the personological model

blurring the distinction with affection and neglecting the attitudinal evaluative powers of individuals.

SKETCHES OF A NORMATIVE PR-THEORY

Finally, we must weave the threads together to form a substantial picture. Identity (imago, self-image and corporate structure and culture), public image and ideality, arguably constitute the main substance of a normative theory of public relations. Given their different origins and their functioning in different scientific domains, we must be aware not to overstretch their meanings. Metaphorical reasoning is powerful, but potentially dangerous. Nevertheless, we will try to develop a consistent proto-theory of PR behaviour and its leading principles.

Every organization strives for (or perhaps should strive for) a consistent and strong identity. A strong identity is a considerable advantage in the public domain where one has to compete for scarce goods such as financial resources, human resources, raw materials (whether substances or political support) and adequate information. A trustworthy identity gives a legitimation to the acts of a company (Jensen 1992). But the question remains of how one can build such an identity, or in more technical terms how can one implement an **identity-programme**? Identity-programmes should be devised to co-orientate the three basic constituing elements of identity: self-image, imago and corporate personality.

Here we must start with the corporate structure. The origin of the firm, the ownership, the company's present performance and the company's overall organizational structure are the most solid elements of the corporate identity. If we were to identify an organization from the outside we would, presumably, start with these aspects (Ind 1992: 63–72). In the daily working routines these aspects are usually taken for granted, unless someone has a reason to doubt the solidity of them. The origin of the firm could be widely misunderstood. The ownership of the firm may still be in the hands of the original founders or their offspring, but their contribution to the daily business may have been reduced to insignificance. Dynamic employees may experience the structure as hampering an adequate exchange of information. The performance may be less than could have been expected in their market, etc.

After an examination of the cultural elements, and if doubts exist, it is necessary to try to bring the various elements in line through a personality programme. The philosophy of Total Quality Management could be such a programme, but other programmes will do as well as long as they allow or stimulate an unconditional dialogue between people considered each other's equal, to paraphrase Habermas. It is a programme of 'getting the basics right' in very direct sense. The next step in the identity programme would be to bring all the external presentations in line with the corporate personality. It is a programme of using a creative concept to symbolize the presentation in an appropriate style. This is the designer's part of an imago-programme.

At the same time there should be ample attention to the external communications. How diverse are all the official utterances, from press-releases to conferences, from answering the telephone to an official letter? Can they be co-ordinated such that the organization gets a monolithic outlook, at least in this respect? The content of the messages should reflect the reality of the firm to a very high degree, even if there is no reason (yet) to be proud of the organization's performance. A careful presentation of the 'ideality' might give some room for a programme of change here. The openness and the honesty of the organization can, in due course, gain the trust of all important audiences.

This programme is also known as 'corporate communications' and need not be discussed here, for there are several excellent studies in this respect (Bernstein 1986: 167–205; Ind 1992: 149–75; Van Riel 1992 Chapters 4–6). Corporate communications is geared towards implementing a fitting corporate image and not a favourable corporate image at all costs. But can the image be influenced significantly? We have seen, that besides the corporate's communication, media, rumour and history, all exert their respective influence and even the cleverest communicator will never succeed in controlling the eventual outcome. The public image stands on its own. This fact urges a third procedure to which we turn now.

The final element over which organizations want to try to exercise control is the set of self-images of all ranks of the corporation. This implies both the perspicuity of the organization as such and of its performance in the world at large. The latter should not be restricted to its financial performance only, but should extend to its social and environmental responsibilities as well. The employees should feel responsible for all the output of the firm, even their waste and pollution. (The Dutch chemical concern DSM (1993) has recently started a programme in this vein.) The resulting self-image should correspond quite closely to the corporate personality and to the corporate imago. A necessary basis for this self-knowledge is the type of systematic external research programme, concerning issues, public opinion and the public relations, called an Environmental Intelligence System (Ferguson 1994: 12–22). Besides this environmental research, there is the need for regular internal readership surveys and research of the corporate morale. But the latter should only be set up after the implementation of the other elements of the identity programme.

The final task should be to balance all three basic factors into a single **strong identity**. A formidable task indeed which asks for much endurance, patience and an open mind. It is the never-ending story of those responsible for the total communication efforts of an organization. It requires the organization of the communication where responsibilities are clear and coherent. Perhaps one could think of what has been called somewhat ironically a 'communication czar' as a central co-ordinator (Schultz *et al.* 1993: 165–8).

With this sketch of a normative theory of corporate communications and public relations we end our overview of the problems connected to a 'grounded' PR theory. Empirical research in this respect does only partially have the quality of 'testing' the theory. An important part of the normative theory consists of a free exchange of views among all 'interested' who will scrutinize its values (to take an Habermasian expression again). Research is indeed intimately connected to the programme suggested above, either as a test for the attitudinal and behavioural explanation in the empirical part or as a necessary carrier of information to, from and within the system in the normative part of the theory.

SOME FINAL REMARKS ON THEORY AND METHOD

In the previous pages we developed a theoretical system for public relations. Because our point of departure was the conceptual structure of the envisaged theory, we were able to connect both epistemological and methodological principles in a single design. The resulting system consists of two aspects: a reasoned proposition and an empirical theory. The empirical theory that can be falsified or corroborated belongs to the domain of psychology. But it can be tested in public relations, as well as in other applied circumstances. Communication science, as the application of both pure social sciences to the domain of the exchange of messages, may thus yield some empirical theories.

But communication science is also characterized by the existence of normative constructions, e.g. public interest theories of the media landscape (Blumler 1992). Public Relations, if it is a science at all, will seldom produce empirical (or basic) theories itself, but will mainly deal with normative questions. That is why we speak of the foregoing normative part of the theory as a reasoned proposition, about which opinions may differ. The main test of this part of our theory then will be a pragmatic one, viz. does it help in understanding, in research and in corporate policy? If it does, it should be added to the range of accepted models. Given the research experience of our students with parts of the system, we are reasonably confident that it will turn out to be a useful approach (Skotnicki 1991; Grote and Labeur 1994).

10 Legitimacy and strategy of different companies: A perspective of external and internal public relations

Inger Jensen

ABSTRACT

In this chapter a conceptual framework is presented for differentiating companies concerning their strategic concept and legitimacy and for focusing on different types of relationships between the employee and the company. It is argued that building up a strategic concept of a company means building up a legitimate field of activities for the company. Moreover, it is stated that the legitimacy of different companies has different kinds of basis in the process of meaning formation. Some companies find their legitimacy referring directly to the quality of human life, whereas other companies have to refer to the legitimacy of a larger system, like the economical system in society or the system of law and administration. Private organizations can be organized on a scale according to whether the prevalent goal is profit making or the usefulness of the products or services offered by the company. Another scale can be described relating to the degree to which the activities of the company are legitimated by referring to substantive qualities of human life conditions or to the functionality of a broader system in society. An analytical model is presented to clarify possible forms of employee involvement in specific companies. It is argued that employee involvement in the social values influenced by the company is of special interest as it links internal and external public relations.

INTRODUCTORY CASE

A private Danish company, 'Falck's Redningskorps' has for generations been recognized as a company specializing in a variety of services like ambulance service and transportation of patients, fire suppression, fire salvage, breakdown and auto assistance service, rescue service and so on. The customers are the public sector as well as private persons who normally pay a subscription for different services adjusted to personal or family needs. The concept of the company has been very clearly defined and connected with helping people in a variety of situations where they would otherwise be helpless. The service delivered by the company has been of high quality and have high credibility. A few years ago, however, the company announced that it was going to introduce an upper age limit for new subscriptions to its services. The public reaction was prompt. If the company was to live up to its own image or concept as a company helping and rescuing people, it was not allowed to exclude a specific segment of customers who could be foreseen to have a special need for assistance. The case was interesting, because it would have been a legitimate decision for a private company to make. And it was not the group of older people, who were directly affected, who started complaining. It was all kinds of citizens who made statements such as if Falck was to enjoy the recognition of being some kind of outstanding company within this field of services, it was not acceptable to exclude a potentially uneconomical group of customers. Economic problems, if any, were to be solved in other ways. The company decided to respond to public opinion and did not implement the strategic change.

This little example can serve as an illustrative point of departure for the subject matter of this chapter. It illustrates that questions of legitimacy are closely connected to the strategic concept of a company; that legitimacy is not identical with legality; that companies are evaluated by other publics than the people directly afflicted and this is at the core of public relations; and as the employees in the case company were influenced by the criticism of the company, even those whose jobs or functions were not at all influenced by the proposed change, it illustrates some aspects of employees' involvement in the strategic goals of the company, which I am going to explore in this chapter.

PREFACE

In service producing companies a great part of the internal communication is concerned with updating the front-line personnel so that they are able to deliver a quality product. For instance, in a bank there are often on-going changes in conditions – interests, new products, new regulations, fiscal changes and events that make it necessary to update every employee. All these events make it necessary to have a well-functioning internal information department. But the examples mentioned are all focused on the employees' relation to the process of service production. To sum up, some part of what is called internal public relations is in fact service management. Another part of what is called internal public relations could be identified as having a human relations function, which means that it focuses on the recognition that employees engage somehow in the social affiliation to colleagues. Another focus point of internal public relations is that employees are a source of information about processes and procedures in the company which could improve effectiveness and productivity. A dialogue about what is really going on and what could be done in much better ways is the core of some theories of internal public relations.[1] Closely related to theories of public relations are some theories of human resource management. A typical focus in this tradition – even if it is not a coherent tradition – is that the more the production is dependent on employees' qualifications, responsibility and initiative, the more important it is to take care of this resource. But theories of human resource management are mostly concerned with developing the right qualifications, the most motivating course of career, motivating employees to take part in decisions concerning the level of organization to which they belong and facilitating knowledge and the flow of information in the company about process and product problems. What is not systematically recognized is that employees potentially are affected by being a member of a company. This means that they can feel proud of, indifferent to, or embarrassed by the overall mission of the firm. In the perspective of public relations it would be important to identify the legitimate field of action that has been built up by the company in interaction with groups and institutions outside the company. And it is important to get an impression of how this legitimate field of activities is rationalized. What are the reasons for the existence of the company? Which groups and institutions accept these reasons as theirs? Do the employees accept these reasons? Do they understand them and would they let their friends and family know these reasons? What happens if they are embarrassed by the general goal of the company? Will employees in the future be content with having a job that gives them money to live on, some satisfaction of being good at something, nice surroundings and good social conditions, but not taking an interest in the ultimate goals of the company of which they are a members. I believe that we are going to witness a future where one of the basic human rights will be to know the meaning of the work that occupies such a considerable part of everyone's life.

It is well documented how professional employees identify with norms and standards formed during their professional education. It is recognized that professionals are attracted to companies that can live up to their professional standards, and it is likewise known that it is a source of conflict if the standards of the company don't fulfil the standards of the professionals. What has not been explored, however, is the degree to which employees in general are involved in the goals of the company.

THE CONCEPT OF LEGITIMACY

It is well known, and a part of western democratic culture, that public institutions must be able to legitimize their policy and operations – although this is not always easily done. It is a more recent phenomenon historically, however, that private companies are held responsible for their existence in society. In accordance with the idea of liberal economy, it was supposed to be a task for the market to decide if a company should survive. Thus, it was thought to be left to investors, suppliers, and customers to make decisions based on private interest and preferences. From this perspective a company was legitimate if it was successful in the market and respected a few regulations of the state. Theories of legitimacy are therefore normally concerned with legitimacy of power exercised by government. The basic assumption in these theories is that legal power is not necessarily supported by custom and general normative ideas. Legal power is not automatically legitimate.[2] To be legitimate, power must be exercised by an agent who is empowered with authority within a certain field of action. This agent is given the authority by the very agents who are at the centre of the exercising of the power. This means that they, based on normative, ideological values, empower an authority within a limited field of action. The empowering agents enable and restrict the legitimate empowered authority.[3] The way the concept of legitimacy is used in this chapter related to private companies is not that closely related to the concept of power. At least not in the narrow meaning of exercising power towards other persons who accept this act of power. The kind of legitimacy concept used in this chapter is a broader one but with the same social mechanisms. A specific company is legitimate to specific groups of actors in society if these actors in general, recognize and accept that the company exercises control over those activities that are related to the concept. This means that the company is an accepted agent within a specific legitimate field of action which at the same time enables and constricts activities. This field of activities is developed through an interaction of, or maybe a struggle about, the concept that the company formulates for its activities and the values which form the basis of the opinion formation process through which the company generally is evaluated.[4] Once a legitimate strategic concept has been established the company is held responsible to be loyal to its own concept and to stick to the legitimate field of actions. It means that for instance a bank, a furniture factory and a humanitarian organization would all have very different, specific legitimate fields of actions. This is common sense, but this tacit knowledge is not explored within the literature of strategic management or public relations. It would be fruitful to develop this knowledge. When the Danish company Falck's Redningscorps wanted to restrict the access of older people to their service, the legitimate field of action connected to the strategic concept was surpassed. A company could not deliberately surpass its field of actions, but the field can be developed actively, if the company is aware of the specific base of values on which the legitimacy should be built. The concept of 'goodwill' is an economic expression of what a buyer is willing to pay for the fact that the company has established a legitimate field of competent action and credibility as a public relationship between the company and relevant groups of agents. Calling it a 'public relationship' refers to the fact that these agents don't act solely on the basis of private preferences, but also as citizens evaluating the company's freedom to act in society. This is an informal public evaluation of private freedom of action. Saying that a company is legitimate in society means that important, relevant and influential groups or institutions accept that the company has a certain field of activities where it is considered a relevant, competent and authorized actor. At the same time it means that they are not able to act legitimately within a completely different field.

Legitimate fields of activities

Building up a successful strategic concept could be considered a process of building up a legitimate field of activities. Figure 10.1 illustrates this field. Within the field of activities different issues or values can be identified, issues or values influenced by the activities of the company. The line around the field marks the limit of accepted activities. It is evident that this limit is not necessarily the same for different publics. Thus in principle a specific field of legitimate activities could be drawn for each of the publics actively involved in the process of meaning formation related to the company. It is important, therefore, to identify the rationales and standards held by

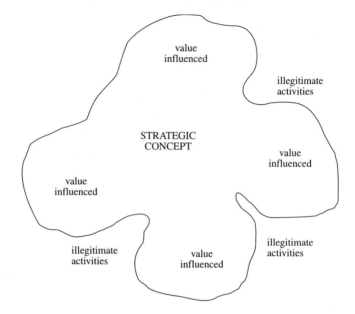

Figure 10.1 Legitimate field of activity

different relevant publics. From my point of view the most interesting way of studying publics is to take specific issues as a departure point and analyse which publics cluster around any one issue, which rationales and standards they hold, and to identify eventual contradictions or consensus. Through this kind of analysis it would become clear where the possibilities for social consolidation of a strategy exist and where the potential crises might emerge. In principle it would be possible to draw the limits of unquestionable or acceptable activities common for every public involved. Maybe this would be a broad field, or on the other hand it may be a very narrow field. Beyond this area of acceptable activities there are more controversial fields where the positions of different publics vary or perhaps conflict with each other. Figure 10.2. illustrates important communicative relationships which could be activated about an issue. The focus in this model is the rationale and standard held by the corporation, different external publics and by different groups of employees. One of the difficulties in making this kind of analysis is that questions of legitimacy can be expressed openly, but it can also be taken for granted as something evident until the moment where the legitimate limit is passed and the limits can be seen. A method of research, ethnomethodology,[5] could

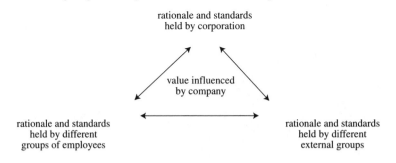

Figure 10.2 Communicative relationships

be used for this type of analysis as some kind of natural experiment before a crisis develops. Within ethnomethodology, imagined critical activities are used in interviewing and it is a sort of verbal testing of the limits.

To understand further the legitimacy of different types of strategic concepts of companies, some analytical distinctions must be made:

- the balance between economic objectives and substantive objectives;
- the reference of legitimacy to systems or to life world;
- the complexity of the base of legitimacy.

The balance of economic and substantive objectives.

Every company produces something or has some kind of function. This could be called the substantive goals or the qualitative side of the company. And every company has some kind of economic goal. Profit can be the dominating objective, whereas the substantive goals are subordinated. Contrary to this, the economic goals can be a subordinated means to the realization of substantive ends and functions. A continuum can be described concerning the relative importance of economic and substantive goals. At one end there are companies where the one and only objective is making a profit, regardless of the specific field of production involved. At the other end are companies where the dominating objective is some kind of mission to which the economic income and economic calculations are completely subordinated to the mission. In between these two extremes a broad variety of companies is found with more or less well-defined products and services as substantive objectives and varying balances between economic and substantive goals characteristic

Figure 10.3 The strategic concepts of companies: the balance between economic and substantive objectives

to the strategic concept (see Figure 10.3). This continuum replaces the dualistic distinction between profit and non-profit organizations.

It is interesting however, that whether a company is legitimate or not is not connected to this scale in a simple way. Very legitimate companies are found close to the abstract profit-making end of the scale and rather illegitimate organizations are found close to the mission end of the scale like, for instance, new Nazi organizations or extreme religious societies. Thus, to understand what constitutes legitimacy of a company it is necessary to go into the kind of reasoning or rationales on which a certain concept is legitimized in society. If we look at a pension fund, it is obvious that the dominating objective for this organization is to ensure that the economic value of the fund will rise or at least not fall until the day the members grow old and will retire from work. It has, however, become common that pension funds make some investment policies based on the position, that is not completely indifferent about where the money comes from. There is for instance a tendency to invest in companies which act in a responsible way towards the environment, or which take employment into consideration. For example, a few years ago pension funds eschewed investment in companies involved in South Africa. With these kinds of investment policies the strategic concept of pension funds can be seen to be moving a little step closer to the mission end of the scale. But it also clear that it would be outside the legitimate field of action if a pension fund spent all the members' money on some otherwise very good and social mission. Thus, to be legitimate a pension fund must stick to a certain position of balance between substantive and economic objectives. It is expected to have profit as the dominating goal. And the rationale is that in the capitalist society the only way of accumulating or augmenting the value of money is to invest them in profit-making activity.

The other end of the scale could be illustrated by a topical Danish case, The Society for the Prevention of Cancer. It is a private fund aiming at curative as well as prophylactic research and information about cancer. The organization has experienced a legitimacy crisis because it has been very successful in fund-raising due to the widespread recognition of the objective of the organization. But the public has criticized it as the fund was growing enormously while the amount of money spent on relevant activities was unacceptably low. There were, however, no accusations of corruption or of persons following private goals. The legitimacy crisis was solely concerned with that economic objectives and substantive objectives were not in harmony with the strategic concept of the organization. By implication this organization should stick rather closer to the mission end of the scale to be legitimate, quite the opposite of the pension fund.

In the middle of the scale a lot of companies are found that make commonly recognized, 'neutral' industrial and consumer goods and services. They are companies whose goods and services have unmistakable quality. Such companies have relatively uncomplicated strategic businesses. They are legitimate in so far as they are responsible to environment and employees and their methods are reliable. The legitimacy of these companies is predominantly determined by the way consumers respond to them in the market.

Within the financial sector a wide diversity of firms is found with strategic concepts ranging from predominantly profit oriented to more substantially defined services, building societies, forms of assurance, financial guarantee etc. The legitimacy of an assurance company is typically dependent on credibility of the services and that the profit goal is combined with objectives of research and prevention of accidents and damages.

Companies and organizations with dominating substantial objectives are held responsible for the ethical and social value of their strategic concept. There are specific demands on harmony between mission and economy. There are public norms of acceptable methods of fund-raising and norms of how competitive humanitarian organizations may be to each other. And there are standards of acceptable financial administration.

By means of a number of examples, it has been shown that the legitimate field of activities for a company with a specific strategic concept implies a certain balance of the economic and substantial objectives. Furthermore, it has been emphasized that legitimate as well as illegitimate strategic concepts can be found all along the described continuum of economic versus substantial goals.

In the section below the substantial objectives of different firms will be discussed a little further.

The reference to system or to life world

Looking at the substantial side of different companies, whatever the content of their activities, it becomes evident that there is an interesting difference in what their legitimacy refers to. Let us compare two firms like the Danish rescue company, Falck, described above and a stock company. They are both specialized service producing firms. In the Falck case the service is directly related to some ideas of welfare and life-saving qualities: they have specialized in giving effective help in emergency situations. Its mission is easy to see and explain. The stock broker company has specialized in the service of selling and buying stocks and shares on behalf of clients. The legitimacy of this kind of service can be explained by the fact that we have a specific kind of financial market that is not easily understood by laymen. This can be a reason for the existence of a company that can analyse the market and mediate between investors and companies, between lenders and borrowers. Thus the legitimacy of the substantive service of a financial company depends on the legitimacy of the economic system in society in general. The justification of the existence of a stock broker company refers to the functionality of the company within a broader system that itself must be justified by explanations as to why this economic system and not another system fulfils the demands of society. It has now become clear that both kinds of services can be justified by reasons that refer to images of human life and the good society. But in the case of the rescue company this connection is much clearer and more direct in the mind of employees who produce the service and of other persons evaluating the legitimacy of the company. In the case of the stock broker company the explanation in everyday thinking will normally end with a technical functional reference to a wider system. It can be pointed out analytically that some strategic concepts get their legitimacy directly by referring immediately to 'life-world values' about human life and society, whereas other strategic concepts – due to an elaborate institutional labour division – are predominantly explained and justified by referring to a wider system, the economic system in society.[6] This difference can be illustrated as an analytical continuum of justifications of the substantive goals of companies indicating whether it refers to system or to life world immediately (see Figure 10.4).

The complexity of the base of legitimacy

In some of the discussion above the matter has been simplified as if the questions of legitimacy are agreed on in general in society. In the description of the legitimate field of actions, however, it was mentioned that different agents and institutions would set the limits of this field differently. Different groups enable and constrain the company in different ways. It might be valuable to make a distinction as follows:

- relatively neutral companies;
- normative but unambiguous fields of business;
- normative and complicated fields of business.

Relatively neutral companies are those in which the process of meaning formation is mainly left to the market decisions, i.e. are considered questions of private preferences.

Normative but unambiguous fields of business are those that are normatively evaluated, positively or negatively, but generally in a homogeneous way.

Normative and complicated fields of business include companies where several and perhaps conflicting normative issues are involved in the strategic concept, or companies where different important groups disagree radically on their normative criteria regarding the legitimacy of the concept.

The pharmaceutical industry has companies varying from neutral to normative complicated fields of business. Production of diet

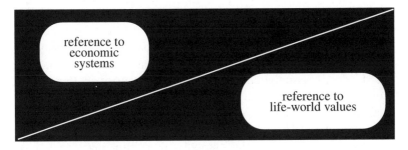

Figure 10.4 The reference of legitimacy to systems or life-world

supplements, for example compressed bran, will normally be left to market decisions. Production of vital medicine, on the other hand, attracts more attention from many sides regarding satisfactory testing, ethical use of animals, gene technology, pricing, marketing etc.

So far this chapter has focused on describing what can be seen as the legitimate field of activities for companies. The balance of economic and substantive objectives has been stressed. It was held that companies, to a varying degrees are justified by referring to their life-world or system. And finally, a variation regarding the complexity of the base of legitimacy has been highlighted. Attention will now be focused on employees' relations to work and to the implication of being a member of a company.

IMAGES OF HUMAN WORK

The relationship between man and his work has been conceived in many different ways in theory and in everyday thinking. Quite contradictory images of work are found simultaneously and a presentation of these images could be useful in understanding what it means to people to be a working member of a company.

Completely instrumental work

In Marxist theories it is held that capitalists, in principle, are not at all interested in the specific field of investment but only in the possibility of accumulating capital. Correspondingly, wage earners are in principle considered not interested at all in the results of the work. What they do in the working process is exclusively a means for them to earn their living. In this view there is no common interest between employers and employees. On the contrary, they are in conflict about the amount of money paid for the work done by the workers. In this conception workers don't work for other reasons than for financial reward. It does not include the possibility that workers could be involved in the working process or in the goals of the company.

For example, Taylor's theories of management are fundamentally based on this assumption. The art of management in this line of thought is therefore to minimize the conflict by inventing scientific methods of measuring the appropriate amount of money for a specific element of work. This principle, payment by the piece or by results, is based on the conception that the only, or dominating incentive, to work is money. And the very implementation of this principle has had a tendency to confirm this assumption like the most militant part of trade unionism.

Empirically, however, not all capitalists are understood to be just capitalists, as not all wage earners are to be understood to be just wage earners. Managers of companies are often well paid employees. Employees can be shareholders and important investors are wage earners. Entrepreneurs can be fascinated by developing their products, and employees can be proud of their professional achievement, or find aesthetic qualities in their working process.

Even Marx was aware that to be successful the capitalist must show some interest in the needs of the customers as an instrument for making profit. Similarly, it was considered necessary for the workers to be aware of the materials they handle, not the least to protect their own body and working abilities. In this way, workers often show, instrumentally, some kind of awareness and interest in the substance of the working process.

Necessary sensitivity

Klaus Ottomeyer (1977) has elaborated this view. According to him, modern working relationships are characterized by increasing labour division and increasing mental work, whereas manual work is declining. His position is that jobs nowadays demand that the employee is willing to engage fundamental parts of his personality as instruments for earning his living. Thus, different jobs demand that different parts of the personality are instrumentally activated. Accountants, sales personnel, air hostesses, social workers, policemen and public relations practitioners must be able to use different parts of their potential personalities instrumentally at their job. This demands a complicated and disciplined regenerating process on the part of the employee to reproduce the ability to present these personality traits day after day. From this perspective, the involvement of the employee in the results of their work is considered an instrumental sensitivity, rather than genuine or personal commitment.

Instrumentally humanized work

The Human Relations school of management is, generally speaking, representative of the idea that money is the primary motivation in work. This school of thought realizes, however, that several additional conditions like the physical and the social environment can provide secondary motivation or compensation for workers. Thus comfortable rooms, social and cultural arrangements, influence or autonomy at the working process level, healthy and clean environment, correct working positions and socially friendly and comfortable arrangements are used as ways of motivating workers. From this perspective good work is work that takes place under conducive social conditions. Such motivating factors may be particularly important where the work is alienating or offers little chance for genuine involvement.

Calling and meaningful occupation

Beside these images of human work described above, quite different images are represented in narratives and historical accounts. We all know of accounts of people who spend, by their own will, all their energy on some impressive, valuable and outstanding mission or achievement. We all know about characters like Florence Nightingale, Jeanne D'Arc, Socrates, outstanding artists, sports heroes, polar adventurers and so on. And we have heard stories about job creation programmes where young people are hired to do quite meaningless jobs. The essence of all these accounts is that we are fascinated by people who have a calling, and meaningless work is generally not seen as worthy for human beings.

In several theories critical of the alienation of work, there is some presumption that within human nature there is the potential for a spontaneous, not alienated involvement in productive activities. Some of these theories refer to descriptions of ancient, so-called natural societies like the kind of social and working system of the Eskimos. Or theories refer to some desired utopia in the future where human work is meaningful, not alienating.

Maslow's theory of motivation assumes that human motivations are hierarchically structured. He holds that when more basic needs of nourishment, physical comfort, social affiliation and trust are steadily satisfied, human beings will develop higher level needs, like the need for achievement and self-realization.

In theories of management it is frequently claimed that in post industrial society manual work is to a high degree overtaken by machines, whereas mental work is concerned with the production of service and knowledge. In this context, companies are clearly more dependent on their employees identifying with the firm.

GENUINE IDENTIFICATION WITH CORPORATE OBJECTIVES?

Is a new relationship developing between employees and the company? Is a new relationship emerging where employees identify genuinely with the objective of the company and not, as previously described, just as a necessary instrumentalization of personality traits? If this is the case, there is no doubt that this would be a source of productivity to an array of companies within service and knowledge industries. Is it true, however, that employees can identify personally with the company, rather than just a management dream aimed at instrumentally by means of charismatic leaders and compensating wage and working conditions?

completely instrumental and alienated work	>>>>> ? >>>>>	genuine involvement and identification with the company

FORMS OF WORK INVOLVEMENT

To be able to give a more detailed answer to this question, it might be valuable to distinguish between different types of work involvement. These types are not mutually exclusive. They are found in a variety of combinations where they influence each other mutually.

Pay

When pay is absolutely the only kind of work involvement, the relation between the employee and the company is a purely instrumental relationship. Dimensions of stability and guarantee of income are included in this category as well as all compensating goods that otherwise must be bought for money.

Skilled or professional achievement

This type of involvement is related to the ability of mastering a specific field of activities and problems, to master the techniques and methods, to be able to solve technical problems and contribute to technically well-functioning products. Here technique should be conceived very broadly and is found in every discipline like skilled work, engineering work, economy, social sciences, medical sciences as well as law, medicine and art.

Aesthetics

This type or aspect of involvement is related to working processes or production that could be a source of fascinating experiences. Aesthetics must be understood in a very broad sense and the criteria is related to the person's individual experience. Thus, an example could be the precision turner's experience of beauty of his material; it could be the smell and the finish of the cabinetmaker's work, the fascination of the composition of a press photo, the absorption in sounds, forms, colours, smell, taste and texture. To this category can be added more abstract, intellectual experiences like 'aha-experiences' when something complicated becomes clear, the elegance of a plot in a drama or a way of doing something.[7]

Working community

Within this type of involvement are included forms of job satisfaction and motivation which are related to a sense of fellowship or community spirit and affiliation to colleagues and fellow workers. Empirically it is evident that community spirit or solidarity among employees is a dimension of involvement of its own character that is not directly connected with the objectives of the company. In fact, in some companies it can be effective directly in opposition to these goals.

Social value

This form includes involvement related to the employee's conception of contributing to something humanistic, ethically or socially important – that problems are solved or something desirable becomes possible. The specific contribution can be of very different kind. It may be midwife work, development of telecommunication, improvement of traffic safety or the work of the dustman or the undertaker. The criterion is that at the psychological level, the employee is involved with his job, due to a conviction of doing something socially meaningful and valuable.

It is important, however, to realize that the forms of involvement mentioned above are of different level and character. In cases when pay is the only form of involvement the working relation is quite abstract. It is an interest in the general power represented by the pay, namely the spending power. That means that when pay is the only form of involvement it does not imply any identification either with the working process itself or with the strategic concept of the company. It is nevertheless evident that pay could never be completely unimportant to a wage earner, as his existence depends on it. Nevertheless, there are considerable variations regarding the relative importance to the individual employee of the five forms of involvement. To some people pay is a priority, others identify with professional or skilled achievement, involvement in the working community, the aesthetics and the social values of work. Correspondingly, companies vary regarding the possibilities of involvement they offer to employees other than pay.

Involvement in skilled or professional achievement or aesthetics is typically related to the employee's own working process and is not necessarily related to any identification with the company. An accountant, for instance, can very well devote himself professionally and aesthetically to the production of perfect accounts without any eye for what the company otherwise makes.

Involvement due to the social meaning or value of the work can be related to the employee's own working process, but this is not necessarily so. The canteen personnel in a factory that produces highly developed plastic equipment for hospitals could identify with the company because they evaluate the products and their purpose positively.

The working community can be detached from the substance of the work and the concept of the company, or it can be closely connected to it. It must be evident that the working community is of a different character whether the sense of fellowship exists in spite of lack of a common working project, or it has emerged as a result of a common project that includes professional achievement, aesthetic qualities or is socially meaningful.

Empirically, some jobs have the potential to offer all five forms of involvement. A biochemist, for instance, who works on developing an enzyme that could make the use of chlorine unnecessary in the chapter mills, could presumably receive reasonable pay, a professional challenge, the satisfaction of belonging to a team that works together on a socially important project, and he could possibly gain some aesthetic experiences through his work. There are other jobs, however, that hardly offer little opportunity for any of the five forms of involvement, like cheap house building on a bad contract.

Figure 10.5 indicates if the five different forms of involvement are necessarily contingent on the employee's identification with the

	Depends on identification with working process	Depends on identification with strategic concept
Pay	no	no
Skilled or professional achievement	yes	no
Aesthetics	yes	no
Working community	no	no
Social value	no	yes

Figure 10.5 The dependency of employee involvement on identification

working process respectively with the strategic concept of the company.

It has now become clear that the question about genuine involvement and identification with work is a complex matter. From the perspective of internal public relations it would be useful to know what kinds of involvement are found in a specific company by different groups of employees and what kinds are lacking. Are the involvement forms related to the working process or not? Are the employees concerned with social values influenced by the activities of the company or why not? If they were, would employees be proud or embarrassed? Involvement in social values is especially important to public relations and is the form that links internal and external public relations, because employees take part in building up the legitimate field of actions of the company.

INVOLVEMENT IN DIFFERENT FORMS OF COMPANIES

Figure 10.6 is an analytical matrix that could be useful in identifying kinds of involvement by different groups of employees in a specific company. The key question is can a specific company with specific strategic objectives invite or demand the different kinds of involvement of its employees?

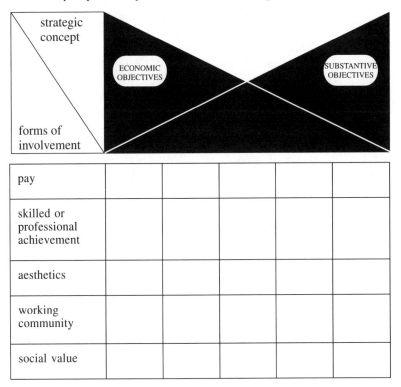

Figure 10.6 Analytical matrix I

As mentioned before, involvement based on pay and on the working community is possible in all kinds of companies and is not necessarily dependent on, or in harmony with, identification with the working process or the objectives of the company. It might be expected that the more dominant the economic objectives are in the corporate strategy the more important becomes involvement in pay on the part of employees. On the other hand, the more dominant the substantive objectives are, the more all the five forms of involvement become a possibility, at least in principle. Examples could be the Society for the Prevention of Cancer, Falck, a private hospital, a theatre and an ornithological society. It might be possible that the priority on pay is relatively low compared to the other forms of involvement. As mentioned before involvement in skilled or professional achievement and in aesthetics is to a high degree related directly to the function and working process of the specific employee.

Contrary to this, involvement in social values is dependent on some degree of identification with the corporate objectives and is not necessarily related to the specific functions and working process of the employee. It is hard to imagine that this kind of company which can survive without some involvement in the social values and identification with the substantive objectives of the company. Potential conflicts between the involvement of employees and the corporate objectives could be fatal to the company. Companies with dominating substantive objectives that are dependent on a high degree of involvement in the social values and identification with the corporate goals, could furthermore be anticipated to be sensitive to public reactions questioning or supporting the legitimacy of the corporate strategy and activities. This does not mean, however, that the sensitivity of employees to public support or critique is simple. At the individual psychological level, as well as at a collective level, there are several possible reactions to normative conflicts with external groups, ranging from pride to indifference, resignation, embarrassment and defence. This is one important perspective of internal and external public relations to investigate.

Involvement in system and life-world related objectives

Earlier in this chapter it was argued that where legitimacy is concerned the substantive objectives and functions of a company which can be analysed to see whether their immediate justification refers to life-world or to economic systems. A matrix figure can be useful in identifying the forms of involvement potentially available in different companies (see Figure 10.7). It would be my assumption that companies with services that are immediately explained by referring to their function within the economic system would possibly represent the involvement forms: pay, skilled or professional achievement, aesthetics and working community, whereas they are less likely to represent involvement in social value and identification with the corporate objectives. In cases of legitimacy crises of the company, however, the ultimate contributions of the company to society and the life-world might be on the agenda of external groups as well as of the employees, and all the above mentioned psychological reactions would be possible. The justifications are, however, more complicated and more indirect than would be the case for companies at the other end of the continuum. This represents another important subject for public relations that should be further investigated.

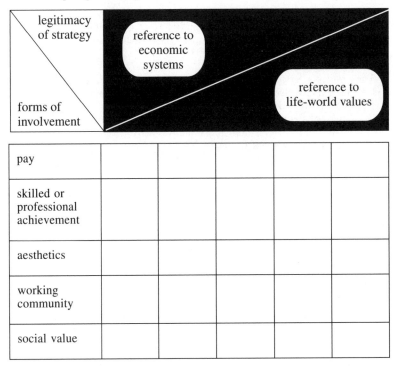

Figure 10.7 Analytical matrix II

CLOSING REMARKS

The focus of this chapter is on strategy and the implications of being a working member of a company. My suggestion is that for strategies and public relations to be sustainable, strategies should be seen as legitimate fields of activities and attention should be paid to the actual and potential forms of employee involvement in the company. Involvement in the social values influenced by the company especially needs attention as it links external and internal public relations.

NOTES

1 See for instance Kreps (1989).
2 Classic theorists in this tradition are Max Weber, Talcot Parsons, more recent contributors include Jürgen Habermas and the school of institutionalism in organizational theory.

3 A recent study on legitimacy and strategy takes this position and is therefore mostly concerned with legitimacy of authority within the strategic managing process in the company. See A. Karlsson (1991).

4 See also Antonsen and Jensen (1992).

5 See Heritage (1984).

6 The concepts System and Life-world are invented by Jürgen Habermas (1989) and are used in the sense that systems ultimately have to be justified by life-world reasons.

7 I should not exclude what could be called the aesthetics of violence, aggression and power which presumably must be a dimension of many film artists' involvement in their work.

11 Communication: magical mystery or scientific concept? Professional views of public relations practitioners in the Netherlands

Betteke van Ruler

INTRODUCTION

Journalists quite regularly engage in, and sometimes instigate, a war of words with PR practitioners (PROs) about the intentions, execution, effects and/or consequences of their actions. Apparently, public relations and related practices are a case of considerable public concern. Contrary to what may be expected though, only the journalists speak a common language. The accumulation of incomprehensible and peculiar public statements by PROs in recent years about what their profession is all about, has led to the question 'what do the leading professionals in the field actually perceive as their occupation?'

The two studies presented in this chapter are so-called communicator research studies. The first study is an open inventory according to the Delphi-technique. This inventory was the basis of a second, more fundamental, study on the theoretical notions behind the views of public relations officers with policy-making responsibilities.

This kind of research is not very common; most of the attention in research is directed at examining the effects of communication. This research project forms a part of a programme aimed at a better understanding of the essential elements of public relations, corporate communication and public affairs, and their theoretical backgrounds.

In his research, Dozier (1984; 1992) found two professional roles of public relations practitioners: that of the technician and the manager. Technicians merely do what others instruct them to do, managers make strategic decisions and are concerned with strategic planning. Although planning and strategy are considered very important in public relations, many researchers have had to conclude that public

relations managers still focus on daily routines and technical procedures (Brody 1985; Cottone *et al.* 1987; Pracht 1991; Reagan 1990).
For juniors and trainees it is quite logical to act as technicians and
according to White and Dozier (1992: 98), even chief executive
officers sometimes act as technicians. That, of course, has nothing
to do with the position they hold but is concerned with the view they
hold.

In many countries, including the Netherlands, there is a seemingly
never-ending discussion about the function of public relations. Practitioners clearly believe that public relations should be one of the
strategic functions within an organization, but in fact many of them
act merely as technicians, which is a non-strategic function.

The members of our research-group at the University of Nijmegen
were interested in this apparent contradiction. Therefore, we started a
research-project to gain insight into basic professional views and
standards of PROs in the Netherlands.

THE DELPHI-STUDY

Research method

To start we chose a panel-research method using the Delphi-
technique (Helmer 1966). This is a type of inductive exploratory
research, based on recurrent consultation with a panel of experts
which produces a condensed but multi-faceted description of a part
of social reality. This kind of research is not theoretically based, but
starts from expressions and responses made by the experts themselves. Methodological critique of the Delphi-technique is understandable, because of, for instance, vaguely formulated questions
and halo-effects, and because of acceptance of snap-judgments in
case of complex issues (Stappers and Nillesen 1985). Nevertheless,
the technique is useful to gain insight into opinions of anonymous
experts and to get group responses (Emmons and Kaplan 1971).

This method allows the researcher to work with the answers provided by panel members. In this method, multiple questionnaires are
sent out in succession, enabling panel members and researchers to
focus on emerging patterns in earlier responses. Delphi questionnaires usually contain in the first round open and rather vaguely
formulated questions and statements. In following rounds the
researcher structures the answers of the panel members and confronts
them with their own words.

The Delphi technique rests on two assumptions. First, because of iterative questioning enhanced with statistical feedback, the ultimate range of answers will decrease. So the opinions expressed by the panel will, after several rounds, converge towards the mid range of the distribution. The second assumption is that the response of the group as a whole will slowly move towards the 'correct' or 'true' answer. But, instead of a single consensus, this method also permits a spread of opinions. At the same time, it highlights the uncertainties which exist around an issue.

We recruited a panel of more than 100 high-ranking experts on public relations and public information, and had an anonymous discussion with them during three rounds. The research-group discussed several distinct items, like the difference between public relations and 'voorlichting' (a typical Dutch question), and the support for certain definitions of public relations. I was responsible for the discussion about the following items:

- What is public relations all about?
- What are the limiting conditions to act as a PRO?
- What should PROs actually do?

In brief, what are the basic professional views of top practitioners in the Netherlands.

Theoretical framework

This large-scale Delphi-research on professional views of top-practitioners (Van Ruler 1994; 1995) showed that most of the practitioners actually claim (and most of the time hold) a management position or a position as a staff member close to the general management; so they want to, and most of the time do, belong to the 'dominant coalition', as Grunig (1992) calls it. They obviously meet the necessary condition (that is to be part of decision making) to act as a manager. The survey also showed that they prefer to be called 'communication manager', and that they view their occupation as a strategic one.

In the Netherlands, as in other countries, public relations seems to have evolved into communication management. However, the object of this management remained unclear. Some of the panel members claimed that communication management is all about technical-professional operations: 'to take care of press contacts', 'to provide good materials'. Others claimed that it is to achieve certain goals and protect a positive image. Others again claimed their job is to bring in ideas from the outside world and build bridges between the organization and public.

The answers to most of our questions resulted in three categories. Dutch literature on professional roles in other occupations (Rozema *et al.* 1983), the theory of Dozier (1992) and the models of public relations by Grunig (Grunig and Hunt 1984) helped me to group these categories and construct three underlying views on the question what public relations – or communication management – is all about.

First, for some respondents, communication management is a function of publicity-seeking and publicity. Following Dozier, I call the type of professional who holds such a view a '**technician**': someone who is tactically concerned with the production and dissemination of communication products or merely maintaining contacts.The technician is busy expressing messages on behalf of the organization. He does not really care to whom he expresses these, and he does not care about the follow-up of his expression. It is a rather unspecific process, because he does not seek his target-groups.

This kind of role is different from the two-way models Grunig and Hunt distinguish for public relations. This type of PRO does not have symmetrical or asymmetrical intentions at all; he just expresses himself and is, therefore, totally self-oriented.

The technician who wants to be a communication manager realizes his management function as the systematic and well-chosen editing of publications and the organization of contacts. Although that is a management function, it has a technical character. It has nothing to do with gaining targets or finding publics; it is not a managerial function.

Second, others claim that the essence of the profession of communication management is the well-organized promotion and the systematic building of a positive image on behalf of the organization. These people are concerned with the effects of their activities and, moreover, of realizing certain goals for the benefit of the organization. This leads to a second type of PROs, whom I call a '**sales manager**': someone who is strategically concerned with 'synchronizing' the behaviour of a public with that of the organization, so that, as Grunig (1992) calls it, the organization can continue to behave in the way it wants without interference.

In this view, communication management consists of repeated cycles of planning, implementation and evaluation of a mix of means of communication. Targets are clearly set, interventions are pre-defined and scheduled, and success or failure determined at the evaluation stage. According to Grunig's PR models, the aim of this kind of communication management can be defined as two-way asymmetrical (Grunig and Hunt 1984). The theory of corporate communication embraces this idea (Van Riel 1992; see also for this kind of view Miller 1989).

A third category of authors and practitioners claim that public relations is all about attuning organization and publics to each other. I therefore typecast PROs of this kind as **'intermediaries'**: people who are strategically concerned with bringing the organization and public in tune with one another, building bridges and trying to stand between an organization and its publics. In this case, communication management is a systematic and strategic exchange to reach mutual understanding, or just to influence both organization and publics. This aim of communication management corresponds with Grunig's symmetrical model of public relations. The outcome is not necessarily for the benefit of the organization; moreover, the main goal is that both parties will be influenced in such a way that they can join forces or at least can live together.

The view of the technician can be called a technical one; he is subservient to the technical demands of the execution of his duties. According to Mintzberg (1983) we can theorize that these people are not concerned with strategic demands on behalf of the organization or fundamental demands of their profession, but only with technical skills and personal experience.

The view of the sales manager can be called an instrumental one (i.e. purely subservient to and instrumental to the demands of the organization) and the view of the intermediary a professional one (i.e. more distanced from the organization and subservient to the demands of the profession).

Analysing the Delphi-research project I constructed these three roles as perceived by the panel of professionals. Dozier's theory must, therefore, be extended, in so far as there are technical and managerial roles, but the latter needs to be devided in two different ones, corresponding with Grunig's asymmetrical and symmetrical models of public relations.

This means that we have to distinguish at least three different kinds of roles of public relations officers:

1 The technician, who has a merely executory orientation towards communication management.
2 The sales manager, who has an instrumental orientation towards communication management.

3 The intermediary, who has a professional orientation towards communication management.

The interpretation of the results

The majority of the aforementioned panel considered themselves to be managers on the strategic level, but on the subject of what they manage, there was great ambiguity. Although the initial outcome of the Delphi-research enabled me to construct the three roles described, it proved quite impossible to assign respondents to any one of the categories on the basis of their answers to further questions. With every new question, opinions (and assigned roles) kept shifting. Asked about the contribution of public relations to the organizational goals, the majority of panel members claimed that their contribution is to lure strategic publics into thinking what they want them to think. But at the same time the majority stressed that the essence of the profession is to attune both organization and publics.

This was rather disturbing: how is it possible to combine this view on the contribution of public relations with such an opposite view on its essence? Moreover, the panel members claimed that all you need for the job are technical skills and a certain personality. Management skills, knowledge of research techniques and knowledge of processes of communication and information did not rank at all. Speech and writing skills, intuition and personality were all that was supposed to be needed. And on top of that, in their daily work they showed themselves to be merely messagemakers instead of communication managers (Van Ruler 1995; Van Ruler *et al.* 1994).

A THEORY-BASED FOLLOW-UP STUDY

New research questions

After the panel research, I analysed the Dutch professional literature on the practice of public relations and 'voorlichting' -in many cases called communication management- and I found the same kind of inconsistencies and rather vague and ill-considered definitions – most of the professional literature on public relations is written by practitioners; there are only a few books of a scholarly nature. It was hard to find out what an author really meant when writing about 'mutual understanding' or 'being an intermediary'. Most of the time these views were explained purely in favour of the organization, with the public in a passive state or not considered at all. But even some of the authors who openly claimed that public relations is about gaining a positive image, appeared to pursue this goal with merely tactical manoeuvres. So the inconsistencies in the panel responses could not be a coincidence; they were obviously structural and therefore they suggested the need for follow-up research and for further, more fundamental, research on the origins of these inconsistencies.

The assumption that 'communication' is the real core of the PRO's occupation led to the presupposition that their understanding of communication is a critical factor in the way they view their professional role. That means that having a clear understanding of how communication works will lead to a consistent view on what public relations is all about.

Conversely, a blurred understanding of how communication works will correspond with an inconsistent view on what public relations is all about. This leads to the presupposition that the different views or inconsistency found in the responses suggests a basic lack of understanding of the concept of communication. If this presupposition is correct, then it is important to investigate the concepts of communication on which the PROs base their daily work, and to pay more attention in professional literature and education to the concept of communication, than has been the case up to now.

The concept of communication

The communication manager has 'to manage the communication', but what is meant by this word 'communication'? Nowadays everybody talks about communication but nobody seems to find it necessary to define what communication is and how they think communication works (Thayer 1968). A classification of understandings of communication can be found in the models of public relations of Grunig (1976). Grunig distinguishes PR models that stress a one-way idea of communication and models that stress a two-way idea. A one-way model of communication can, for instance, be found in the model of Shannon (Shannon and Weaver 1949), in which the stream of signals through a (radio) channel is described. In contrast, a two-way model of communication can, for example, be found in the cybernetica-theory of Wiener (1948), who showed how neurologic processes are a matter of action and reaction, and totally different – for instance in the theory of Watzlawick *et al.* (1970), who describe the circularity of human communicative behaviour.

Furthermore, Grunig, following Thayer (1968), makes a distinction between a synchronic and a diachronic view on the concept of communication. In more recent publications he names these views symmetric and asymmetric, after the idea of co-orientation of Newcomb (1953) and the circular character of communication as described by Watzlawick *et al.* (1970). In his most recent work Grunig (1992) claims that one-way models are always asymmetric. So, in Grunig's theory about public relations we can find three distinct understandings of how communication works: one-way transmission, two-way asymmetric and two-way symmetric.

Looking for a more precise distinction among these concepts, and looking for other communication scientists who make distinctions about the concept of communication concerning public relations, I found the Belgian communication scientist Fauconnier, who claims that in public relations almost every author selects a definition of communication whereby one is not only concerned with the expression of a message, but also with what happens at the side of the receiver, that means whether there are certain effects (1990: 74). Obviously in, Fauconnier's veiw, communication as a concept for public relations has not only to do with expression of messages, but also with effects of these messages. This means that he makes a distinction between communication as expression and communication as a certain process with some kind of effect.

Communication as merely expression is a kind of one-way model, but without concern for the destination of what is expressed. The only concern here is regarding the expression, or 'emission'. This is an 'unaddressed process', so to speak. In such cases it is questionable whether the communication should be defined as a one-way transmission process, because there is no real concern for the effects of the message and any resulting feedback. When there is no attention paid to the audience and no concern about the resulting knowledge of receivers, I prefer to talk about communication as a form of emission or expression. Within the understanding of communication as expression, it is not necessary to do any kind of research, to segment target groups by action or to know something about receivers, let alone about publics (Grunig 1989). As soon as one begins to focus any attention on the effects of the communication process, for example, in terms of the 'reach' of the message transmitted, attention is focused (formally or informally) on some kind of effect. Here, for example, such questions as: 'did the right target-groups notice my messages?' or 'did they hear the signals I sent?' begin to emerge. Where this is the process of communications is no longer 'unaddressed'. The concept of communication as just expression/emission is totally sender-oriented, in so far that effects play no role at all. It is like the idea of communication as a 'magic bullet', as Schramm (1971) describes it. According to Fauconnier, in public relations literature we cannot find support for this concept of communication. It is true that almost all professional authors seem to be concerned with effect, at least at first sight.

During the 1960s, Bauer concluded that one can find two different views on the idea of effects (1964: 319). The first, which he calls the social model:

> held by the general public, and by social scientists when they talk about advertising, and somebody else's propaganda, is one of the exploitation of man by man. It is a model of one-way influence: The communicator does something to the audience, while to the communicator is generally attributed considerable latitude and power to do what he pleases to the audience.

The second model is the scientific model of communication as -what he calls- a transactional process 'in which two parties each expect to give and take from the exchange approximately equitable values'. Although research shows that the scientific model is much more adequate, the social model is the dominant one in practice, according to Bauer.

To put it briefly, we can find at least three different views on the concept of communication regarding public relations and the role of sender and receiver in the communication process:

The receiver does not play any role
Communication is an unaddressed one-sided process with attention given only to the activity of the sender; communication is made equal to expression (emission). It is a concept of communication that is suitable for artists or announcers and is scientifically amateuristic.

Sender $\longrightarrow$ (Receivers)

The receiver plays a passive role
Communication is a linear two-way process with the objective to gain results to synchronize the receiver with the ideas of the sender. This is the communication model Grunig uses for the definition of his asymmetric model of public relations.

Sender $\longrightarrow$ Receiver
$\longleftarrow$
feedback

The receiver plays an active role

The receiver is no longer just receiver. Communication is seen as a two-way process in which sender and receiver are both active and change roles. This is the communication model Grunig uses for the definition of his symmetrical model of public relations.

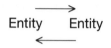

These three models harmonize very well with the three roles of the 'technician', the 'sales manager' and the 'intermediary', I mentioned earlier. The technician suits a concept of communication as expression, the sales manager suits an effect-oriented asymmetric concept, and the intermediary a concept of communication as interaction.

THE RESULTS OF THE SURVEY

The four dimensions of the professional views

Based on the explorative research using the Delphi-technique, the analysis of the professional literature, and the assumption that communication is the core business of the PRO, I designed a construction of professional views, consisting of four dimensions:

1 The essence of public relations.
2 The contribution to the organization.
3 The limiting conditions, i.e. position and skills.
4 The concept of communication.

Every dimension was divided into an explicit view on the dimension and an implicit one. Theoretically, these four dimensions must correspond to secure a consistent view of communication management. The hypothesis that the concept of communication the communication managers utilize is a critical factor in the way they view their professional role, was explained as follows:

- Holding a clear understanding of how communication works will correspond with a consistent view on what communication management is all about.
- Holding a blurred understanding of how communication works will correspond with an inconsistent view on what communication management is all about.

To find evidence to test the hypothesis a survey was held among 75 per cent of the heads of public relations departments of large companies in the Netherlands (more than 500 employees, n=167). Of these 90 per cent said they wanted to co-operate; 67 per cent of them really did (96 respondents). First they had to fill out a questionaire and then in-depth interviews were held with selected respondents to clear up uncertainties of the questionaire.

The dimension 'essence'

First, I asked respondents what they thought was the essence of public relations or communication management. Respondents (n=96) could choose from six possibilities, derived from the three roles discussed earlier. The results were as follows: one per cent selected a technical role, 40 per cent chose an instrumental role, 53 per cent a professional role, 5 per cent could not choose. As in the panel of the delphi-study, almost everybody in the survey chose a managerial role, and the majority the role of the intermediary.

The explicit views on the essence of PR did not, however, seem to have consequences for the way the PROs want to operate. Claiming a professional role should mean that the professional group and/or a scientific basis is important from which to derive the standard of the occupation. Claiming an instrumental role should mean that the demands of the organization are most important. However, when asked from what standard our respondents usually derive their professional decisions, the answers indicated otherwise. The majority (58 per cent) claimed that their standards are based on personal experience and personal skills; 20 per cent said standards are directed by demands of their organization, 15 per cent said their standards are based on the demands of the profession and only 4 per cent chose a scientific basis. So, the managerial role the PROs claim for themselves is based on personal skills and personal experience, and has nothing to do with an instrumental or professional way of working. Instead, a more technical, executory manner prevailed. Consequently, I could find no consistency in the way PROs view the dimension 'essence'.

The dimension 'contribution'

In order to define the dimension 'contribution' I invited respondents to write down what they thought public relations could contribute to the realization of the aims of the organization. Half of the respondents claimed they have to try to reach certain results for the benefit of the organization, and that their job is to 'sell' the organization. Only 17 per cent aim at a more intermediary role, whereby most of these respondents think their function is to 'create a culture of one-big-family', or 'try to synchronize identity and image'. A very small minority said it has to do with mutual influence or exchange of messages between organization and publics.

One can argue that a management role demands having some influence on strategic planning (White and Dozier 1992). In my view such internal influence is essential for an intermediary, because without that it is impossible to influence both parties. It is not that essential for the role of the sales manager; the sales manager just needs to have a reactive influence. It is not at all essential for the technician.

Again, however, I could not find much consistency in the answers of the respondents. Half of the respondents do actually want to have influence, but these are non selectively divided among the different types of PRO's in respect to the contribution they say they want to make. And the wish to have influence on the strategic planning does not correspond with the contribution they say they want to make towards the aims of the organization.

When we compare the open answers to the statements regarding claimed contributions with the (yes-or-no) answers to the question about the essence, there was also considerable inconsistency (see Table 11.1). Less than half of the respondents, who gave a clear answer to the question of the contribution, gave the same type of answers referring to the question of the essence.

The dimension 'conditions'

The third dimension I constructed is that of the conditions, necessary to cope with the job. Although not all of them hold a management position, 82 per cent of the respondents answered that the communication manager should have a position within management or as a staff

Table 11.1 Essence and contribution compared (n=72)

		Contribution		
	Technical	Selling	Interm	
Essence technical	–	–	–	–
Selling	3%	33%	6%	**42%**
Intermediary	10%	35%	14%	**58%**
	13%	68%	19%	**100%**

member very close to the general management; all respondents said they are responsible for communication policy and all of them think this is adequate for such a functionary, as they are. This has led to the conclusion that all of the respondents see their job as a strategic one and all of them see public relations as a function on management level.

Nevertheless, they do not think one needs to have management skills. Almost everyone thought communicative capacities like good speaking and writing are very important (92 per cent) for a job like theirs, just like public relations techniques (85 per cent) and intuition (85 per cent) or intellectual background (77 per cent). Only 53 per cent thought planning skills are essential and only 17 per cent thought research skills are essential. Although all the respondents have strategic responsibilities, very few of them think systematic analytic skills are important. Research skills especially score very low.

Asked what one needs to succeed in this profession, only 12 per cent thought you need specific higher education; 76 per cent claim that personal qualities or just plain common sense are most important, 5 per cent choose a practical PR course.

So, in spite of their self-image of their occupation as a strategic one, hardly any formal qualifications are seen as necessary to engage in it. Any practical skills mentioned are purely technical ones, such as good speaking and writing skills. And to make a career for oneself the skills of a 'steward' will do.

Other characteristics of PROs

Asked to characterize their personal way of acting, the PROs in the survey again showed a mainly technical and 'self-oriented' approach. For instance, 68 per cent said they do not particularly segment target groups per action; 23 per cent do segment, but only on socio-demographic criteria, only 5 per cent said that they bank on opinion-research. Confronted with other questions these 28 per cent said they do not plan their actions using research but on priorities in their organization, and some of them even said they never used research at all. So, even from the respondents who say that they do segment by action, it is questionable that they actually do so.

Asked about how they used their time it became clear that 41 per cent of the departments never devote any time to research; 17 per cent allocate only 1–4 per cent of their time for research. Besides, one third of the respondents who said that they devote time to research, said at a different place in the survey that they never have any research done.

However, it is a mistake to believe these people are unhappy with the way the quality of public relations in general is maintained – 89 per cent rate public relations 6 or 7 on a scale of 10. And they are even more satisfied with their current job: 66 per cent give it an 8 or more; 29 per cent rate their jobs 6 or 7. They all like their profession and almost everybody says that their management thinks public relations is very important. Nevertheless, they rank the status of the communication manager below the status of the financial manager or the marketing manager and even under the personnel manager. So, implicitly, they show that their position is perhaps formally at the same level as of the marketing manager and the other managers, but that practically they see themselves at a lower (more executory) level.

Tentative conclusions about the professional views

According to these findings one might think the respondents did not take my questions seriously and just completed the survey without giving it serious thought. But that was not the case, as shown by a HOMALS analysis of the answers on essence, contribution, internal influence, segmentation criteria and planning skills (Van Ruler 1995). This showed that the respondents were rather consistent in these inconsistencies. So the inconsistency is apparently structural for the way PR professionals view this profession.

My questions on the essence of public relations, on contribution to the organization and on necessary conditions revealed inconsistent patterns when I tried to combine them into a general view on public relations, and the respondents showed very much the same pattern in this inconsistency. For these professionals, at least, the concept of public relations and communication management could not be defined systematically from these three central dimensions.

On the basis of the hypothesis that their understanding of communication is a critical factor in their professional view, it must be that their blurred view of essence, contribution and conditions is consistent with a blurred view of communication.

The dimension 'communication'

The first question asked for the description used for communication in their profession – 11 per cent gave an answer that fitted an action-oriented view of communication ('all the activities we do'); 17 per cent one that fitted an interaction-oriented view ('mutual understanding', or 'listen and tell'); 72 per cent described communication as a process with linear effect ('all the information streams through the organization', or 'transmitting a message and getting feedback on it').

Explicitly, almost three quarters express an effect-oriented concept of communication. Theoretically, this has to have consequences for their choice of a given description of communication policy. I constructed a theory-based range of six possibilities. Here 56 per cent chose an interaction-oriented description, and 38 per cent an effect-oriented one. But I could not find any correlation between the answers on these two questions (see Table 11.2).

Obviously, the definitions the respondents formulated about the concept of communication were not that integrated, in so far that these had consequences for their choice for a certain given definition of communication policy.

Another variable I used to find their implicit view of communication, was 'which characteristic is suitable for communication?'. Most of the respondents chose 'transmission' (81 per cent), and 'contact' (88 per cent) as distinguishing characteristics for communication. 'To make common' or 'to offer a message' (characteristics that belong to an interaction-oriented understanding of communication) did not get much support. In the interviews the respondents said that 'to make common' is too 'soft'. 'To offer' is too weak and too sender-oriented, they said, because they want particular effects and need, therefore, to 'transmit signals to their audiences and collect certain effects'. 'Contact' is seen as the precondition for that.

Seeking effects is not done systematically, however. Only two respondents reported that they scan their environment to find potential

Table 11.2 The description of communication, compared with a description of the essence of communication policy (n=84)

	Description of communication policy				
	Action	*Effect*	*Interact*	*More than one*	*Total*
Description of communication					
Action		5%	6%		**11%**
Effect	4%	26%	41%	1%	**72%**
Inter.		8%	8%		**16%**
Uncertain				1%	**1%**
	4%	39%	55%	2%	**100%**

publics (Brody and Stone 1989) and also only a few respondents said they evaluate their actions (Rice and Paisly 1981; Rice and Atkin 1989).

Other research showed that even large companies seldom evaluate their corporate communication campaigns (Adema *et al.* 1993); and that, if any research is done, the design most used is an unsystematic check of the reach of the message (KS PR 1993). So, the understanding of communication from an effect-orientation that seemed to be dominant among practitioners, is obviously mere lip-service. In practice, almost all respondents saw communication just as expression, although, when asked, they mentioned more effect-oriented definitions.

Again, there was a structural pattern among the respondents. After all, they were rather homogeneous in their (inconsistent) understanding of communication. They showed lip-service to an effect-orientation, but actually they appear to see communication only as unaddressed, sender-driven action.

Because of their blurred understanding of communication or, moreover, their lack of understanding of communication at all, the respondents in this survey were, from a scientific point of view, amateurs.

CONCLUSION OF THE STUDY ON PROFESSIONAL VIEWS

The conclusion of this study is that the respondents of the survey could not be divided on their professional views. The views could be identified, but the gist of their answers changed with the questions.

The respondents appear to have an understanding of communication which deviates wildly from the abstract, sober, clearly defined concept communication science holds it to be. The PROs see themselves at best from a 'less-than-perfect-information-processor-model', as Dervin (1989) calls the effect-oriented models of communication. Many of them are able – when asked – to come up with some subjective variation of the Shannon and Weaver model or with an adaptation of this model with the concepts of effect and feedback.

Although communication science has criticized these linear communication models for about thirty years, it is still the dominant way of thinking about communication in practice. Recent communication theory is not very well implemented in the practice of public relations in the Netherlands. Perhaps it is, as Grunig writes, that 'Practitioners are attracted to the all-powerful view. The academics hold to the limited-effects view.' (Grunig and Hunt 1984: 124). But if Grunig means by an 'all-powerful view' that they are interested in gaining effects, I found that they give only lip-service to that view. Since in their daily work the PROs appear not to take any notice of their receivers (publics) at all. So they actually hold this view only at first sight. They have heard about effect-orientation and they like to talk about well-planned and powerful communication, but confronted with consequences of effect-orientation they show no concern with finding target-groups by action or with following effects at all. So, actually they do not see communication as a problematic process. Moreover, communication is not seen as a concept one should define at all. Communication can be everything you like it to be. Communication is the thing you do and seems to be able to bring what you want it to bring without any doubt or restriction.

The conclusion had to be, therefore, that from a scientific communication point of view, the PROs in the survey were all amateurs. The professional workers' images range from (and shift between) the purely concrete to the intangibly magic. This mutual misunderstanding explains the frustrating fact that PROs say that research takes too much time and money, and that practical education and a certain personality will do.

This research project shows that PROs with a blurred communication concept have blurred professional views and cannot find clear arguments to define their profession. I suppose that this is why they will not surpass the level of the technican, despite their ambitions. This is also why the professional field is still in its infancy and practitioners are not able to cope with abstract strategic planning practices. Professionalization of public relations, therefore, has to go hand-in-glove with conceptualization of communication as a never-ending chain of interactive, most often public, processes.

12 Towards fourth wave public relations: a case study

Dejan Verčič

ABSTRACT

Although public relations is commonly defined as 'relations with publics' there have been practically no methods developed to help organizations when dealing with multiple publics with conflicting interests. Public relations programmes are primarily designed for 'public by public', step-like management. The case study presented in this chapter explores the possible strategies for dealing with multiple publics and a concrete example is used to present a hierarchical placement of two publics with conflicting interests. The chapter discusses the case study of Sostanj steam power station, the second biggest producer of electricity and the biggest air polluter in Slovenia. Its attempts for environmental reconstruction have been unsuccessful due to the lack of adequate public decision-making systems. The research performed (a five-year history of the decision-making involved and situational analysis of publics) concluded with the suggestion that the only rational and ethical alternative left to the plant's management is, by default, to get involved in building Slovenia's public decision-making structure responsible for environmental issues. After examining recent business literature, the final part of the chapter suggests that obstacles in public decision-making systems observed in many countries pose a similar problem to public relations practitioners globally, and not only in former socialist countries which are in the phase of transition. The chapter concludes with a hypothesis that public relations might be facing a new situation that has not been explored yet. This stage of development is termed 'the fourth wave public relations' after the suggestion of Herman Bryant Maynard, Jr. and Susan E. Mehrtens who trace the same type of problems and state: 'Business, by default, must begin to assume responsibility for the whole' (1993: 7).

INTRODUCTION

L. Grunig (1992: 72–3) posed a question relating to the purpose of public relations: 'Are we in the business of persuasion? of information? of negotiation? of co-optation? of co-operation?' The models of public relations first presented by Grunig and Hunt (1984: 21–22) all answer the question differently: for the press agentry model the purpose is propaganda, for the public information model the dissemination of information, for the two-way asymmetrical model scientific persuasion and for the two-way symmetrical model mutual understanding. Grunig and Grunig (1989: 32) summed up those four purposes in two more general forms: control and adaptation. Subsequently, Grunig and Grunig (1992: 312) reconceptualized the models in two continua: one of craft and the other of professional public relations. The latter has two extremes in asymmetry and symmetry and restated purposes in terms of two tactics: compliance-gaining (asymmetry) and problem-solving (symmetry). J. Grunig (1989: 40) argued that: '. . . not only is the two-way symmetrical model a more moral and ethical approach to public relations than the other models, but that it is also a more effective model in practice.'

The Sostanj case discussed in this chapter represents a reopening in scholarly literature of the rarely discussed problem of the purpose of public relations when dealing with multiple publics. The weakness in the theoretical literature was noted by Springston *et al.* (1992: 82) who argued that: 'To date no existing public relations model provides a specific method for measuring and managing the entire field of publics simultaneously.' The problem of managing multiple stakeholder relationships becomes particularly difficult when an organization is squeezed between two (or more) groups of stakeholders/publics with opposing needs and/or wants. Being symmetrical to both sides in all such relationships, while theoretically possible, would mean achieving a balance with all parties; but achieving a balanced relationship is often impossible as one side or the other may be unable to reconcile themselves to the views of the other. Thus, in most cases of multiple relationships, an organization has to take a side and become 'more symmetrical' to (at least) one group. As a result, organizations must consider how they should determine the hierarchy of stakeholders/publics and what policies it should pursue in terms of 'organizational activism'.

Although the case studied occurred in the unique context of 'post-socialism', the chapter concludes by arguing that its implications transcend its geography. The author argues that the public relations profession faces new challenges which are forcing it into a new stage of development, into its **Fourth Wave**.

CONTEXT FOR RESEARCH

In the first book published on public relations more than seventy years ago Edward Bernays noted that 'Public opinion has entered life at many points as a decisive factor' (Bernays 1923: 50). Bernays' comments apply to many Central and Eastern European countries today as they emerge from several decades of communist rule. In the foreword to the first report on public relations in Slovenia (Vreg 1994: 4) the following comment can be found: 'Along with political pluralism, parliamentary democracy, and market economy, new structures of publics and public opinion are becoming relevant.' (for more information on public relations in Slovenia see Gruban, Verčič and Zavrl 1994; Verčič, Grunig and Grunig 1993.) In the original report of the case discussed in this chapter (PR Institut 1993: A2.) it was noted that: 'the Sostanj Steam Plant is the biggest single polluter of air in Slovenia and has been one for years. The reason for this is not in the technology used but in the incomplete investments in its environmental improvements.'

The growing interest within the media about issues relating to ecology, together with the emergence of green social movements and politicization of environmental issues resulted in an enhanced interest amongst the population of Slovenia in the issue of pollution. The Sostanj Steam Plant found itself in the media spotlight and its further operation became dependent on its ability to complete investments in the environmental aspects of its operation. As result of its predicament, the Sostanj Steam Plant contacted the PR Institut of Pristop Communication Group in 1993 to conduct a public relations audit and recommend further action(s).

As Grunig and Hunt (1984: 108) warn in their textbook, public relations practitioners '. . . have, in recent years, used the terms 'public relations audit,' 'communication audit,' and 'social audit' to describe public relations research. They have not used the terms consistently, however.' They defined public relations auditing as '. . . research to define publics and to determine how these publics perceive and evaluate the organizations. Such research determines who the relevant publics are, how the organization stands with these publics, and the power of the publics.' After reviewing the relevant literature, Pavlik (1987: 28) advanced a very similar definition:

The PR audit is designed to evaluate an organization's standing with its relevant publics. . . . A public is considered relevant on the following basis: Does our organization (or may it in the future) have some effects on the public, or does this public (or may it in the future) have some effects on our organization?

Between March and October 1993, a group of researchers led by the author of this chapter executed an audit which consisted of two parts: the first applied Grunig's situational analysis of publics to a representative sample of the population of Slovenia. The decision to use this method to segment publics from the population was based on the core principles of situational theory research: 'An organization seeking to identify and communicate with relevant publics should worry about educated activists and devote most of its effort to communicate with them.' (Anderson 1992: 155.) The second element of the audit was concerned with the decision-making process in the political environment of the plant and sought to identify the relevant publics in this domain. A content analysis of 433 documents used for communication between possible decision-makers produced between 1986 and 1992 has been completed.

The results of this audit were clear. Not only the local population, but also a great part of the Slovenian population as a whole were very concerned with air pollution from the Sostanj Steam Plant. At the same time people feel completely powerless and without any influence on the decision-makers (i.e. parliament). The political process which could provide the solution (the money needed for the environmental improvement) was not legally defined and hence it was impossible for the necessary steps to be taken to resolve the problem. As the report into the situation pointed out:

> The politicization of environmental issues has brought Sostanj Steam Plant into a paradox of conflicting legal requirements: the plant has to operate in order to provide the power that is needed for the stability of the Slovenian electric power supply grid, while at the same time the plant was prohibited from polluting the air above the prescribed level. Yet reconciling these two requirements is impossible at present . . .
>
> (PR Institut 1993: A2.)

On the one hand, the government was interested in having a balanced budget with the smallest possible deficit (ideally with none). On the other hand, the population was more interested in clear air and was even prepared to pay for it from their own pockets (e.g. accept higher prices for electricity). However, the government was not prepared to increase the prices of electricity because of the fear of causing an inflatory spiral, and thus it was impossible to 'close the circle'.

We will first discuss the results of the situational analysis of publics that was conducted, before going on to analyse the communication and decision-making process involved in the situation. Finally, after presenting the outcome of the case studied, we will attempt to identify some general implications.

SITUATIONAL ANALYSIS OF PUBLICS

Grunig and Hunt argue that 'publics develop around problems or issues, differ in the extent to which they are aware of the problem and the extent to which they do something about the problem.' (1984: 147.) Following Dewey (1927) and Blumer's (1966) classic theories of public opinion that issues define publics more than publics define issues, Grunig developed his theory of segmentation of publics (J. Grunig 1994; Grunig and Childers 1988; Grunig and Hunt 1984). Here Grunig and Childers conceptualized communication behaviour as purposive and active: a tool for solving problems (Grunig and Childers 1988.)

Situational theory states that 'the communication behaviours of publics can be best understood by measuring how members of publics perceive situations in which they are affected by such organizational consequences as pollution, quality of products, hiring practices, or plant closing'. (Grunig and Hunt 1984: 148.) The theory operationalizes 'perceptions' with three independent variables: problem recognition, constraint recognition and level of involvement. The three independent variables explain when people will communicate actively or passively. Active communication behaviour is termed 'information seeking' and passive communication behaviour 'information processing'. High problem recognition '. . . increases the likelihood that a member of a public will both seek and process information', whereas constraint recognition '. . . represents the extent to which people perceive that there are constraints – or obstacles – in a situation that limit their freedom to plan their own behaviour'. High constraint recognition decreases the likelihood that a person concerned with an issue would seek or process information. Thus the level of involvement '. . . helps distinguish whether the person's communication behaviour will be active or passive'. (Grunig and Hunt 1984: 151–2.)

Information seeking and information processing are identified as the dependent variables that are explained by these three independent variables. Thus by combining these variables eight possible combinations of variables can be identified (2 X 2 X 2 = 8). 'People whose scores on the measures of the three variables fit into each one of these combinations of variables for any issue – air pollution, for example – can be called public.' (Grunig and Hunt 1984: 153.) Grunig went on to break down these eight kinds of publics according to their level of involvement and obtained four kinds of behaviour: problem-facing behaviour (high problem recognition, low constraint recognition); constrained behaviour (high problem recognition, high constraint recognition); routine behaviour (low problem recognition, low constraint recognition); and fatalistic behaviour (low problem recognition, high constraint recognition).

'Problem facing' describes the behaviour of a public that results when members of that public recognize the problem caused by the consequences of a particular organization's actions and perceive that they face no constraints on their behaviour. Members of a public who fit this type of behaviour will be highly likely to seek and to process information and are likely to be affected by the information. Constrained behaviour occurs when members of a public recognize a problem, but feel constrained from doing anything about it. When members of a public have freedom from constraints – when they can do something about – but still do not recognize the problem, their behaviour can be described as routine behaviour. Fatalistic behaviour describes the behaviour of a public that would seldom, if ever, actively communicate about an issue and that would be least likely to process information that comes to it randomly'. (Grunig and Hunt 1984: 154).

In the case of the Sostanj Steam Plant, problem recognition was measured by asking respondents how much they thought the operation of Sostanj Steam Plant affected the quality of the air in Slovenia. Constraint recognition was measured by asking respondents if they believed that they personally had any influence on parliament with regard to a decision about the environmental improvement of Sostanj Steam Plant. The level of involvement was measured by asking respondents whether they felt personally concerned with the quality of air they breath.

The level of information processing was measured by questioning respondents about whether they would watch a TV programme about the Sostanj Steam Plant that evening. Information seeking was measured by asking respondents if they would contribute to a booklet explaining the plant's environmental improvement programme if the plant would provide one. From 8–19 August 1993, a telephone survey was carried out on two random samples of people selected from the computerized telephone directory. The national sample comprised 500 people, and a second control sample of 50 telephone subscribers in the town of Sostanj (local district) was constructed. The response rates were 81.2 per cent on the Slovenian sample and 92 per cent for the Sostanj sample. The results of the survey in terms of the probabilities of different forms of communication behaviour are summarized in Table 12.1

Table 12.2 shows the probabilities of communication behaviour obtained on the control (local) sample.

The figures in the first columns show how many respondents fit into

Table 12.1 Probabilities of communication behaviour obtained on the Slovenian sample.

	Population number	%	Process number	Seek number
High involvement				
Problem-facing behaviour	19	4.7	18	9
Constrained behaviour	252	62.1	191	72
Routine behaviour	0	0	0	0
Fatalistic behaviour	41	10.1	25	7
Low involvement				
Problem-facing behaviour	3	0.7	3	0
Constrained behaviour	57	14	38	5
Routine behaviour	2	0.5	1	0
Fatalistic behaviour	32	7.9	24	6
Totals	406	100	300	99

Table 12.2 Control sample

	Population number	%	Process number	Seek number
High involvement				
Problem-facing behaviour	2	4.3	2	2
Constrained behaviour	42	91.3	39	28
Routine behaviour	0	0	0	0
Fatalistic behaviour	1	0.2	1	1
Low involvement				
Problem-facing behaviour	0	0	0	0
Constrained behaviour	1	0.2	0	0
Routine behaviour	0	0	0	0
Fatalistic behaviour	0	0	0	0
Totals	46	100	42	31

a particular category of publics. The second columns show the percentages of persons in each category. The third columns show how many respondents indicated that they would process information. And the fourth columns show how many respondents would be likely to undertake information seeking behaviour. The row 'totals' in the third and fourth columns show how many respondents in the sample would process information and how many would seek it. The results clearly support the theoretical model. The results of the control sample also support those obtained for the national sample.

What is notable in these findings is the very high problem recognition scores supported also by other questions. With regard to the responses about whether the quality of air in Slovenia is a serious problem, 83 per cent of respondent stated that it was 'very serious' or 'serious' (100 per cent on the control sample of the Sostanj population). At the same time 64.3 per cent of respondents indicated that they would be prepared to pay a higher price for electricity (84.8 per cent of the control sample). However, only 5.9 per cent of respondents felt that they could influence their representatives in parliament (4.3 per cent of the control sample). The small sample size made it difficult to predict problem-facing behaviour and a majority of the population exhibited constrained behaviour.

ANALYSIS OF THE COMMUNICATION AND DECISION-MAKING PROCESS

The first decision to start environmental improvements at the Sostanj Steam Plant was made in 1986 following the political conference 'Ecology, Energy and Preservation' and the Slovenian government accepted the need to take action under the pressure of the newly emerging green movement in Slovenia. The fact the government at that time agreed to the 'polluter pays principle' was already a sign of the weakness of the old regime. Since 1986, communication process concerning the problem of Sostanj Steam Plant had been progressing without any indication that it might result in a firm decision from government. The question of financing a public utility (and investments in its environmental improvement) was above the level of the plant management. Throughout this period Slovenia was (and still is) unable to finance the total investment required in the short term. The only solution was a form of delayed payment – i.e. involve foreign capital and repay the debt with money collected over the years by higher electricity prices. However, no government had been willing to make such a decision because of the fear of inflation. In the meantime, the political regime changed from socialism to a parliamentary democracy. Slovenia gained independence and the new political parties on the scene were more concerned with 'historical themes' (privatization, etc.) than common everyday issues, such as the quality of air.

An analysis of the communication and decision-making process was based on Luhmann's (1982: 226) 'central problem of communication theory': '. . . the problem of irrepressible contingency of the acceptance/rejection of communicated messages . . .' between Sostanj Steam Plant, ministries, banks, and other relevant organizations. All together more than thirty different public and private, domestic and foreign (e.g. World Bank) formal organizations engaged in the communication process were identified. They were analysed as thirty entities (the last one being a group of other, 'peripheral points', in the language of the network theory; Scott 1991: 91). The researchers were seeking the location of power. 'Power exists whenever a decision maker chooses one specific possibility from among many and when this selection is in turn accepted by others as a premise for their own decision making – even though it is obviously based on a selective decision.' (Luhmann 1982: 151.)

The communication process was defined as starting with the initial information in written form – a document. The recipient

> . . . accepts the selective content of the communication (the information) as a premise of his own behaviour, thus joining further selections to the primary selection and reinforcing its selectivity in the process. In this context, acceptance as a premise of one's own behaviour can mean acting in accordance with corresponding directives, but also processing experiences, thoughts and other perceptions on the assumption that a certain piece of information is correct
>
> (Luhmann 1981: 125).

Thus the recipient of the document (information) wrote his decision on the paper or not. In the case of the Sostanj Steam Plant, the decision had not been formally written down or had been written and not sent ahead, thus communication was defined as being 'stopped'.

The researchers were reading documents and searching for trails of decisions that could fit the given definition of power or conflicts which were defined again after Luhmann (1992: 82): 'We can speak of conflict whenever one participant in an interaction refuses to accept the choices or selection of another, and communicates this refusal.'

All together 433 documents (information) were found with no clear conflict and no real decision based on power. The whole communication process was meaningless in terms of arriving at a viable decision. As the original report stated (PR Institut 1993: B56): 'It is obvious from the analysis carried out that the communication and decision-making process operated at different levels according to different rules with different notions of rationality and with different time perspectives.' Furthermore, the report concluded that 'We can conclude that all the actors involved in this communication and decision-making process covering environmental improvement went through a process that should be brought up to the level of consciousness as a collective experience'. The problem was in the political system which was unable to produce a number of possible alternative solutions that would solve the problem for its voters. And here another problem emerged: the publics that were affected by the pollution from Sostanj Steam Plant were also the voters who had brought the government to power and it was the government which was the only authority that could (but did not) produce a solution. The management of the plant was squeezed between two powerless (contingent to this particular problem) groups of its stakeholders/publics: the local population and the politicians.

RESULTS

The public relations audit performed for Sostanj Steam Plant in 1993 identified eight publics from the population of Slovenia and also identified the immobility in the political system that had failed to produce a necessary decision concerning the improvement of the impact of the plant on the environment. The common sense approach would suggest the management should have engaged in lobbying within the political system and amongst grass root pressure groups in order to put strong pressure on individual politicians.

One simple argument against this proposal was that Sostanj Steam Plant was a public utility and as such it was not in a position to engage in lobbying and pressure politics. A more important reason for the lack of action can be traced to the tradition of the Slovenian green movement which was at least partially responsible for the failure to resolve the situation. In 1986, the green movement was more concerned with 'the politics of deconstruction of the governing codes and symbolic meanings, than with politics in the sense of goal oriented rationality' (PR Institut 1993: C4). In 1989, the green movement transformed itself into a political party and entered the first Slovenian post-socialist government. Thus, as part of the political system, it was not in its interest to 'get its hands dirty' (PR Institut 1993: C9) with lobbying for the management of the plant that survived a change of regime. Finally, the party split into a left and right wing and engaged in the popular 'politics of morality as the substitute for political programmes' (PR Institut: C6). After such a debacle of the civil society green movement, any grass root pressure tactics would immediately be instrumentalized in the national (left-right) political strategies.

As Windahl and Signitzer (1992: 34) pointed out: 'The question of who is blamed has great influence on a communication planner's choice of solutions to a problem'. The public relations audit showed that there is nobody personally responsible for the situation described. The problem lay in the undeveloped system of public decision-making. The only viable alternative left to the management was to engage in the development of the political system itself. And that implied two things: first, the supremacy of the citizens' interests (one group of stakeholders/publics) over politicians (the other group of stakeholders/publics), and second, 'organizational activism'. Although the first consequence (the supremacy of interests of citizens over politicians) can be seen as a simple one, it is possible to conceive of situations where a hierarchy of stakeholders/ publics is not so easily identified. In such situations, there are no obvious public relations strategies that can be employed. This is one field in which there is clearly a need for further detailed research.

Grunig and Grunig (1989: 47) predicted that when there is a low level of constraint, organizations will use asymmetrical communication to try to dominate the environment. In the Sostanj case, that would have meant asymmetrical communication directed towards the local community (politicians have more power, particularly when a public utility is in the question.) However, this did not happen. The second consequence of this situation also seems an obvious one, but holds even greater potential dangers. This concerns the interpretation placed on the use of public relations by private formal organizations to influence public policies. Such practices have been condemned in some quarters (e.g. Olasky 1987).

Here we come back to the initial question: what is the purpose of public relations?

HISTORY REVISED: TOWARD FOURTH WAVE PUBLIC RELATIONS

Maynard and Mehrtens (1993) have used Alvin Toffler's concept of waves of change as the framework for rethinking where the business is heading into the new millennium. The First Wave of change was the agricultural revolution. The Second Wave was industrialization. The Third Wave is post-industrialization. And the Fourth Wave is seen as still emerging at present. Maynard and Mehrtens (1993: xiv, 6, 38) have excluded the First Wave from their analysis, and for the remaining three offered the following worldviews:

- Second Wave – We are separate and must compete.
- Third Wave – We are connected and must co-operate.
- Fourth Wave – We are one and must choose to co-create.

We can see a very clear correspondence between the purposes of public relations as suggested by J. Grunig and L. Grunig, and world-views of Maynard's and Mehrten's Second and Third wave. Further-more: J. Grunig (1989) argued against the prevailing worldview that sees public relations as persuasive and manipulative. Rather, he proposed a symmetrical view of public relations. In course of developing a theory of excellence in public relations and communications management, Grunig and White (1992) argue against an asymmetrical and in favour of a symmetrical worldview. Here their arguments for symmetry are very similar to those advanced by Maynard and Mehrtens (1993: 7–8):

> The transition between the Second and the Third Wave entails the corporation to see itself as a creator of value. Its philosophy of doing business undergoes a profound shift as it focuses more on serving the needs of its various stakeholders (now defined as all parties who have a relationship to the firm, not just its owners) than on production per se.

Maynard and Mehrtens go on to argue (1993: 10): 'The Third Wave corporation will be more supportive of social and resource accounting as it begins to change its underlying value system. Fourth Wave business will have wider agenda, reflecting its leadership role and its acceptance of responsibility for the whole.' In this way, we could place classical public relations (Bernays 1923; 1986) in the time of industrialization (modernization; and press agentry, and public infor-mation model at the premodern stage) and two-way symmetrical model in the era of postindustrialization (postmodernism). But the question arises what is Fourth Wave public relations?

As we have seen in the Sostanj case, symmetry, understanding, or adaptation as strategies for problem solving might be impossible (at least for all groups of stakeholders/publics). In that case, Naisbitt's (1994: 24) dictum: 'Think Locally, Act Globally,' might apply. The organization has to decide which are the groups of stakeholders/publics that are most important and which need to be served first.

The problem acquires its broader implication when considered in the light of the arguments of several researchers that 'democratic political systems are becoming slower and slower in their decision-making processes, postponing what should be done as far as they can' (Drucker 1990: 98; Kennedy 1993: 121; Smith 1989). Politicians have recognized this phenomena, and Ronald Reagan stated on his inauguration as President '. . . government is not the solution to our problem; government is the problem.' (Quoted in Tulis 1987: 191.) The implications of modern political systems are summed up by Naisbitt (1994: 149): 'Politics as usual, like business as usual, is no longer acceptable'. And so 'business, by default, must begin to assume responsibility for the whole'. (Maynard and Mehrtens 1993: 7 and 48.). 'Taking responsible, proactive, aggressive action to serve the whole is good business.' (Maynard and Mehrtens 1993: 59.) Both Maynard and Mehrtens and Naisbitt argue that as a result of such changes in attitude towards the role of business, businesspeople will become leaders also outside their organizations. What is more in question is whether public relations is prepared to participate in such a new game? Maynard and Mehrtens (1993: 48) maintain that: 'The business of business is not only business.' Does that mean that also public relations is becoming more than 'relationship management'? (Pavlik 1987: 118.) Pearson (1990: 232) offers a more far-reaching proposal: '. . . public relations as a particular kind of collaborative decision-making process.'

Whichever way the profession goes, we have to agree with L. Grunig (1992: 70): 'We are beginning to understand the far-reaching consequences of public relations to society, yet few of our presuppositions have been scrutinized and evaluated.'

This chapter does not have a positive answer to the question of what the actual purpose of Fourth Wave public relations would be. The author has simply sought to highlight some questions that were faced while working on a concrete case. Further research is needed to search for the answers to the question of the (possible) hierarchy of stakeholders/publics and to the question of required 'organizational activism'. It might well be that we shall be forced to find the purpose of public relations at a more philosophical level.

POSTSCRIPT

The case study presented in this chapter fits in with the well-established line of using case studies in public relations both for pedagogic (e.g. Black 1993; Cole 1981; Culbertson *et al.* 1993; Moss 1990) and research purposes (e.g. Anderson 1992; Coombs 1992; Moffitt 1994; Murphy and Dee 1992; Serini 1993). But the concrete use of the methodologies in the case reported follows the notion that 'there is nothing neutral about programme research. Seeking rational and apolitical optimization of organizational responses to environmental pressures, as suggested by systems theory, is naive and ineffective'. (Dozier 1990: 13). In writing a case study, the author describes 'one particular solution to the problems presented,' fully aware that 'there is rarely one way in which any particular problem could have been tackled.' (Moss 1990: 3–4.). 'In fact, one of the chief benefits of the cases lies in their examination of the underlying strategic thinking that lay behind the programmes that were developed and implemented.' (Moss 1990: 2.)

The first question to be answered here is: why were two methodologies used to investigate two types of publics (the Slovenian population and decision-makers; situational analysis of publics and content analysis)? Following 'the law of requisite variety' that 'the diversity of ideas and viewpoints within a manager's self-regulating system should equal diversity of the environment' (Culbertson *et al.* 1993: 23) the designers of the project adopted two kinds of variety: first, in the research team, part of which were also two independent Slovenian environmentalists, and second, in the research design (on full elaboration on the need for requisite variety in public relations research see: L. Grunig 1994). Opinion formation problem (of the Slovenian population) demanded a method that can capture its logic and dynamics – and for that reason, Grunig's situational analysis of publics was selected (on situational analysis of publics see: J. Grunig 1994). Political decision-making, on the other hand, which in a democratic society is primarily a procedural problem (Luhmann 1982), demanded a methodology that could follow documented communication, and for that reason a content analysis with some elements of a grounded theory approach was selected (on content analysis see: Broom and Dozier 1990: 139–41; on case analysis and content analysis see: Patton 1987: 147 *passim*; on grounded theory approach see: Easterby-Smith, Thorpe and Lowe 1991: 35–37, 104–115).

The second question emerges from the introductory statement to this case study, that the problem of dealing with multiple publics is rarely discussed in public relations scholarly literature; is this true? While this may be true, it does not negate the awareness of the existence of multiple publics found in public relations handbooks, textbooks and introductory materials to the profession. As many writers have observed, public relations is probably a misnomer. As one author has commented: 'It is not "public relations", but "publics relations."' (Cole 1981: 4.)

The man, who named the profession in the 1920s, Edward L. Bernays, defined it: 'Public relations means exactly what it says, relations of an organization, individual, idea, whatever, with the publics on which it depends for its existence.' (Bernays 1986: 35.) Similarly Jon White argues: 'Public relations is, quite literally, about the relationship between organization and various "publics."' (White 1991: ix.) George Cheney and George N. Dionispoulos went even further, questioning the name itself: 'Public Relations? No, Relations with Publics . . .' (Cheney and Dionispoulos 1989.) But despite this widespread awareness that public relations managers deal with multiple publics, there are no clearly developed methods to solve public relations problems in such settings. Even texts that promise such an approach in their titles (e.g. Caywood and Ewing 1992), do not provide an adequate answer.

A final question to be addressed in this chapter, concerned whether the programme/solution presented in this study (direct organizational involvement into the development of a country's political system) can be considered as a public relations programme or whether it transcends this domain ? Here again the author suggests that the answer is 'yes'. Professional public relations has evolved beyond the phase of exclusively symbolic relations management (if there indeed was such a narrow defined phase of public relations development) into behavioural relations management (see Grunig 1993). And as Marx (1990) argued several years ago, public relations (or public affairs, as he calls the same process) should not only engage in behavioural (interactive, relational, responsive) relations, but even plan them in advance (cocreate). That is essential for what the author in this chapter has termed 'fourth wave public relations'.

NOTES

(eds C. L. Caywood and R. P. Ewing).
(eds C. H. Botan and V. Hazleton, Jr.).
(eds C. H. Botan and V. Hazleton, Jr.).
(ed. J. E. Grunig).
(eds J. E. Grunig and L. A. Grunig).

Concluding remarks

What insights and lessons emerge from the collection of chapters presented in this volume? The first and most immediate impression is of the considerable diversity and breadth of research interests of scholars working in this field. At one extreme, we find a strong emphasis on fundamental research and theorizing about the essential nature of public relations (e.g. chapters by Gunter Bentele and Betteke van Ruler) while elsewhere the emphasis is placed firmly on applied research, exploring how public relations is practised in different contexts (e.g. chapters by Danny Moss and Gary Warnaby, Barbara Baerns and Dejan Verčič). Other major themes that emerge within the chapters contained in this volume include the concept of image and identity (Henrik Rebel), how the theory of publics has evolved (Jim Grunig), how the concept of legitimacy may be applied in public relations (Inger Jensen), the extent to which practitioners should recognize and embrace a moral role (Jon White) and how the practice of public relations may differ between national cultures (Toby MacManus).

What these chapters clearly demonstrate is that research in public relations can and does follow many different paths – perhaps reflecting the very breadth of the domain of public relations itself. As these chapters reveal, scholars throughout both Europe and the USA have chosen to focus on quite different, yet equally relevant, dimensions of what is still an emerging discipline. Undoubtedly, this diversity of research interests can be attributed, at least in part, to the varied backgrounds and specialist interests of scholars who have chosen to work within this relatively new disciplinary field.

Such diversity of interests can be seen to be both a strength as well as a potential weakness in the future development of the discipline. On one hand, diversity brings with it fresh perspectives and challenges to existing conceptualizations of the public relations function.

On the other hand, it can present problems for those attempting to define the parameters of the discipline and create a coherent body of knowledge.

At this stage, as was suggested in the introduction to this book, it is impossible to claim that a coherent European body of knowledge exists in the field of public relations and it may well be some time before such a claim can be justified. However, as this volume of chapters suggests, scholarly interest in public relations is alive and growing in Europe and over the coming years promises to emerge as a major force to challenge the traditional dominance of North America.

References

1 A SITUATIONAL THEORY OF PUBLICS

Abugov, M. B. (1985) 'The board's communication dilemma: An analysis of a public communication dilemma as experienced by Alberta's Energy Resources Conservation Board.' Unpublished master's thesis, University of Calgary, Calgary, Alberta, Canada.

Al-Doory (aka Ramsey), S. A. (1974) 'An analysis of information seeking parameters of the blind and physcially handicapped.' Unpublished master's thesis, University of Maryland, College Park, MD.

Anderson, J. R. (1983) *The Architecture of Cognition*, Cambridge, Mass.: Harvard University Press.

Anderson, J. R. (1985) *Cognitive Psychology and its Implications* (2nd edn), New York: W. H. Freeman.

Anderson, J. R. and Reder, L. M. (1979) 'An elaborative processing explanation of depth of processing,' in *Levels of Processing in Human Memory,* (eds L. S. Cermak and F. I. M. Craik) pp. 385–403, Hillsdale, N.J.: Lawrence Erlbaum.

Anderson, R. B. (1989) 'Reassessing the odds against finding meaningful behavioural change in mass media health promotion campaigns,' in *Public Relations Theory,* (eds C. H. Botan and V. Hazleton, Jr.) pp. 309–22, Hillsdale, NJ: Lawrence Erlbaum Associates.

Atwood, L. E. and Cheng, P. (1986) 'Public opinion and media use in Hong Kong: The '1997' question,' Occasional chapters no. 15, Centre for Hong Kong Studies, Institute of Social Studies, The Chinese University of Hong Kong, Shatin, New Territories, Hong Kong.

Baldwin, W. R. (1989) 'Situational Publics of the Federal Reserve System.' Unpublished master's thesis, University of Maryland, College Park, MD.

Bandura, A. (1977) 'Self-efficacy: Toward a unifying theory of behavioural change,' *Psychological Review*, 84, pp. 191–215.

Bartholomew, C. M. (1973) 'Cognitive effects from using analogies to communicate physics to audiences in different decision situations.' Unpublished master's thesis, University of Maryland, College Park.

Bernays, E. L. (1923) Crystallizing Public Opinion, New York: Boni and Liveright.

Bishop, W. B. (1983) Communication from a scientific meeting. Unpublished master's thesis, University of Maryland, College Park, MD.

Blumer, J. (1966) (originally published in 1946) 'The mass, the public, and public opinion,' in *Reader in Public Opinion and Communication* (eds B. Berelson and M. Janowitz) (2nd edn) pp. 43–50, New York: Free Press.

Cameron, G. T. (1992) 'Memory for investor relations messages: An information-processing study of Grunig's situational theory,' *Journal of Public Relations Research*, 4, pp. 45–60.

Cameron, G. T. and Yang, J. (1990) 'Refining Grunig's situational theory: The addition of valence of support as a key variable.' Paper presented to the Association for Education for Education in Journalism and Mass Communication, Minneapolis (August).

Cantrill, J. G. (1993) 'Communication and our environment: Categorizing research in environmental advocacy.' *Journal of Applied Communication Research,* 21, pp. 66–95.

Carter, R. F. (1965) 'Communication and affective relations.' *Journalism Quarterly*, 42, pp. 203–12.

Clarke, P. and Kline, F. G. (1974) 'Mass media effects reconsidered: Some new strategies for communication research.' *Communication Research*, 1, pp. 224–70.

Clarke, P. B. and Wilson, J. Q. (1961) 'Incentive systems: a theory of organizations.' *Administrative Science Quarterly*, 6, pp. 219–66.

Conley, J. L. (1977) 'Government communication: A study of the communication behaviour of citizen publics with their local government.' Unpublished master's thesis, University of Maryland, College Park, MD.

Converse, P. E. (1964) 'The nature of belief systems in mass publics,' in D. E. Apter (ed.), *Ideology and Discontent* pp. 206–61, New York: Free Press.

Covello, V. T. (1992) 'Risk communication: An emerging area of health communication research.' in *Communication Yearbook 15,* (ed. S. A. Deetz) pp. 359–73, Newbury Park, CA: Sage.

Craik, F. I. M. (1979) 'Levels of processing: overview and closing comments,' in *Levels of Processing in Human Memory,* (eds L. S. Cermak and F. I. M. Craik) pp. 447–61, Hillsdale, N.J.: Lawrence Erlbaum.

Craik, F. I. M. and Lockhart, R. S. (1972) 'Levels of processing: a framework for memory research.' *Journal of Verbal Learning and Verbal Behavior*, 11, pp. 671–84.

Cutlip, S. M. and Center, A. H. (1958) *Effective Public Relations* (2nd edn), Englewood Cliffs, NJ: Prentice-Hall.

Davis-Belcher, P. O. (1990) 'Communication behaviours and the management of public policy issues.' Unpublished master's thesis, University of Maryland, College Park, MD.

Dewey, J. (1927) *The Public and its Problems,* Chicago: Swallow.

Dewey, J. (1938) *Logic: The Theory of Inquiry,* New York: Henry Holt.

Dewey, J. (1939) *Theory of Valuation, Chicago: University of Chicago Press.*

Essich, T. (1984) 'Environmental communication behaviour of industry managers.' Unpublished master's thesis, University of Maryland, College Park, MD.

Fishbein, M. and Ajzen, I. (1975) *Belief, Attitude, Intention, and Behaviour,* Reading, Mass.: Addison-Wesley.

Fisher, R. and Brown, S. (1988) *Getting Together: Building a Relationship that Gets to Yes,* Boston: Houghton Mifflin.

Fisher, R. and Ury, W. (1981) *Getting to Yes: Negotiating Agreement Without Giving In,* New York: Penguin Books.

Flora, J. A., Maccoby, N. and Farquhar, J. W. (1989) 'Communication campaigns to prevent cardiovascular disease: The Stanford community studies,' in *Public Communication Campaigns* (eds R. E. Rice and C. K. Atkin) (2nd ed.) (pp. 233–252). Newbury Park, CA: Sage.

Gibbs, J. D. (1986) 'An evaluation of Grunig's decision-situation theory of communication,' Unpublished master's thesis, University of Florida, Gainesville, FL.

Graber, D. A. (1984) *Processing the News,* New York: Longman.

Grunig, J. E. (1968) 'The role of information in economic decision making,' *Journalism Monographs,* No. 3.

Grunig, J. E. (1969) 'Information and decision making in economic development,' *Journalism Quarterly,* 46, pp. 565–75.

Grunig, J. E. (1971) 'Communication and the economic decision making processes of Colombian peasants,' *Economic Development and Cultural Change,* 19, pp. 580–97.

Grunig, J. E. (1974a) 'A case study of organizational information seeking and consumer information needs.' Paper presented to the Association for Education in Journalism and Mass Communication, San Diego (August).

Grunig, J. E. (1974b) 'Three stopping experiments on the communication of science,' *Journalism Quarterly,* 51, pp. 387–99.

Grunig, J. E. (1975) 'Some consistent types of employee publics,' *Public Relations Review,* 1(4), pp. 17–36.

Grunig, J. E. (1976) 'Communication behaviours occurring in decision and nondecision situations,' *Journalism Quarterly,* 53, pp. 252–63.

Grunig, J. E. (1977a) 'Review of research on environmental public relations,' *Public Relations Review,* 3(3), pp. 36–58.

Grunig, J. E. (1977b) 'Evaluating employee communication in a research operation,' *Public Relations Review,* 3(4), Winter, pp. 61–82.

Grunig, J. E. (1978) 'Defining publics in public relations: The case of a suburban hospital,' *Journalism Quarterly,* 55, pp. 109-118.

Grunig, J. E. (1979a) 'Time budgets, level of involvement, and use of the mass media,' *Journalism Quarterly,* 56, pp. 248–61.

Grunig, J. E. (1979b) 'A new measure of public opinions on corporate social responsibility,' *Academy of Management Journal,* 22, pp. 738–64.

Grunig, J. E. (1979c) *Membership Survey and Communication Audit.* Washington: American Alliance for Health, Physical Education, Recreation, and Dance.

Grunig, J. E. (1982a) 'The message-attitude-behaviour relationship: Communication behaviours of organizations,' *Communication Research,* 9, pp. 163–200.

Grunig, J. E. (1982b) 'Developing economic education programs for the press,' *Public Relations Review,* 8(3), pp. 43–62.

Grunig, J. E. (1983a) 'Communication behaviours and attitudes of environmental publics: two studies,' *Journalism Monographs* No. 81.

Grunig, J. E. (1983b) 'Washington reporter publics of corporate public affairs programs,' *Journalism Quarterly,* 60, pp. 603–15.

Grunig, J. E. (1985) 'A structural reconceptualization of the organizational communication audit, with application to a state department of education,' Paper presented to the International Communication Association, Honolulu (May).

Grunig, J. E. (1987) 'An audit of organizational structure, job satisfaction, and the communication system in the Allegany County School System.' Cumberland, MD: Allegany County School System (July).

Grunig, J. E. (1989a) 'A situational theory of environmental issues, publics, and activists,' in *Environmental Activism Revisited: The Changing Nature of Communication through Organizational Public Relations, Special Interest Groups, and the Mass Media,* (ed. L. A. Grunig) pp. 50–82, Troy, Ohio: North American Association for Environmental Education.

Grunig, J. E. (1989b) 'Sierra club study shows who become activists,' *Public Relations Review*, 15(3), pp. 3–24.

Grunig, J. E. (1989c) 'Symmetrical presuppositions as a framework for public relations theory,' in *Public Relations Theory,* (eds C. H. Botan and V. Hazleton, Jr.) pp. 17–44, Hillsdale, NJ: Lawrence Erlbaum Associates.

Grunig, J. E. (1992) 'Communication, public relations, and effective organizations: An overview of the book,' in *Excellence in Public Relations and Communication Management,* (ed. J. E. Grunig) pp. 1–30, Hillsdale, NJ: Lawrence Erlbaum Associates.

Grunig, J. E. (1993) 'Image and substance: From symbolic to behavioural relationships,' *Public Relations Review*, 19, pp. 121–39.

Grunig, J. E. and Childers (aka Hon), L. (1988). 'Reconstruction of a situational theory of communication: Internal and external concepts as identifiers of publics for AIDS.' Paper presented to the Association for Education in Journalism and Mass Communication, Portland, OR (July).

Grunig, J. E. and Disbrow, J. B. (1977) 'Developing a probabilistic model for communication decision making,' *Communication Research*, 4, pp. 145–68.

Grunig, J. E. and Grunig, L. A. (1992) 'Models of public relations and communication,' in *Excellence in Public Relations and Communication Management,* (ed. J. E. Grunig) pp. 285–326 Hillsdale, NJ: Lawrence Erlbaum Associates.

Grunig, J. E. and Hunt, T. (1984) *Managing Public Relations*. New York: Holt, Rinehart and Winston.

Grunig, J. E. and Ipes, D. A. (1983) 'The anatomy of a campaign against drunk driving,' *Public Relations Review*, 9(2), pp. 36–53.

Grunig, J. E., Nelson, C. L., Richburg, S. J. and White, T. J. (1988) 'Communication by agricultural publics: internal and external orientations,' *Journalism Quarterly*, 65, pp. 26–38.

Grunig, J. E., Ramsey, S. and Schneider (aka L. Grunig), L. A. (1985) 'An axiomatic theory of cognition and writing,' *Journal of Technical Writing and Communication*, 15, pp. 95–130.

Grunig, J. E. and Repper, F. C. (1992) 'Strategic management, publics, and issues,' in *Excellence in Public Relations and Communication Management,* (ed. J. E. Grunig) pp. 117–58, Hillsdale, NJ: Lawrence Erlbaum Associates.

Grunig, J. E. and Stamm, K. R. (1979) 'Cognitive strategies and the resolution of environmental issues: A second study,' *Journalism Quarterly*, 56, pp. 715–26.

Grunig, L. A. (1985) 'Meeting the information needs of employees,' *Public Relations Review*, 11(2), pp. 43–53.

Grunig, L. A., Dozier, D. M. and Grunig, J. E. (1994) *IABC Excellence in Relations and Communication Management, Phase 2: Qualitative Study, Initial Analysis: Cases of Excellence*, San Francisco: IABC Research Foundation.

Hamilton, P. K. (1992) 'Grunig's situational theory: A replication, application, and extension,' *Journal of Public Relations Research*, 4, pp. 123–50.

Harwood, R. (1994) 'So what do polls signify?' *Washington Post*, June 25, p. A21.

Hunt, T. and Grunig, J. E. (1994) *Public Relations Techniques*, Fort Worth, TX: Harcourt Brace.

Jeffers, D. W. (1989a) 'Putting the "public" first in public relations: An exploratory study of municipal employee public service attitudes, job satisfaction, and communication variables,' *Public Relations Research Annual*, 1, pp. 197–214.

Jeffers, D. W. (1989b) 'Using public relations theory to evaluate specialized magazines as communication channels,' *Public Relations Research Annual*, 1, pp. 115–24.

Jenkins, L. (1976) 'Prison communication: A study of the public perception of Lorton Prison.' Unpublished master's thesis, University of Maryland, College Park, MD.

Jennings, M. K. (1992) 'Idelogical thinking among mass publics and political elites,' *Public Opinion Quarterly*, 56, pp. 419–41.

Kelly, K. S. (1979) 'Predicting alumni giving: An analysis of alumni donors and non-donors of the College of Journalism at the University of Maryland.' Unpublished master's thesis, University of Maryland, College Park, MD.

Kotler, P. and Andreasen, A.R. (1987) *Strategic Marketing for Nonprofit Organizations* (3rd edn), Englewood Cliffs, N.J.: Prentice-Hall.

Krugman, H. E. (1965) 'The impact of television advertising: learning without involvement,' *Public Opinion Quarterly*, 29, pp. 349–56.

Lang, G. E. and Lang, K. (1983) *The Battle for Public Opinion*. New York: Columbia University Press.

Major, A. M. (1993a) 'Environmental concern and situational communication theory: Implications for communicating with environmental publics,' *Journal of Public Relations Research*, 5, pp. 251–68.

Major, A. M. (1993b) 'A test of situational communication theory: Public response to the 1990 Browning earthquake prediction,' *International Journal of Mass Emergencies and Disasters*, 11, pp. 337–49.

Markus, M. and Zajonc, R. B. (1985) 'The cognitive perspective in social psychology,' in *Handbook of Social Psychology* (eds G. Lindsey and E. Anderson) (Vol. 1) pp. 137–230, New York: Random House.

Moe, T. M. (1980) *The Organization of Interests*, Chicago: University of Chicago Press.

Myers, Jr., R. E. (1985) 'Communication behaviours of Maryland farmers: An analysis of adopters and nonadopters of innovations to reduce agricultural pollution of the Chesapeake Bay.' Unpublished master's thesis, University of Maryland, College Park.

O'Keefe, G. J. (1985) '"Taking a Bite Out of Crime": The impact of a public information campaign,' *Communication Research*, 12, pp. 147–78.

Olson, M. (1971) *The Logic of Collective Action*, Cambridge, Mass.: Harvard University Press.

Pavlik, J. V. (1983) 'The effects of two health information campaigns on the complexity of cognitive structure: An information processing approach.' Unpublished doctoral dissertation, University of Minnesota, Minneapolis.

Pelham, K. L. (1977) 'Using communication at the Naval Surface Weapons Center: An analysis using Grunig's multi-system theory.' Unpublished master's thesis, University of Maryland, College Park, MD.

Petty, R. E. (1981) *Attitudes and Persuasion: Classic and Contemporary Approaches*, Dubuque, Iowa: Wm. C. Brown.

Petty, R. E. and Cacioppo, J. T. (1986). *Communication and Persuasion: Central and Peripheral Routes to Attitude Change*. New York: Springer-Verlag.

pr reporter (1990) 'Behavioral model replacing communication model as basic theoretical underpinning of pr practice: Key is stimulating latent readiness & creating triggering events; (July 30).

Price, V. (1992) *Public Opinion*. Newbury Park, CA: Sage.

Ray, M. L. (1973) 'Marketing communication and the hierarchy of effects,' in P. Clarke (ed.), *New Models for Mass Communication Research*, pp. 147–76, Beverly Hills: Sage.

Rice, R. E. and Atkin, C. K. (eds) (1989). *Public Communication Campaigns* (2nd edn). Newbury Park, CA: Sage.

Rogers, E. M. (1983) *The Diffusion of Innovations* (3rd edn) New York: Free Press.

Rothschild, M. L. and Ray, M. L. (1974), 'Involvement and political advertising effect: an exploratory experiment,' *Communication Research*, 1, pp. 264–85.

Salmon, C. T. (1986), 'Perspectives on involvement in consumer and communication research,' in *Progress in Communication Sciences* (eds B. Dervin and M. J. Voigt) (Vol. VII), pp. 243–69, Norwood, N. J.: Ablex.

Sandman, P. M. (1982), 'Motivating change: Psychological jujitsu and the environmental movement,' *Not Man Apart*, (May) 19, p.22.

Sandman, P. M. (1985) 'Getting to maybe: Some communication aspects of hazardous waste facility siting,' *Seton Hall Legislative Journal*, 9, pp. 442–65.

Sauerhaft, S. and Atkins, C. (1989) *Image Wars: Protecting Your Company When There's No Place to Hide*. New York: Wiley.

Schneider (aka L. Grunig), L. A. (1978) 'Employee communication at a university-based R & D centre: An analysis using Grunig's theory of communication behaviour.' Unpublished master's thesis, University of Maryland, College Park, MD.

Schneider (aka L. Grunig), L. A. (1985) 'Implications of the concept of the schema for public relations,' *Public Relations Research & Education*, 2(1), pp. 36–47.

Sheriff, C. W., Sheriff, M. and Nebergall, R. E. (1965). *Attitudes and*

Attitude Change: The Social Judgement Approach. Philadelphia: Saunders.

Slater, M. D., Chipman, H., Auld, G., Keefe, T. and Kendall, P. (1992) 'Information processing and situational theory: A cognitive response analysis,' *Journal of Public Relations Research,* 4, pp. 189–204.

Spicer, S. R. (1985) 'Effectiveness of a fire department public information campaign.' Unpublished master's thesis, University of Maryland, College Park, MD.

Springston, J. K., Keyton, J., Leichty, G. B. and Metzger, J. (1992) 'Field dynamics and public relations theory: Toward the management of multiple publics,' *Journal of Public Relations Research,* 4, pp. 81–100.

Stamm, K. R. and Bowes, J. E. (1972) 'Environmental attitudes and reaction,' *Journal of Environmental Education,* 3, pp. 56–60.

Stamm, K. R. and Grunig, J. E. (1977) 'Communication situations and cognitive strategies for the resolution of environmental issues,' *Journalism Quarterly,* 54, pp. 713–20.

Tesh, S. (1984) 'In support of "single-issue" politics,' *Political Science Quarterly,* 99, pp. 27–44.

Turner, D. (1981) 'Communication behaviour of linking agents in the Maryland Cooperative Extension Service,' Unpublished master's thesis, University of Maryland, College Park, MD.

Ury, W. (1991) *Getting Past No: Negotiating with Difficult People,* New York: Bantam Books.

Van Leuven, J. K. and Slater, M. D. (1991) 'How publics, public relations, and the media shape the public opinion process,' *Public Relations Research Annual,* 3, pp. 165–78.

Vasquez, G. M. (1993) 'A homo narrans paradigm for public relations: Combining Bormann's symbolic convergence theory and Grunig's situational theory of publics,' *Journal of Public Relations Research,* 5, pp. 201–16.

Vasquez, G. M. (1994) 'Testing a communication theory-method-message-behaviour complex for the investigation of publics,' *Journal of Public Relations Research,* 6, pp. 267–91.

Vaugan, E. (1994) 'The significance of socioeconomic and ethnic diversity for the risk communication process,' Paper presented to the conference on addressing agencies' risk communication needs: A symposium to discuss next steps, sponsored by the Center for Environmental Communication, Rutgers University, Annapolis, MD (June).

Waddell, D. G. (1979) 'Employee communication at a multi-campus community college: An analysis using Grunig's communication behaviour theory.' Unpublished master's thesis, University of Maryland, College Park, MD.

Wallack, L. M. (1993) *Media Advocacy and Public Health: Power for Prevention,* Newbury Park, CA: Sage.

Weick, K. (1979) *The Social Psychology of Organizing* (2nd edn), Reading, Mass.: Addison-Wesley.

Wilson, J. Q. (1973) *Political Organizations,* New York: Basic Books.

Winett, R. A. (1986) *Information and Behaviour: Systems of Influence,* Hillsdale, N.J.: Lawrence Erlbaum Associates.

2 REQUISITE VARIETY IN PUBLIC RELATIONS RESEARCH

Babbie, E. (1992) *The Practice of Social Research*, (6th edn.) Belmont, CA: Wadsworth.

Bantz, C.R. (1990) 'Organizing and enactment: Karl Weick and the production of news', in *Foundations in Organizational Communication: A Reader*, (eds S.R. Corman, S.P. Banks, C.R. Bantz and M.E. Mayer) pp. 133–41. New York: Longman.

Bantz, C.R. (1993) 'Cultural diversity and group cross-cultural team research', *Applied Communication Research*, 21(1): pp. 1–20.

Bergen, J. (1994) '2010 PR agencies: Borderless consultancies', *IABC Communication World*, (January/February) pp. 46–7.

Biker, B.D. and Hovgaard, U. (1994) 'Rational relations: The rationality of organizations in a communication-theoretical perspective', *International Public Relations Review*, 17(1): pp. 16–26.

Clifford, J. (1986) 'Introduction: Partial truths', n J. Clifford and G.E. Marcus (eds), *Writing culture: The Poetics and Politics of Ethnography*, pp. 1–26, Berkeley: University of California Press.

Cohen, A. A., Adoni, H. and Bantz, C.R. (1990). *Social Conflict and Television News*, Newbury Park, CA: Sage.

Cox, T. (1994) 'The effects of diversity and its management on organizational performance', *The Diversity Factor*, (Spring) pp. 16–22.

Dobzhansky, T., Ayala, F.J., Stebbins, G.L., and Valentine, J.W. (1977) *Evolution*, San Francisco: W.H. Freeman.

Eadie, W.F. (1994) 'Research on more than a shoestring', *Spectra*, (June) pp. 5–15.

Everett, J.L. (1994) 'Communication and sociocultural evolution in organizations and organizational populations', *Communication Theory*, 4(2): pp. 93–110.

Geertz, C. (1988) *Works and Lives: The Anthropologist as Author*, Stanford, CA: Stanford University Press.

Gruban, B., Verčič, D. and Zavrl, F. (1994) Public relations in Slovenia. Special Issue, *pristop* (January).

Grunig, J. E. (ed) (1992) *Excellence in Public Relations and Communication Management*. Hillsdale, NJ: Lawrence Erlbaum Associates.

Grunig, L.A. (1988) 'A research agenda for women in public relations', *Public Relations Review*, 14(3): pp. 48–57.

Grunig, L.A., Grunig, J.E. and Ehling, W.P. (1992) 'What is an effective organization?' in *Excellence in Public Relations and Communication Management*, (ed J.E. Grunig) pp. 65–90. Hillsdale, NJ: Lawrence Erlbaum Associates.

Hofstede, G. (1984) *Culture's Consequences: International Differences in Work-related Values* (abridged edn), Beverly Hills: Sage.

Huang, Y. (1990) 'Risk communication, models of public relations and anti-nuclear activism: A case study of a nuclear power plant in Taiwan'. Unpublished master's degree thesis, University of Maryland, College Park.

IABC Research Foundation (1991) *Initial Data Report and Practical Guide*, San Francisco: Author.

Kauffman, B.J. (1992) 'Feminist facts: Interview strategies and political subjects in ethnography, *Communication Theory*, 2(3): pp. 187–206.

Kuhn, T. (1962) *The Structure of Scientific Revolutions*, Chicago: University of Chicago Press.

Laufenburger, A. (Forthcoming) *Excellence in Public Relations in France*, Paris.

Lincoln, Y.S. and Guba, E.G. (1985) *Naturalistic Inquiry*, Beverly Hills: Sage.

Locke, L.F., Spirduso, W.W. and Silverman, S.J. (1987) *Proposals That Work: A Guide for Planning Dissertations and Grant Proposals*, (2nd edn) Newbury Park, CA: Sage.

Lyra, A. (1991) 'Public relations in Greece: Models, roles and gender'. Unpublished master's degree thesis, University of Maryland, College Park.

Marshall, C. and Rossman, G.B. (1989) *Designing Qualitative Research*, Newbury Park, CA: Sage.

Miles, M.B. and Huberman, A.M. (1984) *Qualitative Data Analysis: A Sourcebook of New Methods*, Newbury Park, CA: Sage.

Nemeth, C. (1985) 'Dissent, group process and creativity', *Advances in Group Processes*, Vol. 2, pp. 57–75.

Putnam, L.L. (1983) 'The interpretive perspective: An alternative to functionalism', in *Communication and Organizations: An Interpretive Approach*, (eds L.L. Putnam and M.E. Pacanowsky) pp. 31–54, Newbury Park, CA: Sage.

Smircich, L. (1981) 'The concept of culture and organizational analysis'. Paper presented at the Speech Communication Association/International Communication Association Conference on Interpretive Approaches to Organizational Communication (June).

Smith, L.M. (1978) 'An evolving logic of participant observation, educational ethnography and other case studies', in *Review of Research in Education*, (ed. L. Shulman) Vol. 6. Itasca, IL: Peacock.

Smith, M.J. (1988) *Contemporary Communication Research Methods*, Belmont, CA: Wadsworth.

Sriramesh, K. (1991) 'The impact of societal culture on public relations: An ethnographic study of South Indian organizations'. Unpublished doctoral dissertation, University of Maryland, College Park.

Weick, K.E. (1969) *The Social Psychology of Organizing*, Reading, MA: Addison-Wesley.

Weick, K.E. (1977a) 'Cognition in organizations: An analysis of the Utrecht Jazz Orchestra', *Administrative Science Quarterly*, 22: pp. 606–639.

Weick, K.E. (1977b) 'Enactment processes in organizations', *New Directions in Organizational Behavior*, 1, pp. 267–300.

Weick, K.E. (1979a) 'Cognitive processes in organizations', *Research in Organizational Behavior*, 1, pp. 41–74.

Weick, K.E. (1979b) *The Social Psychology of Organizing* (2nd edn). Reading, MA: Addison-Wesley.

Weick, K.E. (1983) 'Organizational communication: Toward a research agenda', in *Communication and Organizations: An Interpretive Approach*, (eds L.L. Putnam and M.E. Pacanowsky) pp. 13–30, Newbury Park, CA: Sage.

Weick, K.E. (1984) 'Toward a model of organizations as interpretation systems', *Academy of Management Review*, 9, pp. 284–95.

Woolf, V. (1929) *A Room of One's Own*, London: Hogarth Press.

Yin, R.K. (1989) *Case Study Research: Design and Methods*, (rev. edn) Newbury Park, CA: Sage.

3 PUBLIC RELATIONS AND REALITY: A CONTRIBUTION TO A THEORY OF PUBLIC RELATIONS

BDW (1993) *Ergebnisbericht der Erhebung des Deutschen Kommunikationsverbandes BDW zur Bedeutung–Planung–Durchfuhrung von EVENTS.* Bonn: BDW.

Becher, M. (1993) *Public Relations und Ethik. Eine empirische Studie zu ethisch relevanten Bereichen im Berufsfeld PR*. Bamberg: unveröff. Diplomarbeit.

Bernays, E.L. (1923/1929) *Crystallizing Public Opinion*. New York: Liveright.

Bernays, E.L. (1952) *Public Relations*. Norman: University of Oclahoma Press.

Boorstin, D.J. (1963) *The Image or What Happened to the American Dream*. Harmondsworth: Penguin.

Gross, H. (1951) *Moderne Meinungspflege. Für die Praxis der Wirtschaft*. Düsseldorf: Droste.

Grunig, J.E. (1993) 'World View, Ethics, and the Two-Way Symmetrical Model of Public Relations.' in *Normative Aspekte der Public Relations. Grundlegende Fragen und Perspektiven. Eine Einführung*. (hrsg. W. Armbrecht & U. Zabel) Opladen: Westdeutscher Verlag, S. 69–89.

Hundhausen, C. (1951) Werbung um öffentliches Vertrauen. 'Public Relations.' Essen: Girardet.

Jarchow, K. (1992) *Wirklichkeiten, Wahrheiten, Wahrnehmungen*. Bremen: WMIT-Druck und Verlags-GmbH.

Kalt, G. (1993) 'Viele inszenierte Anlässe. Zur Auswahl aktueller Wirtschaftsthemen bei ARD, RTL und dpa.' in *Medien-Kritik*, Nr. 36 vom 6.9. 1993, S. 7–10.

Lippmann, W. (1922) *Public Opinion*. New York: Macmillian.

Merten, K. (1992) 'Begriff und Funktion von Public Relations.' in *PR-Magazin*, Nr. 11 (1992), S. 35–46.

Neske, F. (1977) *PR-Management*. Gernsbach: Deutscher Betriebswirte-Verlag.

Newsom, D., Scott, A. and VanSlyke Turk, J. (1989) *This is PR. The Realities of Public Relations*. Belmont, Cal.: Wadsworth.

Nitsch, H. (1975) *Dynamische Public Relations. Unternehmerische Öffentlichkeitsarbeit – Strategie für die Zukunft*. Stuttgart: Taylorix.

Oeckl, A. (1960) Öffentlichkeitsarbeit in Theorie und Praxis. Veröffentlichungen der Wirtschaftshochschule Mannheim. Reihe 2: Reden, Heft 5. Stuttgart usw.: Kohlhammer.

Oeckl, A. (1976) *PR-Praxis. Der Schlüssel zur Öffentlichkeitsarbeit*. Düsseldorf/Wien: Econ.

Ronneberger, F. and Rühl, M. (1992) *Theorie der Public Relations. Ein Entwurf.* Opladen: Westdeutscher Verlag.

Zedtwitz-Arnim, G.V.G. von (1996) *Tu Gutes und rede darüber. Public Relations für die Wirtschaft.* Berlin/Frankfurt/Wien: Ullstein.

4 COMMUNITY PUBLIC RELATIONS IN GERMANY

Baerns, B. (1993a) 'Understanding and Development of Public Relations in Germany, East and West', in *Communication Management. The Role for Public Relations in Organizational Communication.* Proceedings of the second European Seminar for Teachers, Practitioners and Researchers. Prague, May 6–8, pp. 63–74.

Baerns, B. (1993b) 'Informationsrechte and Auskunftspflichten', in *Handbuch fur Offentlichkeitsarbeit (PR) von Wirtschaft, Verbanden, Behorden und Institutionen.* (ed. G. Schulze-Furstenow) Founded by Werner Muhlbradt. Neuwied 31993, Vol. 1, Group I, 3, pp. 1–26.

Bockelmann, F. (1991) Die Pressestellen der Öffentlichen Hand. Munchen 1991 (= Arbeitsgemeinschaft fr Kommunikationsforschung 35).

Hoffmann-Riem, W. (1991) 'Die Entwicklung der Medien and des Medienrechts im Gebiet der ehemaligen DDR', in *Archiv fur Presserecht* 1991, pp. 472–81.

Kauffmann. W-D. (1987) 'Presse- and Offentlichkeitarbeit 1987', in *Statistisches Jahrbuch deutscher Gemeinden* (ed. D. Stadtetag) Vol. 75, Kôln 1988, pp. 409–19.

Kutscher-Klink, A. (1994) 'Kommunale Offentlichkeitsarbeit in der Bundesrepublik Deutschland. Bestandsaufnahme und Kritik'. MA. Thesis, Free University of Berlin 1994.

Nimmo, D. (1977) 'Political Communication and Research. An Overwiew', in Communication Yearbook I (ed. D. Ruben) An Annual Review Published by the International Communication Association. New Brunswick and New Jersey 1977, pp. 441–52.

Rober, M. (1988) 'Moglichkeiten und Grenzen des offentlichen Marketing. Anmerkungen aus verwaltungswissenschaftlicher Sicht', *Die Offentliche Verwaltung*, Vol. 41, pp. 1029–35.

5 TOWARDS A TYPOLOGY OF MA AND PHD THESES PROJECTS IN PUBLIC RELATIONS

Angerer, U. (1990) Public Relations 1980 bis 1990: Ein Jahrzehnt deutschsprachiger PR-Forschung. PhD thesis. University of Salzburg.

Cooper, H.M. (1989) *Integrating Research. A Guide for Literature Reviews* (2nd edn.), Newbury Park: Sage.

Larson, M.S. (1977) *The Rise of Professionalism. A Sociological Analysis*, Berkely: University of California Press.

Pavlik, J.V. (1987) *Public Relations. What Research Tells Us*, Newbury Park: Sage

Signitzer, B. (1994) Professionalisierungstheoretische Anstze und Public Relations: Oberlegungen zur PR-Berufsforschung, in *Normative Aspekte der Public Relations* (eds W. Ambrecht and U. Zabel), Opladen: West-deutscher Verlag.

Windahl, S. and Signitzer, B. (1992) *Using Communication Theory: An Introduction to Planned Communication*, London: Sage.

Yin, R.K. (1989) *Case Study Research. Design and Methods*. (rev. edn) Newbury Park: Sage.

6 PUBLIC RELATIONS OR SIMPLY PRODUCT PUBLICITY

Cutlip, S.M. Center, A.H. and Broom, G.M. (1985) *Effective Public Relations*, Englewood Cliffs, NJ: Prentice Hall International.

Davidson, W.R and Doody. A.F. (1966) *Retailing Management*, New York: Ronald Press.

Davies, G. (1992) *Positioning Strategy in Retailing*, London: Paul Chapman Publishing Ltd.

Ferguson, M.A. (1984) Building a theory of public relations: Interorganizational relationships. paper presented at the Association of Education in Journalism and Mass Communication (August) Gainsville, Florida.

Gilligan, C. and Sutton, C. (1987) Strategic planning in grocery and DIY retailing, in *Business Strategy and Retailing* (ed. G. Johnson) Chichester: John Wiley & Son, pp. 172–92.

Greenley, G. and Shipley, D. (1991) 'A comparative study of operational marketing practices among British department stores and supermarkets', *European Journal of Marketing*, 26 (5), pp. 22–35.

Grunig, J.E. and Hunt, T. (1984) *Managing Public Relations*, New York: Holt Rheinhart Winston.

Grunig, J.E. (ed.) (1992) *Excellence in Public Relations and Communications Management*, Hilldale NJ: Lawrence Erlbaum Associates.

Grunig, J.E. and Grunig, L.A. (1992) Models of public relations and communications, in *Excellence in Public Relations and Communications Management* (ed. J.E. Grunig) pp. 285–325, Hillsdale, NJ: Lawrence Erlbaum Associates.

Grunig, J.E. (1992) 'What is Excellence in Management?', in *Excellence in Public Relations and Communications Management* (ed. J.E. Grunig) pp. 219–50, Lawrence Erlbaum Associates, Hillsdale, NJ.

Hickman, C.R. and Silva, M.A. (1984) *Creating Excellence*, New York: Plume.

Kanter R.M. (1989) *When Giants Learn to Dance*, New York: Simon & Schuster.

Kotler, P. (1982) *Marketing for Non-profit Organizations*, Englewood Cliffs N.J: Prentice Hall.

Kotler, P. (1986) 'Megamarketing', *Harvard Business Review*, 64, 2, March–April.

Kotler, P. (1988) *Marketing Management* (5th edn), Englewood Cliffs, NJ: Prentice Hall.

Kotler, P. and Mindak, W. (1978) 'Marketing and public relations', *Journal of Marketing*, (4) October.

Lees, R. and Worthington, S. (1989) 'Achieving above average profitability in retailing', *International Journal of Retailing*, 4, (2) pp. 17–34.

McGee, J. (1987) Retailer strategies in the UK, in *Business Strategy and Retailing*. (ed. G. Johnson) Chichester: John Wiley & Son.

Miller, G.R. (1989) 'Persuasion and public relations: Two 'Ps' in a pod', in Public Relations Theory (eds. C.H. Botan and V. Hazelton Jnr) Lawrence Erlbaum Associates, Hillsdale, NJ, pp. 44–66.

Moore, H.F. and Kalupa, F.B. (1985) *Public Relations: Principles, Cases, and Problems* (9th edn) Homewood, Ill.; Richard D. Irwin.

Murphy. P. (1991) 'The limits of symmetry: A game theory approach to symmetric and asymmetric public relations', in *Public Relations Research Annual* (eds J.E. Grunig and L.A. Grunig) (Vol 3) (pp. 115–132) Hillsdale, NJ: Lawrence Erlbaum Associates.

Peters, T.J and Waterman, R.H (1982) *In Search of Excellence: Lessons From America's Best Run Companies*, New York: Harper & Row.

Piercy, N. (1987a) 'Marketing in UK retailing part 1', *Retail and Distribution Management March/April*, pp. 52–55.

Piercy, N. (1987b) 'Marketing in UK retailing part 2', *Retail and Distribution Management May/June*, pp 58–60.

Piercy, N. and Alexander, N. (1988) 'The status quo of the marketing organization in UK retailing: A neglected phenomenon', *The Service Industries Journal*, 8 (2), pp. 155–75.

Porac, J. F., Thomas, H., and Emme, B. (1987) 'Knowing the competition: The mental models of retailing strategists' in *Business Strategy and Retailing* (ed. G. Johnson) Chichester: John Wiley & Son.

Robbins, S.P. (1990) *Organisational Theory: Structure Design and Applications* (3rd edn), Englewood Cliffs, N.J: Prentice Hall.

Schwartz, G. (1982) 'Public relations gets short shrift from new managers', *Marketing News*, October 15 1982, p. 8.

Shimp, T.A. and Delozier, M.W. (1986) *Promotion Management and Marketing Communications*, New York, Dryden

Van der Meiden, A. (1993) 'Public relations and other modalities of professional communication', *International Public Relations Review*, 16 (3), 1993, pp. 8–12.

Walters, D. and White, D. (1987) *Retail Marketing Management*, Basingstoke, Macmillan.

Wortzel, L.H., (1987) 'Retailing strategies for todays mature market place', *Journal of Business Strategy*, 7 (4), pp. 45–56.

7 BUSINESS AND ORGANIZATIONAL CONSEQUENCES OF THE MORAL ROLE OF THE PUBLIC RELATIONS PRACTITIONER

Bovet, S. F. (1993) 'The burning question of ethics: the profession fights for better business practices,' *Public Relations Journal*, 49, (11).

Budd, J. F. Jnr (1991) 'Ethical Dilemmas in Public Relations,' Gold Paper No 8, International Public Relations Association, Geneva.

Business International (1991) 'New Directions in Corporate Governance' Report No 2137 Economist Group, London.

Department of Trade and Industry, CBI, (1993) Innovation – the Best Practice, London.

Department of Trade & Industry (1993) 'Competitiveness,' Memorandum, DTI, London.

Finn, D. (1959) 'The struggle for ethics in public relations,' *Harvard Business Review*, (January – February) 37, (1) pp. 49–58.

Frederick, W. C. Davis, K, Post J. (1988) *Business and Society: Corporate Strategy, Public Policy, Ethics*, McGraw-Hill, New York.

Gallup Organization (1990) 'Managers' expectations of public relations advisors,' Study carried out for the International Public Relations Association, London Seminar.

Grunig, J. (1992) (ed.) *Excellence in Public Relations and Communications Management*, Lawrence Erlbaum Associates, Hillsdale, New Jersey.

Grunig, J. and Hunt, T. (1984) *Managing Public Relations*, Holt Rinehart and Winston, New York.

Grunig, J. and White, J. (1992) 'The effect of worldviews on public relations,' in *Excellence in Public Relations and Communications Management* (ed. J. Grunig) Lawrence Erlbaum Associates, Hillsdale, New Jersey.

Hampden-Turner, C. and Trompenaars, F. (1993) *The Seven Cultures of Capitalism*, Piatkus, London.

Harrison, S. L. (1990) 'Ethics and moral issues in public relations curricula,' *Journalism Educator*, (Autumn) 45, 3.

Hedron Consulting, (1993) *Communication: Why Managers Must Do More,* Hedron Consulting, London.

Hofstede, G. (1980) 'Angola coffee – or the confrontation of an organisation with changing values in its environment,' *Organisation Studies*, 1(1) pp. 21–40.

Olasky, M. (1984) 'The 1984 public relations scam awards,' *Business and Society Review*, 51, pp. 42–6.

New Directions in Corporate Governance (1991), Report No 2137, Business International, Economist Group, London.

Royal Society for the encouragement of the Arts, Manufacture and Commerce (1994) 'Tomorrow's Company: the role of business in a changing world,' interim report, RSA, London.

Walton, D. (1987) *British Petroleum*, Government and Public Affairs Department, London.

White, J. and Blamphin, J. (1994) 'Priorities for research in UK public relations practice: the results of a Delphi study,' *The Research Network*, University of Stirling and City University Business School.

8 A COMPARATIVE ANALYSIS OF PUBLIC RELATIONS IN AUSTRIA AND THE UNITED KINGDOM

Ang, I. (1990) 'Culture and communication: towards an ethnographic critique of media consumption in the transnational media system', *European Journal of Communication*, Vol. 5, pp. 239–60, Sage.

Baerns, B. (1994) '*Understanding the development of public relations in Germany, East and West in communication management*': Proceedings of

296 *References*

the Second European Seminar for Teachers Practitioners and Researchers. Gent. CERP Education.

Baskin, O. and Aronoff, C. (1992) *Public Relations: the Profession and the Practice*, Dubuque, Iowa: W.C. Brown.

Black, S. (1990) 'Public relations in China today', *International Public Relations Review*, 13 (4) pp. 6–7.

Botan, C. (1990) 'Public relations as a science: implications of cultural differences and international events'. Paper presented at the Quandt Foundation Communication Group. Salzburg.

Botan, C. (1992) 'International Public Relations Critique and Reformulation', *Public Relations Review* 18, (12) pp. 149–59.

Bourdieu, P. (1984) *Distinction: A Social Critique of the Judgement of Taste*, London: Routledge, Kegan Paul.

Carroll, J. C. (1956) *Language, Thought and Reality: Selected Writings of Benjamin Lee Wharf*, MIT Cambridge, MA.

Carey, J. W. (1989) *Communication as Culture*, Unwin Hyman.

Coombs, W. T, Holladay, S. Signitzer, B. and Hasenauer, G. (1994) 'A comparative analysis of international public relations: identification interpretation of similarities and differences between professionalisation in Austria, Norway and the USA', *Journal of Public Relations Research.*, 6 (1) pp. 23–39.

Crable, R.E. and Vibbert, S.A. (1986) *Public Relations as Communication Management*, Edina, MN: Bellwether Press.

Cuff, E., Sharrock, W., and Francis, D. (1990) *Perspectives in Sociology* (3rd edn) London: Routledge.

Curran, J. (1990) 'The new revisionism in mass communication research: a reappraisal', *European Journal of Communication*, 5, (2–3) pp. 135–64, Sage.

Fiske, J. (1989) *Understanding Popular Culture*, Unwin Hyman.

Flieger, H. (1988) *Public Relations – Berater. Curriculum Für eine Akademische Ausbildeng*.

Foucalt, M. (1980) *Power/Knowledge*, Brighton: Harvester.

Garreau, J. (1981) *The Nine Nations of North America*, Houghton Mifflin.

Granovetter, M. (1985) 'Economic action and social structure: the problem of embeddedness,' *American Journal of Sociology*, 91 (3) pp. 481–510.

Grunig, J. E. and Hunt, T. (1984) *Managing Public Relations*, New York: Holt Rinehart and Winston.

Grunig, J. E. and Grunig, L. A. (1992) 'Models of public relations and communications,' in *Excellence in Public Relations and Communication Management* (ed. J. Grunig), pp. 285–325, Hillsdale, NJ: Lawrence Erlbaum Associates.

Gunn, J. (1994) Environmental Public Relations: Consultancy Practice in Bangkok. Unpublished BSc. Dissertation. Bournemouth University.

Gurevitch, M., Bennett, T. Curran, J. and Woollacott, J. (eds) (1982) *Culture, Society and the Media*, Methuen.

Hall, S. (1986) 'Cultural studies: two paradigms', in *Media, Culture and Society: A Critical Reader* (eds R. Collins, J Curran, N. Garnham, P. Scannell, P. Schlesinger, and C. Sparks) London: Sage.

Hofstede, G. (1984) *Cultures' Consequences: International Differences in Work Related Values*, (Abridged edn), London: Sage.

Hofstede, G. (1991) *Cultural and Organisations: Software of the Mind*, London: Harper Collins.

Honey, P. and Mumford, A. (1986) *Using Your Learning Styles*, T. Honey, Maidenhead.

Ivanov, V. (1994) *Exemples der structures de Relations Publiques naissantes en Europe de L'Este: La Russie*. Communication Management: Proceedings of the Second European seminar for Teachers, Practitioners and Researchers. Gent. CERP Education.

Jenks, C. (ed) (1993) *Cultural Reproduction*, London: Routledge.

Lindenmann, W. K. (1993) 'An "effectiveness yardstick" to measure public relations success,' *Public Relations Quarterly*, Spring, pp. 7–9.

MacManus, T. (1990) 'Public Relations in the Swedish Health Service.' Unpublished report to the National Association of Health Service Public Relations Officers.

MacManus, T. (1992) *Some Methodological Issues and Opportunities in Cross Cultural Public Relations Research*. Communication Management: Proceedings of the Second European seminar for Teachers, Practitioners and Researchers. Gent. CERP Education.

Mackey, S. (1994) 'A Theory of Public Relations Theory.' Paper to the ICA section of the ICA/ACA conference (July) Sydney.

Malinowski, B. (1926) *Crime and Custom in Savage Society*, London: Routledge and Kegan Paul.

Maloney, K. (1994) 'Lobbyists for Hire.' Doctoral Dissertation. Bournemouth University. United Kingdom.

Moores, S. (1993) *Interpreting Audiences: the Ethnography of Media Consumption.* London: Sage.

Morley, D. (1986) *Family Television: Cultural Power and Domestic Leisure*, London: Comedia.

Namenwirth, J. Z and Weber R. P. (1987) *Dynamics of Culture*, Allan and Unwin.

Newman, W. (1993) 'New Words For What We Do?' *Institute of Public Relations Journal*, 12 (4) pp. 12–13.

Ohashi, S. (1984) 'Public relations in Japan', *Public Relations Journal*, 40, pp. 15–17.

Oyen, E. (1990) 'The Development of Comparative Research: Towards Casual Explanations', in *Comparative Methodology* (ed. E. Oyen), London: Sage.

Scheuch, E. (1992) 'The Development of Comparative Research: Towards Casual Explanations' in *Comparative Methodology* (ed. E. Oyen), London: Sage.

Scannell, P. Schlesinger, P. and Sparks (1992) *Culture and Power*, Ch. 14, London: Sage.

Sigal, L (1987) 'Sources make the news', in *Reading the News* (eds R. Manholt and M. Schudson) New York: Pantheon.

Søndergaard, M. (1994) 'Research note: Hofstede's consequences: a study of reviews, citations and replications,' *Journal of Organisational Studies*, 15 (3), pp. 447–56.

Sriramesh, K. Grunig, J. and Buffington, J. (1992) 'Corporate Culture and Public Relations' in *Excellence in Public Relations and Communication*

Management (ed. J. Grunig) pp. 577–95, Hillsdale, N. J.: Lawrence Erlbaum Associates.

Sriramesh, K. (1992) 'Societal Culture and Public Relations: Ethnographic evidence from India', *Public Relations Review,* 18 (12) pp. 201–11.

Sriramesh, K. and White, J. (1992) 'Societal Culture and Public Relations', in *Excellence in Public Relations and Communication Management* (ed. J. Grunig) Hillsdale, N. J.: Lawrence Erlbaum Associates.

Toth, E. L. and Heath, R. L. (eds) (1992) *Rhetorical and Critical Approaches to Public Relations,* Hillsdale, N. J.: Lawrence Erlbaum.

Tunstall J. (1981) *Journalists at Work,* Constable.

Usunier, J-C. (1993) *International Marketing: A Cultural Approach,* Hemel Hempstead: Prentice-Hall.

Verčič, D., Grunig, L. and Grunig, J. (1993) *Global and Specific Principle of Public Relations: Evidence from Slovenia.* Paper presented to the Association for the Advancement of Policy, Research and Development in the Third World, Cairo.

Watson, T. (1994) 'Public Relations Evaluation: Nationwide Survey of Practice in the United Kingdom'. Paper presented to the International Public Relations Research Symposium, Slovenia (July).

White, J. (1991) *How to Understand and Manage Public Relations,* London: Business Books.

Whittington, R. (1993) *What is Strategy and Does it Matter?* London: Routledge.

Whyte, W. F. (1943) *Street Corner Society: The Social Structure of an Italian Slum.* University of Chicago Press.

9 TOWARDS A METAPHORICAL THEORY OF PUBLIC RELATIONS

Anderson, J.R. (1981) 'Concepts, Propositions and Schemata: What are the Cognitive Units?,' in *Cognitive Processes* (ed. J. H. Flowers) (Nebraska Symposium on Motivation 1980, Lincoln, Nebraska), University of Nebraska Press, pp. 121-61.

Anderson, N.H. (1990) 'Personal Design in Social Cognition', in *Research Methods in Personality and Social Psychology,* (eds C. Hendrick and M. S. Clark), London and Newbury Park: Sage, pp. 243–78.

Armstrong, D.M. (1988), 'Perception and Belief', in *Perceptual Knowledge,* (ed. J. Dancy) Oxford: Oxford University Press, pp. 127–44.

Baskin, O. and Aronoff, C. (1988) *Public Relations: the Profession and the Practice,* Dubuque, Iowa: Brown Publishers.

Bernstein, D. (1984) *Company, Image, and Reality:, A Critique of Corporate Communications,* Eastbourne: Holt, Rhinehart & Winston.

Blauw, E. (1986) *Het Corporate Image,* Amsterdam: De Viergang.

Blumler, J.G. (ed.) (1992) *Television and the Public Interest: Vulnerable Values in West European Broadcasting,* London and Newbury Park: Sage.

Boorstin, D.J. (1962) *The Image or What Happened to the American Dream?,* Harmondsworth: Penguin.

Boulding, K.E. (1956) *The Image: Knowledge in Life and Society*, Ann Arbor: University of Michigan Press.

Boyd, R. (1981) 'Metaphor and Theory Change: What is "Metaphor" a Metaphor for?,' in *Metaphor and Thought*, (ed. A. Ortony), Cambridge: Cambridge University Press, pp. 356-408.

Burns R.B. (1981) *The Self Concept*, Harlow: Longman.

Dauzat, A., Dubois, J. and Mitterand, H. (1971) *Nouveau Dictionnaire Etymologique et Historique*, Paris: Larousse.

Denis, M. (1991) *Image and Cognition*, Hemel Hempstead: Harvester Wheatsheaf.

Denzin, N.K. (1978) *The Research Act (A Theoretical Introduction to Sociological Methods)*, New York: McGraw Hill.

Donnellan, K. (1977) 'Speaking of Nothing', in *Naming, Necessity and Natural Kinds* (ed. S. P. Schwartz), Ithaca and London: Cornell University Press, pp. 216-245.

Dovidio, J.F and Fazio, R.H. (1994) 'New Technologies for the Direct and Indirect Measurement of Attitudes', in *Questions About Questions, Inquiries into the Cognitive Bases of Surveys*, (ed. J. M. Tanur), New York: Russell Sage, pp. 204-40.

Dretske, F.I. (1981) *Knowledge and the Flow of Information*, Oxford: Basil Blackwell.

DSM (1993) *DSM En Het Milieu*, Waar Staan We Voor, Heerlen: CPR/DSM.

Emmons, R.A. (1989) 'The Personal Striving Approach to Personality', in *Goal Concepts in Personality and Social Psychology*, (ed. L. A. Pervins), Hillsdale (N.J): Lawrence Earlbaum Ass. pp. 87-127.

Evans, G. (1977) 'The Causal Theory of Names', in *Naming, Necessity and Natural Kinds* (ed. S. P. Schwartz), pp. 192-216.

Fazio, R., Sanbonmatsu, D.M., Powell, M.C. and Kardes, F.R. (1986), 'On the Automatic Activation of Attitudes,' *Journal of Personality and Social Psychology*, 50 2, pp. 229-38.

Ferguson, S.D. (1994) *Mastering the Public Opinion Challenge*, Burr Ridge, New York: Richard D. Irwin.

Festinger, L. (1957) *A Theory of Cognitive Dissonance*, Stanford: University Press.

Fishbein, M. and Ajzen, I. (1975) *Beliefs, Attitudes, Intentions, and Behaviour*, Reading (Mass.): Addison Wesley.

Fodor, J. (1983) *The Modularity of Mind - An Essay on Faculty Psychology*, Cambridge (Mass.): MIT-Press.

Frijda, N. (1986) *The Emotions*, Cambridge (UK): Cambridge University Press.

Garbett, T. (1988) *How to Build a Corporation's Identity and Project its Image*, Massachussets/Toronto: Lexington Books.

Goffman, E. (1959) *The Presentation of Self in Everyday Life*, Harmondsworth (Middlesex): Penguin.

Grote, B. and Labeur, S. (1994) *Operationalisering van het Identiteitsbegrip*, Utrecht: HE and M.

Grunig, J.E. (1993) 'Image and substance: from symbolic to behavioral relationships,' *Public Relations Review*, 19 (2), pp. 121-39.

Hawkes, T. (1972) *Metaphor*, London/New York: Methuen.

Hefting, P. (1990) *In Search of an Identity, so Obvious and yet so Complex*, in The Image of a Company, (C. De Jong, *et al.*) London: The Architecture, Design and Technology Press, pp. 2-12.

Hofstede, G. (1980; 1984) *Cultures Consequences, International Differences in Work-Related Values* (abridged edition), Newbury Park: Sage.

Holbrook, M. (1978) 'Beyond attitude structure: toward the informational determinants of attitudes,' *Journal of Marketing Research,* 15, pp. 545-56.

Ind, N. (1992) (rev. ed.), *The Corporate Image, Strategies for Effective Identity Programmes,* London: Kogan Page.

Jensen, I. (1992) *Legitimacy - an Essential Concept of Public Relations.* Paper presented to the CERP-Education Research Committee Meeting (June), London.

Kotler, P. and Fox, K.F.A. (1985) *Strategic Marketing for Educational Institutions,* Englewood Cliffs (N.J.): Prentice Hall.

Krosnick, J.A. and Abelson, R. (1994) 'The case for measuring attitude strength in surveys,' in *Questions About Questions, Inquiries into the Cognitive Bases of Surveys* (ed. J. M. Tanur), New York: Russell Sage pp. 177-203.

Lee, T.W., Locke, E.A. and Latham, G.P., 'Goal setting theory and job performance,' in *Goal Concepts in Personality and Social Psychology,* (ed. L. A. Pervin), Hillsdale (N.J.): Lawrence Earlbaum Ass., pp. 291–326.

Levy, S. (1990) The Mapping Sentence in Cumulative Theory Construction: Wellbeing as an Example, in *Operationalization and Research Design,* (eds. J. J. Hox and J. De Jong Gierveld), Lisse/Amsterdam: Swets and Zeitlinger, pp. 155–78.

Lippman, W. (1922) *Public Opinion,* New York: Harcourt, Brace and World.

Mead, G.H. (1934) *Mind, Self and Society (From the Standpoint of a Social Behaviorist),* Chicago: University of Chicago Press.

Merton, R. K. (1949) *On Theroetical Sociology,* New York: Macmillan.

Minsky, M. (1986) *The Society of Mind,* New York: Simon and Schuster.

Mish, F. C. (ed.) (1985) *Webster's Ninth New Collegiate Dictionary,* Springfield (Mass.): Merriam-Webster Inc.

Muller, F., Renkema, E. H. and Heyde, K. (1963) *Short Dictionary Latin-Dutch,* Groningen: Wolters.

Pervin, L. A. (ed.). (1989), *Goal Concepts in Personality and Social Psychology,* Hillsdale (N.J.): Lawrence Earlbaum Ass.

Pruyn, A. T. H. (1992) Imago: een analytische Benadering van het Begrip, in *Handboek Corporate Communication,* Deventer: Van Loghum Slaterus. (eds. C. B. M. Van Riel and W. H. Nijhoff).

Putnam, H. (1977) 'Meaning and Reference', in *Naming, Necessity and Natural Kinds* (ed. S. P. Schwartz), Ithaca and London: Cornell University Press. pp. 119–33.

Rajecki, D. W. (1982) *Attitudes, Themes and Advances,* Sunderland, Mass.: Sinauer.

Rebel, H. J. C. (1991) Modelling Personal Opinions, A New Paradigm for Political Psychology, 1–3 (unpublished doctoral dissertation), The Hague: Department of Defense.

Rebel, H. J. C. (1993) 'Images, Imago's, Identiteiten en Idealen', in *Jaarboek Public Relations en Voorlichting 1993,* (eds. J. Katus and A. Van der Meiden) Bussum: Dick Coutinho, pp. 39–51.

Rebel, H. J. C., Postma, M. and Snellen, M. A. (1993) *Theoriegestuurde Protokolanalyse*, Utrecht: HE and M (internal publication).

Rokeach, M. (1969) *Beliefs, Attitudes and Values*, San Francisco: Jossey Bass.

Schadé, J. P. (1984) *Onze Hersenen*, Utrecht/Antwerp: Het Spectrum.

Schiffman, S., Reynolds, M. L. and Young, F. W. (1981) *Introduction to Multidimensional Scaling, Theory, Methods and Applications*, New York/ London: Academic Press.

Schlenker, B. R. and Weigold, M. F. (1989) 'Goals and the self-identification process: constructing desired entities,' in *Goal Concepts in Personality and Social Psychgology*, (ed. L. A. Pervin), Hillsdale, N.J.: Lawrence Earlbaum Ass. pp. 243–290.

Schultz, D. E., Tannenbaum, S. I. and Lauterborn, R. F. (1993), *Integrated Marketing Communications, Pulling It Together and Making It Work*, Lincolnwood (Ill.): NTC Business Books.

Shanteau, J. (1988) 'Consumer impression formation: the integration of verbal and visual information,' in *Nonverbal Communication in Advertising*, (eds. S. Hecker and D. W. Stewart), Lexington, Mass: D. C. Heath and Company, pp. 43–57.

Silverman, D. (1994) *Interpreting Qualtative Data, Methods for Analysing Talk, Text and Interaction*, London: Sage.

Skotnicki, E. (1991) *Dimensies Van Het Imago* (bach. th.), Utrecht: HE and M.

Snodgrass, J. G. (1984) 'Concepts and their Surface Representations', *Journal of Verbal Learning and Verbal Behavior*, 23, pp. 3–22.

Szalay, L. B. and Mir-Djalali, E., (1991) 'Image of the enemy: critical parameters, cultural variations,' in *The Psychology of War and Peace, The Image of the Enemy*, (ed. R. A. Rieber), New York/London: Plenum, pp. 213–50.

Van der Meiden, A. (1993) Identiteit en Imago, Het beeld in Gods diensthistorische Zin, in *Jaarboek Public Relations en Voorlichting 1993* (eds. Katus and Van der Meiden), Bussum: Dick Coutinho, pp. 52–56.

Van der Meiden, A. (1994a) *Met Raad Verlegen, Aspecten van morele legitimatie van het PR-advies*, Bussum: Dick Coutinho.

Van der Meiden, A. (1994b) *The Embarrassment of Advice, Aspects of Moral Legitimation of Public Relations Advice* (Eng. ver.), Amersfoort: Vandermeiden Consultancy.

Van Doorn, J. A. A. and Lammers, C. J. (1979) *Moderne Sociologie, Een Systematische Inleiding*, Utrecht/Antwerpen: Het Spectrum.

Van Riel, C. B. M. (1992) *Identiteit en Imago, een Inleiding in de Corporate Communication*, Schoonhoven: Academic Service.

Vélu, H. (1988) *Aperitief (Voor Managers)*, The Hague: Winkelman and Van Hessen.

Vos, M. F. (1992) 'The Corporate Image Concept, a Strategic Approach' (unpublished doctoral dissertation), Wageningen: Agricultural University.

Williams, R. (1981) *Keywords, A Vocabulary of Culture and Society*, Glasgow: Fontana/Croom Helm.

Wright, R. A. and Brehm, J. W. (1989) 'Energization and goal attractiveness,' in *Goal Concepts in Personality and Social Psychology*, (ed. L.A. Pervin), Hillsdale, N.J.: Lawrence Earlbaum Ass., pp. 169–210.

10 LEGITIMACY AND STRATEGY OF DIFFERENT COMPANIES

Antonsen, M. and Jensen, I. (1992) 'Forms of legitimacy essential to public relations', in *Business Annals* (ed. M.K. Pedersen) Roskilde: FS&P.

Habermas, J. (1989) *The Theory of Communicative Action*, Cambridge: Polity Press.

Heritage, J. (1984) *Garfinkel and Ethnomethodology*, Cambridge: Polity Press.

Karlsson, A. (1991) *Om Strategei och Letgitimitet*, Lund: Lund University Press.

Kreps, G.L. (1989) Reflexivity and internal public relations: the role of information in directing organisational development, in *Public Relations Theory* (eds C.H. Botan and V. Hazleton), New Jersey: Lawrence Erlbaum Associates.

Ottomeyer, K. *Ökonomische Zwänge und menschliche Beziehungen*, Reinbek bei Hamburg: Rohwohlt Taschenbuch Verlag.

11 COMMUNICATION: MAGICAL MYSTERY OR SCIENTIFIC CONCEPT?

Adema, R.L.A., C.B.M. van Riel and B. Wierenga (1993) *Kritische succesfactoren bij management van corporate communication*, Delft: Oburon.

Bauer, R.A. (1964) 'The obstinate audience: the influence process from the point of view of social communication', *American Psychologist*, 19, pp. 319–28.

Brody, E.W. (1985) 'Changing roles and requirements of public relations', *Public Relations Review*, 11, pp. 22–8.

Brody, E.W. and Stone, G.C. (1989) *Public Relations Research*, New York: Praeger.

Cottone, L. (1987) 'Public relations roles and functions by organization', *Public Relations Review*, 13, pp. 24–32.

Dervin, B. (1989) 'Information as non-sense; information as sense: the communication technology connection', in *Tussen vraag en aanbod* (eds H. Bouwman, P. Nelissen and M. Vooijs). pp.44–59, Amsterdam: Cramwinckel.

Dozier, D.M. (1984) 'Program evaluation and the roles of practitioners', *Public Relations Review*, 10, pp. 13–21.

Dozier, D.M. (1992) 'The organizational roles of communication and public relations practitioners', in *Excellence in Public Relations and Communication Management* (ed. J.E. Grunig). pp. 327–256. Hillsdale: Lawrence Erlbaum.

Emmons, J.F. and L.M. Kaplan (1971) 'The delphi method and decision making: a futuristic technique'. Paper for the International Communication Association, Phoenix, Arizona, April 22–24.

Fauconnier. G. (1990) 'Communicatietheorie', in *Profiel en professie, inleiding in de theorievorming van public relations* (eds A. van der Meiden and G. Fauconnier), pp. 69–81, Leiden: Martinus Nijhoff.

Grunig, J.E. (1976) *Organizations and Public Relations: Testing a Communication Theory*, Journalism Monographs, 46.

Grunig, J.E. (1989) 'Publics, audiences and market segmenets: segmentation principles for campaign', in *Information campaigns: managing the process of social change* (ed. C.T. Salmon). pp. 199–228, Beverly Hills: Sage (Annual Review XVIII).

Grunig, J.E. (1992) *Public Relations as a Two-way Symmetrical Process*, Culemborg: Phaedon (School of Journalism and Communication, Utrecht).

Grunig, J.E. and Hunt, T. (1984) *Managing Public Relations*, New York: Holt, Rinehart and Winston.

Helmer, O. (1966) *Social Technology*, New York: Basic Books.

KS PR (1993) PR: Meten of Passen . . . Amersfoort (internal research paper).

Miller, G.R. (1989) 'Persuasion and public relations: Two 'Ps' in a pod', in *Public Relations Theory* (eds C.H. Botan and V. Hazleton Jr.), pp. 45–66, Hillsdale: Lawrence Erlbaum.

Mintzberg, H. (1983) *Structures in Fives: Designing Effective Organizations*, Englewood Cliffs: Prentice-Hall.

Newcomb, T.M. (1953) 'An approach to the study of communicative acts', *Psychological Review*, 60, pp. 393–404.

Pracht, P. (1991) 'Zur Systematik und Fundierung praktischer Oeffentlichkeitsarbeit, Ein Soll-Ist-Vergleich', *PR Magazin*, 5, pp. 39–46.

Reagan, J. (1990) 'A factor analysis of Broom and Smith's public relations roles scale', *Journalism Quarterly*, 67, pp. 177–83.

Rice, R.E. and Atkin, C.K. (eds) (1989) *Public Communication Campaigns*, Newbury Park: Sage.

Rice, R.E. and Paisley, W.J. (eds) (1981) *Public Communication Campaigns*, Beverly Hills: Sage.

Riel, C.B.M. van (1992) *Identiteit en Imago, een Inleiding in de Corporate Communication*, Schoonhoven: Academic Service.

Rozema, R., Visser, A.Ph. and Boekestijn, C. (1983) 'Roloriëntatie en rolgedrag in een brugpositie', in *Rollen, Persoonlijke en Sociale Invloeden op het Gedrag* (ed A.Ph. Visser) pp. 243–59, Meppel: Boom.

Ruler, A.A. van (1995). Communicatiemanagement in Nederland. Houten: Bohn Stafleu Van Loghum (dissertation).

Ruler, A.A. van, Stappers, J.G., Evers, W.J.M. and Nillesen, A.B. (1994) 'Communicatoren op de pijnbank. Een onderzoek naar de werkvisie en werkwijze van voorlichtings en pr-functionarissen', *Massacommunicatie*, 22, vol. 4.

Ruler, A.A. van, Stappers, J.G., Evers, W.J.M. and Nillesen, A.B. (1995) *Public Relations Officers in the Netherlands: Standards, Ambitions and Daily Routines* (in press).

Schramm, W. (1971) 'The nature of communication between humans', in *The Process and Effects of Mass Communication* (eds W. Schramm and D.F. Roberts). pp. 3–53, Urbana: University of Illinois Press.

Shannon, C.E. and Weaver, W. (1949) *The Mathematical Theory of Communication*, Urbana: University of Illinois Press.

Stappers, J.G. and Nillesen, A.B (1985) 'Voorlichters in informatieverschaffers onderzocht Voorlichters doorgelicht', *Massacommunicatie*, 9, pp. 186–99.

Thayer, L. (1968) *Communication and Communication Systems in Organization, Management and Interpersonal Relations*, Homewood Ill.: Richard D. Wirwin.

Watzlawick, P., Beavin, J.H. and Jackson, D.D. (1970) *De Pragmatische Aspecten van de Menselijke Communicatie*, Deventer: Van Loghum Slaterus.

White, J. and Dozier, D.M. (1992) 'Public relations and management decision making', in *Excellence in Public Relations and Communication Management* (ed. J.E. Grunig). pp. 91–108, Hillsdale: Lawrence Erlbaum.

Wiener, N. (1948) *Cybernetics or Control and Communication in the Animal and the Machine*, New York: Wiley & Sons.

12 TOWARDS FOURTH WAVE PUBLIC RELATIONS: A CASE STUDY

Anderson, D. S. (1992) Identifying and responding to activist publics: a case study. *Journal of Public Relations Research* 4(3), pp. 151–65.

Bernays, E. L. (1923) *Crystallizing Public Opinion*, New York: Boni and Liveright.

Bernays, E. L. (1986) *The Late Years: Public Relations Insights, 1956–1986*, Rhinebeck, NY: H&M Publishers.

Black, S. (ed.) (1993) *International Public Relations*, London: Kogan Page.

Blumer, H. (1966) 'The Mass, the public and public opinion,' in *Reader in Public Opinion and Communication* (eds B. Berelson and M. Janowitz), (2nd edn) New York: Free Press.

Broom, G. M. and Dozier, D. M. (1990) *Using Research in Public Relations: Applications to Program Management*, Englewood Cliffs, NJ: Prentice Hall.

Caywood, C. L. and Ewing, R. P. (1992) 'Communication strategies and tactics: all the stakeholders', in *The Handbook of Communications in Corporate Restructuring and Takeovers*, Englewood Cliffs, NJ: Prentice-Hall.

Cheney, G. and Dionispoulos, G. N. (1989) 'Public relations? No, relations with publics: a rhetorical-organizational approach to contemporary corporate communications', in *Public Relations Theory*, Hillsdale, NJ: Lawrence Erlbaum, pp. 135–57.

Cole, R. S. (1981) *The Practical Handbook of Public Relations*, Englewood Cliffs, NJ: Prentice-Hall.

Coombs, W. T. (1992) 'The failure of the task force on food assistance: a case study of the role of legitimacy in issue management'. *Journal of Public Relations Research*, 4(2), pp. 101–22.

Culbertson, H. M., Jeffers, D. W. Stone, D. B. and Terrell, M. (1993) *Social, Political, and Economic Contexts in Public Relations: Theory and Cases*. Hillsdale, NJ: Lawrence Erlbaum Associates.

Dewey, J. (1927) *The Public and Its Problems*, Chicago: Swallow.

Dozier, D. M. (1990) 'The innovation of research in public relations practice: review of a program of studies', in *Public Relations Research Annual* (eds J. E. Grunig and L. A. Grunig) Vol. 2, pp. 3–28.

Drucker, P. F. (1990) *The New Realities: In Government and Politics . . . In*

Economy and Business . . . *In Society* . . . *and In World View*, London: Mandarin.

Easterby-Smith, M., Thorpe, R. and Lowe, A. (1991) *Management Research: An Introduction*, London: Sage.

Gruban B., Verčič, D. and Zavrl, F. (1994) 'Public relations in Slovenia: research report 1994. Ljubljana: Pristop special issue, pp. 4–6.

Grunig, J. E. (1994) 'A situational theory of publics: conceptual history, recent challenges, and new research'. Paper presented to the International Public Relations Symposium, Bled, Slovenia (July).

Grunig, J. E. (1993) 'Image and substance: from symbolic to behavioral relationships', *Public Relations Review*, 19(2), pp. 121–39.

Grunig, J. E. (1989) 'Symmetrical presuppositions as a framework for public relations theory', in *Public Relations Theory*, Hillsdale, NJ: Lawrence Erlbaum, pp. 17–44.

Grunig, J. E. and Childers L. (1988) 'Reconstruction of a situational theory of communication: internal and external concepts as identifiers of publics for Aids'. Paper presented to the Communication Theory & Methodology Division, Association for Education in Journalism & Mass Communication, Portland, OR (July).

Grunig, J. E. and Grunig, L. A (1992) 'Models of public relations and communication', in *Excellence in Public Relations and Communication Management*, Hillsdale, NJ: Lawrence Erlbaum, pp. 285–325

Grunig, J. E. and Hunt, T. (1984) *Managing Public Relations*, New York: Holt, Rinehart and Winston.

Grunig, J. E. and Grunig, L. A. (1989) 'Toward a theory of the public relations behaviour of organizations: review of a program of research', in *Public Relations Research Annual* (eds J. E. Grunig and L. A. Grunig) Vol. 1. Hillsdale, NJ: Lawrence Erlbaum, pp. 27–63.

Grunig, J. E. and White, J. (1992) 'The effect of worldview on public relations theory and practice', in *Excellence in Public Relations and Communication Management* (ed. J. E. Grunig) Hillsdale, NJ: Lawrence Erlbaum, 31–64.

Grunig, L. A. (1994) 'Requisite variety in public relations'. Paper presented to the International Public Relations Symposium, Bled, Slovenia.

Grunig, L. A. (1992) 'Toward the philosophy of public relations', in *Rhetorical and Critical Approaches to Public Relations* (eds E. L. Toth and R. L. Heath) Hillsdale, NJ: Lawrence Erlbaum, pp. 65–91.

Kennedy, P. (1993) *Preparing for the Twenty-First Century*. London: Fontana Press.

Luhmann, N. (1992) *Legitimacija kroz proceduru*. Trans. I. Glaser. Zagreb: Naprijed. N. Luhmann. (1975) Legitimation durch Varfahren. Frankfurt/ Main: Suhrkamp Verlag.

Luhmann, N. (1982) *The Differentiation of Society*, Transl. S. Holmes and C. Larmore. New York: Columbia University Press.

Luhmann, N. (1981) 'The improbability of communication'. *International Social Science Journal*, 33(1), pp. 122–32.

Marx, T. G. (1990) 'Strategic planning for public affairs'. *Long Range Planning*, 23(1), pp. 9–16.

Maynard, H. B., Jr. and Mehrtens, S. E. (1993) *The Fourth Wave: Business in the 21st Century*, San Francisco: Berrett-Koehler.

Moss, D. (ed.) (1990) *Public Relations in Practice: A Casebook*, London: Routledge.

Moffitt, M. A. (1994) 'A cultural studies perspective toward understanding corporate image: a case study of state farm insurance'. *Journal of Public Relations Research*, 6(1), pp. 41–66.

Murphy P. and Dee, J. (1992) 'Du Pont and Greenpeace: the Dynamics of Conflict between Corporations and Activist Groups'. *Journal of Public Relations Research* 4(1), pp. 3–20.

Naisbitt, J. (1994) *Global Paradox: The Bigger the World Economy, the More Powerful its Smallest Players*, London: Nicholas Brealey.

Olasky, M. N. (1987) *Corporate Public Relations: A New Historical Perspective*, Hillsdale, NJ: Lawrence Erlbaum.

Patton, M. Q. (1987) *How to Use Qualitative Methods in Evaluation*, Newbury Park, CA: Sage.

Pavlik, J. V. (1987) *Public Relations: What Research Tells Us*, Newbury Park, CA: Sage.

Pearson, R. (1990) 'Ethical values or strategic values? Two faces of systems theory in public relations' in *Public Relations Research Annual*, Vol. 2, pp. 219–34.

PR Institut (1993) *Raziskava komunikacijskih vidikov ekoloske sanacije TE Sostanj, 1. del.* (Research on communication aspects of the environmental improvement of SP Sostanj, Vol. 1.) Ljubljana, Slovenia: PR Institut, Pristop.

Scott, J. (1991) *Social Network Analysis: A Handbook*, London: Sage.

Serini, S. A. (1993) 'Influences on the power of public relations professionals in organizations: a case study'. *Journal of Public Relations Research*, 5(1), pp. 1–25.

Smith, H. (1989) *The Power Game: How Washington Works*, New York: Ballantine Books.

Springston, J. K., Keyton, J. Leichty, G. B. and Metzger, J. (1992) 'Field dynamics and the public relations theory: toward the management of multiple publics'. *Journal of Public Relations Research* 4(2), pp. 81–100.

Tulis, J. K. (1987) *The Rhetorical Presidency*, Princeton, NJ: Princeton University Press.

Verčič, D., Grunig, L. A. and Grunig, J. E. (1993) 'Global and specific principles of public relations: evidence from Slovenia'. Paper presented to the International Conference on The State of Education and Development, New Directions, Association for the Advancement of Policy, Research, and Development in the Third World, Cairo, Egypt (November).

Vreg, F. (1994) 'Foreword', in Pristop, special issue: public relations in Slovenia: research report 1994 (eds B. Gruban, D. Verčič and F. Zavrl) Ljubljana: Pristop, pp. 4–6.

White, J. (1991) *How to Understand and Manage Public Relations: A Jargon-free Guide to Public Relations Management*, London: Business Books.

Windahl, S. and Signitzer, B. (1992) *Using Communication Theory*, London: Sage.

Index

Abugov, M. B. 14
Adema, R. L. A. *et al.* 262
advertising, community 114–15
AIDS study 27, 28, 33–5, 40
Al-Doory, S. A. 14
American Institute of Public
  Relations (IPRA) 161
American Opinion Research
  Corporation 214
Anderson, D. S. 267, 277
Anderson, J. R. 32, 211–212; and
  Reder, L. M. 32
Anderson, R. B. 47
Ang, I. 170, 175–176
Angerer, U. 123
Antonsen, M. and Jensen, I. 246
Armstrong, D. M. 212
attitudes 7–8, 9, 20–1, 22, 31,
  216–217; inclusion/prediction of
  38–9
Atwood, L. E. and Cheng, P. 14, 30
Austria, comparison with UK
  176–191

Babbie, E. 66
Baerns, B. 111, 170
Baldwin, W. R. 14
Bandura, A. 27
Bantz, C. R. 66–8, 70–1, 81–2
Barnum, P. T. 93
Bartholomew, C. M. 26
Baskin, O. and Aronoff, C. 178, 212
Bauer, R. A. 255
BDW 108
Becher, M. 95

behaviour 7–8, 9, 20–1, 24, 38,
  218–219, 221, 268, 270
Bergen, J. 80
Bernays, E. L. 3, 89, 90, 92, 275,
  278
Bernstein, D. 203, 214, 222
Bishop, W. B. 14
Black, S. 277
Blauw, E. 200
Blumer, H. 5, 268
Blumler, J. G. 223
Bockelmann, F. 116
Boorstin, D. J. 96–7, 106, 200
Botan, C. 170, 171
Boulding, K. E. 211, 218
Bourdieu, P. 179
Bovet, S. F. 168
Boyd, R. 202
British Gas 166–167
Brody, E. W. 248; and Stone, G. C.
  262
Broom, G. M. and Dozier, D. M. 277
Budd Jnr, J. F. 165
Buller, D. 52
Burns, R. B. 204
Business International 161, 162

Cadbury Committee on Corporate
  Governance 162
Cameron, G. T. 23; and Yang, J. 38
Cantrill, J. G. 20
Carey, J. W. 175
Carroll, J. C. 174
Carter, R. F. 11

Caywood, C. L. and Ewing, R. P. 278
Cheney, G. and Dionispoulos, G. N. 278
Clark, P. B. and Wilson, J. Q. 19
Clarke, P. and Kline, F. G. 9
Clifford, J. 59
Co-op Wholesale Society (CWS) 147–148; study findings 148–158
Code of Athens 95
Code of Lisbon 186
cognition 7–8, 9, 20–1, 38, 216–221; hedging and wedging 22–3; structures of 31–7
Cohen, A. A. *et al.* 67
Cole, R. S. 277, 278
communication: active/passive 9, 11, 20, 22, 23–5, 31–2; concept of 253–255; conditions of 258–259; contribution of 257–258; corporate 222–223; and depth/breadth of processing 32–5; dimensions of 256–262; essence of 257; false 89; indirect counterinformation 90; intermediaries 251, 252; internal 226–227; as magic bullet 255; process 271–273; professional views on 260–263; research *see* Delphi-Study; sales manager 250–251; sender/receiver 255–256; situational theory of 7–8, 10–19, *see also* situational theory of publics; technicians 250, 251
Confederation of British Industry (CBI) 167
conflict resolution 35–7, 60–1; and best alternative to a negotiated agreement (BATNA) 36
constraint recognition 9–11, 24, 25, 29–30, 37, 39, 43–6, 268–269
Converse, P.E. 20
Coombs, W.T. 277; *et al.* 170, 171, 181
corporate: communication programme 222–223; culture 206; identity 204–211; objectives 239; personalities 205, 206; structure 206

corporate sector: developments in 137–139; and evolution of professional practice 140–141; and excellence 143–145, 156–157, 158; ideality 214–216; identity-programmes 221; image 211–214; legitimacy and strategy in 225–245; marketing in 141–143, 154–156; personality programmes 221–222; and product/image branding 136, 138; and responsibility 276; *see also* retail sector UK study
Cottone, L. *et al.* 248
Covello, V. T. 35
Cox, T. 81
Crable, and Vibbert, 178
Craik, F. I. M. 32; and Lockhart, R. S. 32
Cuff, E. *et al.* 179
Culbertson, H. M. *et al.* 277
cultural dimensions 67, 171, 173–174, 190–191; individualism 67–8; masculinity 70–1; power distance 68–70, 83, 191; uncertainty avoidance 70, 190
culture 209; concept of 172–176, 189
Curran, J. 175
Cutlip, S. M., and Center, A. H. 3; *et al.* 140

data analysis: 'analyse as we go' 63; interpretation 62–3; reduction 62
Dauzat, *et al.* 202
Davidson, W. R. and Doody, A. F. 138
Davies, G. 136, 138; and Brooks, 138
Davis-Belcher, P. O. 14
decision-making process 267, 271–273, 274, 277
Delphi-Study 169, 262–263; follow-up study 252–256; interpretation of results 252; research method 248–249; results of survey 256–262; theoretical framework 249–251; *see also* Excellence Project; international research; research design

Delphi-technique 247, 248–249, 256
Denis, M. 202, 211–212
Denzin, N. K. 209
Department of Trade and Industry (DTI) 167
Dervin, B. 262
Dewey, J. 5, 9, 10, 268
disposition terms 213
Dobzhansky, T. *et al.* 71
Donnellan, K. 201
Dozier, D. M. 63, 247, 250, 251, 277
Dretske, F. I. 212
Drucker, P. F. 276

East Germany, comparison with West Germany 120–1
Easterby-Smith, M. *et al.* 278
'Ecology, Energy and Preservation' conference (1986) 271
effect, social/scientific models 255
Ego 204, 205
Emmons, J. F. and Kaplan, L. M. 248
Emmons, R. A. 204
employees: and identification with corporate objectives 239; relationship with company 225–228; and work involvement 239–244
Environmental Intelligence System 223
epistemological principles 201
Essich, T. 14
ethnography 179
ethnomethodology 230–231
European Code 186
Evans, G. 201
events 89–91; management 107; media 106–9; natural 96–7, 104–5; rules governing 103–4; social 96–7, 105–6; types of 99–109
excellence criteria 143–144, 154, 155–158, 275
Excellence Project 49–50, 135–136; as comparative study 50–4; conclusions for 76–81; and requisite variety 71–6; variety in interviewees' perspectives 54–9; and variety in team research

59–71; *see also* Delphi-Study; international research; research design

facts 101–3; rules governing 103
Falck's Redningskorps 225–226, 229, 234, 243
Fauconnier, G. 254
Fazio, R. *et al.* 217
Federal Building Act (1977) 111
Ferguson, S.D. 219, 223
Finn, D. 160
Fishbein, M. and Ajzen, I. 21, 31, 212
Fisher, R., and Brown, S. 36; and Ury, W. 36
Fiske, J. 175
Flieger, H. 182
Flora, J.A. *et al.* 40
Fodor, J. 206
Foucalt, M. 175
Foundation of the International Association of Business Communicators (IABC) 49–50, 59, 68–9, 76, 77, 84, 85
fourth wave PR 275–277
Frederick, W. C. *et al.* 165
Freimuth, V. 52
Frijda, N. 217

Garbett, T. 200
Garreau, J. 188
Geertz, C. 64
Gibbs, J. D. 14
Gilligan, C. and Sutton, C. 138
Graber, D. A. 47
Granovetter, 172
Greenley, G. and Shipley, D. 137, 145
Gross, H. 94
Grote, B. and Labeur, S. 224
Gruban, B. *et al.* 51
Grunig, J.E. 8, 10–14, 15–17, 19, 21–4, 26, 31, 48, 53–4, 75, 79, 85, 136, 144, 154, 162, 211, 212, 249, 250, 253, 265, 268, 277, 278; and Childers, L. 14, 27, 30, 268; and Disbrow, J.B. 11–12, 14; *et al.* 13, 14, 48, 135, 143–144, 155–158; and Grunig, L. A. 8, 35, 141, 146,

152, 158, 171, 265, 266, 268, 274, 275; and Hunt, T. 4, 9, 13, 30, 46, 93, 135, 140, 141–142, 145, 152, 160, 171, 178, 182, 191, 250–251, 262, 265; and Ipes, D.A. 10, 14, 23, 24, 31, 41; and Repper, F.C. 8; and Stamm, K.R. 22, 31; and Theus, 14; and White, J. 162, 168, 275
Grunig, L. A. 14, 77, 265, 276, 277; *et al.* 47, 72
Gunn, J. 171
Gurevitch, *et al.* 175
Guttman, L. 213

Habermas, J. 174, 222, 223, 246
Hamilton, P. K. 14
Hampden-Turner, C. 161–162; and Trompenaars, F. 161
Harrison, S. L. 160
Harrods 146; study findings 148–158
Harvard Negotiation Project 36
Harwood, R. 5–6
health-care study 27, 29, 35–7, 40
Hedron Consulting 167
Hefting, P. 200
Heritage, J. 246
Hickman, C. R. and Silva, M. A. 157
Hofstede, G. 67, 70–1, 133, 159, 160, 171, 173, 174, 178, 187–188, 190, 209
Holbrook, M. 217
Honey, P. and Mumford, A. 181
Huang, Y. 51
human resource management 227
Hundhausen, C. 94
Hunt, T. and Grunig, J. E. 41

IABC Research Foundation *see* Foundation of the International Association of Business Communicators (IABC)
ideality 214–215, 221, 222; measurement of 216
identity 200, 203–204, 206, 210, 221; as core-personality 207; programmes 221; split 208; strong 207, 221, 223; weak 207
imagenem 202
images 200–201, 202–203, 211; and attitudes 216–217; and behaviour 218–219, 221; and cafeteria technique 214; as cognitive phenomena 212, 216–221; as container-concept 212; and facet designs 213–214; of human work 236–238; imagination 212; impression 212; measurement of 213–214; personological model *220*; and scaling methods 214; and semantic differential 214
imago 201, 202–203, 205, 213, 221; deeds 208; physical presence 208–209; work 208
Ind, N. 207, 208, 221, 222
information: as comprehensive and objective 94; fictional/authentical 98; freedom of 110; indirect counterinformation 90; negative/positive 41; processing 9, 42–3, 71–6, 268–269; seeking 9, 43, 268–270; theory of 99–109
Institute of Public Relations (IPR) 180, 185, 186, 191–192
interest groups 17–19
international research 170–172; differences between doing and thinking 189; and mutual understanding/goodwill 189–190; objectives and methodology 176–182; preliminary findings 182–189; and public view of PR 190; questionnaires 180–182; UK questionnaire 192–196; *see also* Delphi-Study; Excellence Project; research design
Ivanov, V. 170

James, W. 203–204
Jarchow, K. 97
jargon 200
Jeffers, D. W. 14
Jenkins, L. 14
Jenks, 174
Jennings, M. K. 20
Jensen, I. 221
Journal of International Studies of Management and Organisation 171

Journal of Public Relations Research 25
journalism 111, 247; norms of 91–2; and truth 92–3, 95

Kalt, G. 108
Kant, I. 211
Kanter, R. M. 143
Karlsson, A. 246
Kauffman, B.J. 60
Kauffmann, W.-D. 115
Kelly, K. S. 14
Kennedy, P. 276
Kotler, P. 142; and Andreasen, A.R. 8; and Mindak, W. 135, 142, 146, 154, 155
Kreps, G. L. 245
Krosnick, J. A. and Abelson, R. 217
Krugman, H. E. 11
KS PR 262
Kutscher-Klink, A. 115

Lang, G. E. and Lang, K. 47
language 174
Laufenburger, A. 51
Lee, I. L. 92, 93, 103
Lee, T. W. *et al.* 215
Lees, R. and Worthington, S. 138
legitimacy 225–226; and balance of economic and substantive objectives 231–234; complexity of the base of 235–236; concept of 228–236; and fields of activity 229–231; and identification with corporate objectives 239; and images of work 236–239; and the reference to system or to life world 234–235, 244; and work involvement 239–244
level of involvement 9–11, 25, 29–30, 37, 39, 40, 42–7, 268–269
Levy, S. 213
Lincoln, Y. S. and Guba, E. G. 53–4
Lippmann, W. 5, 92, 202, 211
Locke, L. F. *et al.* 59
logical principles 201
Luhmann, N. 272, 277
Lyra, A. 51

McGee, J. 138
McGrath, J. 48
Mackey, S. 171
MacManus, T. 171, 174
Major, A. M. 14, 30, 40
Maloney, K. 188
marketing 110–14, 141–143, 154–156, 186
Marks and Spencer 147; study findings 148–158
Markus, M. and Zajonc, R. B. 31, 33
Marshall, C. and Rossman, G. B. 54
Marx, Karl (Marxism) 175, 236, 237
Marx, T. G. 278
Maynard Jnr, H. B. and Mehrtens, S. E. 275–276
Mead, G. H. 204
meaning development, questions concerning 201–204
media 39–41, 92, 99, 174, 175; reality 102–3
Merten, K. 97
Merton, R. K. 206
metaphorical reasoning 202
Miles, M. B. and Huberman, A. M. 63
Miller, G. R. 140
Minsky, M. 217, 218
Mintzberg, H. 251
Mish, F. C. 202, 203
Moe, T. M. 18
Moffitt, M. A. 277
Moore, H. F. and Kalupa, F. B. 139
Moores, S. 179, 176
Moss, D. 277
Muller, F. *et al.* 202
Murphy, P. 140; and Dee, J. 277
Myers, R. E., Jr 24

Naisbitt, J. 276
Namenwirth, J. Z. and Weber, R. P. 172–173
Nemeth, C. 61
Neske, F. 94
Newcomb, T. M. 254
Newman, W. 189
Newsom, D. *et al.* 97
Nitsch, H. 94
normative theory 197, 199, 221–223

Oeckl, A. 94
O'Keefe, G. J. 32
Olasky, M. N. 165, 274
Olson, M. 18–19
open-systems theory 201
opinion 7; and conflict resolution
  35–7; and possible
  communication outcomes 20–5;
  see also publics; situational theory
  of publics
Ottomeyer, K. 237
Oyen, E. 176

Patton, M. Q. 278
Pavlik, J. V. 33, 123, 266, 276
Pearson, R. 276
Pelham, K. L. 14
perception *see* constraint
  recognition; level of involvement;
  problem recognition
personality 205, 206, 219, *220*;
  culture 209; programme 221–222;
  structure 209
Pervin, L. A. 215
Peters, T. J. and Waterman, R. H.
  143
Petty, R. E. and Cacioppo, J. T. 21,
  31, 34, 47
Piercy, N. 145; and Alexander, N.
  145
politics 276
Porac, J. F. *et al.* 138
PR Institut of Pristop
  Communication Group 266, 267,
  273–274
PR practitioners 141, 159–160;
  codes of conduct 161–163, 186;
  development of 168–169;
  implications for business/
  organization 166–168;
  professional views of *see* Delphi-
  Study; role of 160, 163–166
PR Week 168
Pracht, P. 248
press offices 115–16; organization
  116–17; tasks/objectives v. actual
  activities 117–20
press-agentry 140, 141, 152, 158
Price, V. 4–5, 7, 39, 47
problem facing 269

problem recognition 9–11, 24, 26,
  29–30, 37, 39, 40, 41, 43–6,
  268–269, 271
Pruyn, A. T. H. 211, 212
pseudo-events 96, 106–7
psychology 202–204, 223
public opinion 266; cultivation of
  94; defined 3–4; and mass media
  39–40; research on 7–8
public relations 136–137; breadth of
  280; conceptions of 91–6,
  199–201; defined 97–8, 192;
  diversity of research interests in
  280; and evolution of professional
  practice 140–141; purpose of
  265–278; role of 135–136; v.
  public marketing 110–14; world-
  view 156, 158
Public Relations Association of
  America 181
Public Relations Society of America
  (PRSA) 93–4
Public Relations Verband Austria
  (PRVA) 180
publics 4–7; activist 17–19, 25–9,
  31; corporate 15–17, 22–3;
  environmental 14–15, 17, 21, 22,
  23, 26; hot-issue 40–1;
  identification of 12–13;
  intellectual 25–9; internal/external
  components 25–9; multiple 265,
  273, 278; *see also* opinion;
  situational theory of publics
Putnam, H. 201
Putnam, L. L. 74

Rajecki, D. W. 212
Ray, M. L. 11
Reagan, J. 248
reality 89–91; concept of 91–6;
  constructions of 99–109; and
  events 96–9
Rebel, H. J. C. 200, 204, 219; *et al.*
  216
referent criterion 11–12, 32
requisite variety 50, 71–4, 83–4,
  277; and adaptation 73, 75, 80, 84;
  and breadth of perspective 72–3;
  and enactment 73–4; implications

of 81–4; as necessary 74–5; and time 75–6

research design 64–71, 84–6; and avoidance of bias 77–8; blueprint for 59–62; and cultural dimensions 60–1, 67–71; and data analysis 62–3; as dependable, confirmable, transferable and credible 53–4, 78; and dissemination of results 76; in-depth interviewing 209; and international dimension 79–80; multiple-case 52; qualitative/ quantitative approaches to 51–2, 76, 77; questionnaires 248; and requisite variety 71–6, 81–4; and researcher effects 65–6; and response bias 77–8; sampling methods 54–9, 84; and Sostanj Steam Plant 269–271; and standards for evaluation 52–4, 78–9; student theses on PR 122–131; and time 51, 76–7; triangulation method 76, 77, 84, 209; and two-way symmetrical communication 79; *see also* Delphi-Study; Excellence Project; international research

retail sector UK study; aims of 136–137; dominant PR models 148–153; excellence criteria 156–157, 158; findings 146–148; marketing and PR 154–156; methodology 145–146; PR objectives 153–154; PR as tactical publicity function 158; *see also* corporate sector

Rice, R. E.; and Atkin, C. K. 48, 262; and Paisly, W. J. 262

Riel, C. B. M. van 200, 222, 251

risk situation study 27, 28–9, 35

Rober, M. 112

Rogers, E. M. 24

Rokeach, M. 212

Ronneberger, F. 91; and Rüh, M. 98

Roskilde University 85–6

Rothschild, M.L. and Ray, M.L. 11

Royal Society of Arts (RSA) 159–160, 161, 167, 168

Rozema, R. *et al.* 250

Rühl, M. 91

Ruler, A. A. van 249, 252, 260; *et al.* 252

Russell and Bromley 147; study findings 148–158

Salmon, C. T. 27

Sandman, P. M. 18, 35

Sauerhaft, S. and Atkins, C. 3

Scannell, P. 175

Schadé, J. P. 217

schemas 32–3

Scheuch, E. 177–178

Schiffman, S. *et al.* 213

Schlenker, B. R. and Weigold, M. F. 204

Schneider, L. A. 14, 48

Schramm, W. 255

Schultz, D. E. *et al.* 212, 223

Schwartz, G. 142

Scott, J. 272

self-image 205, 210, 222

semantic principles 201

service management 227

Shannon, C. E. and Weaver, W. 253, 262

Sheriff, C. W. *et al.* 27

Shimp, T. A. and Delozier, M. W. 142

Sierra Club study 17–19

Sigal, L. 175

Signitzer, B. 180

Silverman, D. 201

situational theory of publics 8–10, 267, 268–271, 277; and communication outcomes 20–5; examples of applied studies 13–17; extension of to activist groups 17–19; intellectual history of 10–13; new research on 25–37; questions to measure variables of 42–7; research challenges to 37–41; *see also* communication; opinion; publics

Skotnicki, E. 224

Slater, M. D. *et al.* 24, 38, 48

Smircich, L. 74

Smith, L. M. 78

Smith, M. J. 65, 77

Society for the Prevention of Cancer (Denmark) 233, 243
Sondergaard, 173–174
Sostanj Steam Plant 259, 265, 266–268, 269–274
Springston, J. K. *et al.* 37, 265
Sriramesh, K. 51, 170; *et al.* 171; and White, J. 171
Stamm, K. R.; and Bowes, J. E. 22; and Grunig, J. E. 22, 31
Stappers, J. G. and Nillesen, A. B. 248
strategic: concepts 225, 234; management theory 8
student research theses 122–123; basic 123–124; empirical on aspects of PR process 128; empirical on people doing PR 129; empirical on PR programme areas 126–127; empirical on PR techniques 127; empirical sector-based 125; largely empirical on PR industry as such 129–130; largely practical resulting in real-life PR proposals 130–131; theoretical on aspects of PR process 127–128; theoretical on people doing PR 128–129; theoretical on PR programme areas 125–126; theoretical on PR techniques 127; theoretical sector-based 124
Szalay, L. B. and Mir-Djalali, E. 213

Tarde, G. 5
teamwork: and comparability 59–60; and cultural dimensions 67–71, 82; disadvantages of 66–7, 82; diverse qualities of 77, 83; and effect of pluralism 82; and flexibility 60–2; and importance of listening 83; and learning by doing 81–2; and overcoming disadvantages of 82; problems concerning 64–6; and published work on 65–71; and qualitative data analysis 62–3; and requisite variety 83–4; and responsibility/ leadership 82–3; and writing up results 63–4

Tesh, S. 19
Thayer, L. 253
Toffler, A. 275
Total Quality Management (TQM) 58, 77, 221–222
Toth, E. L. and Heath, R. L. 175
truth 94–5, 97
Tulis, J. K. 276
Tunstall, J. 175
Turner, D. 14
two-way symmetrical model 8, 79, 140, 144, 152, 158, 275

United Kingdom: comparison with Austria 176–191; questionnaire 192–196; retail sector study 145–158
Usunier, J.-C. 172, 174, 191

Van der Meiden, A. 140, 200, 203, 204
Van Doorn, J. A. A. and Lammers, C. J. 206
Van Leuven, J. K. and Slater, M. D. 39, 47
Vasquez, G. M. 39, 47
Vaughan, E. 48
Vélu, H. 214
Vercic, D., *et al.* 171, 266; and Zavrl, 266
Vos, M. F. 200, 207, 211, 214
Vreg, F. 266

Waddell, D. G. 14
Wallack, L. M. 48
Walters, D. and White, D. 137, 138
Walton, D. 163
Watson, T. 181
Watzlawick, P. *et al.* 253–254
Weick, K. E. 26, 50, 61, 71, 73–5, 80–1, 83
West Germany; comparison with East Germany 120–1; PR in 114–20
Wharf-Sapir hypothesis 174
White, J. 178, 278; and Blamphin, J. 169; and Dozier, D.M. 248, 258
Whittington, 172
Whyte, W. F. 176
Wiener, N. 253

Williams, R. 172, 173, 200
Wilson, J. Q. 19
Windahl, S. and Signitzer, B. 274
Winett, R. A. 32
Woolf, V. 62
work: calling and meaningful occupation 238; completely instrumental 236–237; images of 236–238; instrumentally humanized 237–238; necessary sensitivity 237
work involvement: and aesthetics 240; in different forms of companies 242–244; and pay 239; and skilled/professional achievement 239–240; and social value 240–242; in system and life-world related objectives 244; and working community 240
Wortzel, L. H. 138
Wright, R. A. and Brehm, J. W. 215

Yin, R. K. 52, 84

Zedwitz-Arnim, Graf von 94